To Busy Women Everywhere—

Good and easy. It's an unbeatable combination of the best of both worlds. And with this cookbook in hand, you can prepare 365 breakfasts, lunches and dinners every year, in a hurry—without skimping on quality or any of the nice little touches that make mealtime a pleasure.

Consider this latest edition of *Good and Easy* your ultramodern shortcut to this kind of mealtime pleasure. We show you how to use the latest convenience foods in new and unusual ways; how to serve nourishing food without being ho-hum; how to plan menus that will make your family sit up and take notice. We offer ingredient substitutions to help you use what you have on hand. We suggest splendid revivals for leftovers. And for instant decision-making, we have main-meal meats at the beginning—because they're the starting point for most of your meal planning.

We hope you'll use these recipes as guides to branch out and create ideas of your own—that's part of the fun of cooking. And we'd like to think that our *Good and Easy Cookbook* will give you extra time for the many other good things in your life.

Cordially,

Betty Crocker

P.S. Each and every recipe has been tested, of course in our Kitchens and in the kitchens of busy women across the country.

Betty Crocker's Good and Easy Cookbook

· BANTAM BOOKS ·
® TORONTO · NEW YORK · LONDON

BETTY CROCKER'S GOOD AND EASY COOKBOOK

*A Bantam Book / published by arrangement with
Western Publishing Company, Inc.*

PRINTING HISTORY

*Golden Press edition published April 1971
Eight printings through 1974
Bantam edition / February 1975*

4th printing

Published simultaneously in the United States and Canada

PRINTED IN THE UNITED STATES OF AMERICA

Contents

Meats and Main Dishes

Beef 3
Pork 26
Lamb 47
Veal 55
Chicken 61
Turkey 70
Fish and Seafood 77
Cheese, Eggs and Beans 87

Serve-Withs and Side Dishes

Salads 93
Vegetables 107
Potatoes 123
Noodles and Spaghetti 129
Rice 134
Dinner Breads 140

Desserts and Confections

Fruit Desserts 146
Puddings 153
Chilled and Frozen Desserts 156
Cookies 161
Candies 172
Cakes 177
Pies 193
Beverages 205

Breakfasts and Brunches

Fruits 211
Cereals 216
Eggs 220
Meats 228
Breads 233
Beverages 242

Lunches and Munches

Soups 248
Sandwiches 253
Main Dishes 264
Snacks 276

Good and Easy Guidelines

Planning Your Meals 285
Freezing 290
Carving 295
Approximate Metric Equivalents 298
Index 299

MEATS AND MAIN DISHES

∎

Stop! Here's where the road to good and easy meal-times begins. You probably start thinking about the meat you're going to serve for dinner first. Right? Well, we do too. Why? Because until that decision has been made, you can't even begin to think intelligently about side dishes and desserts. And besides, you'll have a much better idea of what you can do with the rest of the food budget. It only stands to reason, then, that the main-meal meat becomes the natural starting point for your over-all menu plot, be it daily or weekly.

So choose your entree from this chapter—depending on the week's best buys, or what you have in the freezer. Then move on to the following chapters and round out the three daily meals—remembering snack-time, of course. You'll find some interesting menu clues with many of these main dish recipes. (And if you feel you need to brush up on the basics of meal planning, take our refresher course on pages 285–289.)

BE CHOOSEY

Eye those meat cuts like a pro. Look for flecks of fat within the lean; it's called marbling, and it increases juiciness, flavor and tenderness. Take note of the U.S. stamp of approval, too, which tells you all is well. And where grading is concerned, remember this: U.S. Prime and Choice offer deluxe quality but the less expensive grades, if properly cooked, give you the same good nutrition.

Be bright about bargains. Ask questions about the day's best buys. If your meat retailer has a special on a new cut, go ahead and try it—for variety and for savings. When you spot a particularly good buy on roast lamb, for example, think ahead: Sunday's dinner, Tuesday's casserole. Then buy for two meals at a time and plan to combine the leftovers with speedy, easy

1

convenience foods. Take a clue from Shepherds' Pie (page 54). If you're not looking to "planned overs," buy in exact amounts. Meat that you don't need or won't eat is an expensive loss.

HOW MUCH IS ENOUGH?

As a rule of thumb, figure on 3 ounces of *cooked* meat or 4 ounces of *uncooked* meat for each serving. Here are some guidelines to follow:

Meats with large bone	1 or 1½ servings per pound
Meats with medium bone (pot-roast, ham, chicken, rib roast, dressed fish)	2 or 3 servings per pound
Meats with small or no bone (ground meat, fish fillets, boneless roast)	3 or 4 servings per pound

With main dish combinations like Dried Beef Casserole (page 17), however, the meat protein is supplemented by that of other foods; so you can get by with less meat.

STORING MEAT

Store fresh meat uncovered or loosely covered in the coldest part of the refrigerator. Keep the temperature as low as possible without actually freezing the meat. Plan on using fresh meats within 2 or 3 days, ground meats and variety meats within 24 hours. Cured or smoked meats can be stored 1 to 2 weeks.

Take special care with cooked meats and casseroles. Cool *quickly*, then cover or wrap tightly; they, too, go in coldest part of the refrigerator. You can speed the cooling of a main dish casserole by placing it in a pan of ice and water.

And lucky you, if you own a freezer. You can really shop and cook for the good and easy life. See pages 290–294 for specific information for freezing and thawing meats and main dishes.

Beef

TO ROAST BEEF

Select roast from those listed in chart on page 4. Allow about ½ pound per person—less for boneless roasts, more for roasts with a bone. If desired, season with salt and pepper before, during or after roasting.

Place meat fat side up on rack in open shallow roasting pan. The rack keeps the meat out of the drippings. (In roasts such as standing rib, the ribs form a natural rack.) It is not necessary to baste.

Insert meat thermometer so tip is in center of thickest part of meat and does not touch bone or rest in fat. Do not add water. Do not cover.

Roast meat in 325° oven. (It is not necessary to preheat oven.) Roast to desired degree of doneness (see Timetable), using thermometer reading as final guide.

Roasts are easier to carve if allowed to set 15 to 20 minutes after removing from oven. Since meat continues to cook after removal from oven, if roast is to "set," it should be removed from oven when thermometer registers 5 to 10° lower than the desired doneness.

You'll find some guidelines for carving a standing rib roast on page 295.

HORSERADISH SAUCE

In chilled bowl, beat ½ cup chilled whipping cream until stiff; stir in 3 tablespoons horseradish and ½ teaspoon salt. Refrigerate until serving time.

1 cup.

TIMETABLE

Cut	Approximate Weight	Meat Thermometer Reading	Approximate Cooking Time (Minutes per Pound)
Rib	6 to 8 pounds	140° (rare)	23 to 25
		160° (medium)	27 to 30
		170° (well)	32 to 35
	4 to 6 pounds	140° (rare)	26 to 32
		160° (medium)	34 to 38
		170° (well)	40 to 42
Boneless Rib	5 to 7 pounds	140° (rare)	32
		160° (medium)	38
		170° (well)	48
Rib Eye (Delmonico)*	4 to 6 pounds	140° (rare)	18 to 20
		160° (medium)	20 to 22
		170° (well)	22 to 24
Rolled Rump (high quality)	4 to 6 pounds	150° to 170°	25 to 30
Tip (high quality)	3½ to 4 pounds	140° to 170°	35 to 40
Tenderloin (whole)**	4 to 6 pounds	140° (rare)	45 to 60 minutes (total)
Tenderloin (half)**	2 to 3 pounds	140° (rare)	45 to 50 minutes (total)

*Roast at 350°   **Roast at 425°

CALIFORNIA ROAST

4-pound beef rolled rump roast or tip roast
1 cup orange juice
1 cup tomato juice
¼ cup salad oil
2 teaspoons salt
½ teaspoon allspice
¼ teaspoon chili powder
⅛ teaspoon instant minced garlic
Tangy California Gravy (below)

Place meat in deep glass bowl or plastic bag. Mix remaining ingredients except Tangy California Gravy; pour on meat. Cover; refrigerate at least 4 hours, turning meat occasionally. Remove meat from marinade; reserve 2 cups of the marinade for the gravy.

Place meat fat side up on rack in open shallow roasting pan. Insert meat thermometer so tip is in center of thickest part of meat and does not rest in fat. Roast in 325° oven to desired degree of doneness, about 2 hours. (Meat thermometer should register 150° for rare, 160° for medium, 170° for well.) Place meat on warm platter; keep warm while making gravy.

8 to 10 servings.

TANGY CALIFORNIA GRAVY

Heat reserved marinade to boiling. In tightly covered jar, shake ¼ cup water, 2 tablespoons vinegar and 3 tablespoons flour; stir into hot marinade. (If you prefer a less tangy gravy, omit vinegar and shake flour with ⅓ cup water.) Heat to boiling, stirring constantly. Boil and stir 1 minute. If necessary, season with salt and pepper.

To Cook on a Rotisserie: Insert spit rod lengthwise through center of roast; secure with holding forks. Check balance by rotating spit in palms of hands. Insert meat thermometer in center of thickest part of meat, making sure it does not touch fat or spit. Set oven control to rotisserie. Cook roast until thermometer registers 5 to 10° below desired doneness, about 2 hours.

CRANBERRY-PEPPER ROAST

4-pound beef tip roast
2 tablespoons cracked pepper
3 tablespoons salad oil
2⅔ cups cranberry cocktail
Cranberry Gravy (below)

Score meat (cut lightly in a crisscross pattern). Rub all sides but not ends with pepper. Brown meat in oil over medium heat, about 15 minutes.

Reduce heat; pour cranberry cocktail on meat. Cover tightly; simmer on top of range or in 325° oven 2½ hours or until tender. Place meat on warm platter; keep warm while making gravy.   *8 servings.*

CRANBERRY GRAVY

Strain hot broth; measure 3 cups and heat to boiling. In tightly covered jar, shake ¾ cup cranberry cocktail and ⅓ cup all-purpose flour; stir into hot liquid. Heat to boiling, stirring constantly. Boil and stir 1 minute. Season with salt.

Substitutions

For tip roast: 4-pound beef rolled rump roast.
For cranberry cocktail: 2⅔ cups water with the roast and ¾ cup water in the gravy.

POT-ROAST IN FOIL

4-pound beef chuck pot-roast
1 envelope (about 1½ ounces) onion soup mix
1 can (10½ ounces) condensed cream of
mushroom soup

Place 30x18-inch piece of heavy-duty aluminum foil in baking pan, 13x9x2 inches; place meat on foil. Sprinkle soup mix on meat and spread with cream of mushroom soup. Fold foil over meat and seal securely. Cook in 300° oven 4 hours.

Menu-mate: Orange-Cauliflower Salad (page 104).
8 to 10 servings.

Substitution

For chuck pot-roast: 4-pound beef rump, top round or bottom round roast.

TO BROIL BEEF

For each serving, allow about 1 pound of any steak with a bone, about ½ pound for boneless cuts.

Diagonally slash outer edge of fat on steak at 1-inch intervals to prevent curling (do not cut into lean). Set oven control at broil and/or 550°. Place meat on rack in broiler pan so tops of ¾- to 1-inch steaks are 2 to 3 inches from heat, 1- to 2-inch steaks are 3 to 5 inches from heat. Broil until brown. The meat should be about half done (see Timetable).

If desired, season brown side with salt and pepper. (Always season after browning as salt tends to draw moisture to surface and delay browning.) Turn meat; broil until brown.

TERIYAKI STEAK

2-pound beef sirloin steak, 1 to 1¼ inches thick
½ cup soy sauce
½ cup water
1 tablespoon brown sugar
1½ teaspoons ginger

Diagonally slash outer edge of fat on steak at 1-inch intervals to prevent curling (do not cut into lean). Score meat (cut lightly in a crisscross pattern) and place in shallow glass dish. Heat remaining ingredients to boiling, stirring occasionally; pour on meat.

Cover; refrigerate at least 2 hours, turning meat occasionally.

Set oven control at broil and/or 550°. Remove meat from marinade. Broil 3 to 4 inches from heat about 10 minutes on each side for rare, about 12 minutes for medium. Cut meat across grain at a slanted angle into ¼-inch slices.

Play up the Oriental origin and serve with Snow Peas and Carrot Nuggets (page 117), buttered rice and, as dessert, lemon sherbet and Polynesian Cookies (page 170).   8 *servings*.

Substitution

For sirloin steak: 2 pounds beef round steak, ¾ inch thick; broil 8 minutes for medium, 10 minutes for well.

TIMETABLE

Cut	Approximate Cooking Time per Side	
	Rare	Medium
Rib, Rib Eye or Top Loin Steak		
1 inch	8 minutes	10 minutes
1½ inches	12 minutes	15 minutes
2 inches	17 minutes	22 minutes
Sirloin, Porterhouse or T-bone Steak		
1 inch	10 minutes	12 minutes
1½ inches	15 minutes	17 minutes
Tenderloin (Filet Mignon)		
(4 to 8 ounces)	5 to 7 minutes	8 to 10 minutes
Chuck Eye Steak (high quality)		
1 inch	12 minutes	15 minutes
1½ inches	20 minutes	22 minutes
Ground Beef Patties		
(1 inch)	7 minutes	12 minutes

Charcoal-grilled Steak

Whether you're splurging with sirloin or going the way of a round steak and meat tenderizer, you'll want to do it right. So choose steaks 1 to 2 inches thick. Trim off excess fat (to cut down on flare-ups). Slash rest of fat every 2 inches; this keeps steak from curling. Check timetable below; check coals to be sure they're hot (If you can hold your hand near the grid 3 seconds, they're *not!*) When you're ready to go, grill steaks 4 inches from coals; use tongs to turn. Season after turning and after grilling. To test for doneness, make a knife slit along the bone.

	1 Inch Thick Minutes per Side	2 Inches Thick Minutes per side
Rare	4 to 5	12 to 13
Medium	7 to 8	15 to 17
Well	10 to 11	22 to 25

BARBECUED ROUND STEAK

2-pound beef round steak, ¾ inch thick
2 tablespoons salad oil
3 tablespoons instant chopped onion
1 cup barbecue sauce
½ cup water

Cut meat into 6 serving pieces. In large skillet or Dutch oven, brown meat in oil over medium heat. Stir in remaining ingredients. Cover tightly; cook on top of range or in 325° oven 1½ hours or until meat is tender.

Suggested accompaniments: green beans, Carrots Bouillon (page 113) and Macaroni Fruit Salad (page 105).   *6 servings.*

Substitutions

For round steak: 2-pound beef tip steak.
For instant onion: ½ cup chopped onion.

PEPPER STEAK BORDELAISE

1½ pounds sirloin steak, ½ inch thick
2 tablespoons salad oil
½ teaspoon salt
½ teaspoon freshly ground pepper
1 clove garlic, minced
1 green pepper, cut into 1-inch pieces
  (about 1 cup)
1 can (13¼ ounces) Bordelaise sauce
2 tomatoes, peeled and cut into eighths
3 to 4 cups hot cooked rice

Trim fat and bone from meat; cut into 4 to 6 serving pieces. In large skillet, brown meat on one side in oil over medium-high heat. Turn meat; season with ¼ teaspoon salt and ¼ teaspoon pepper. Brown other side of meat; turn. Season with remaining salt and pepper. Remove meat from skillet.

In same skillet, cook and stir garlic and green pepper until tender. Stir in Bordelaise sauce. Add meat; cook uncovered 10 minutes. Add tomatoes; heat through. Serve on rice.

Orange and Onion Salad (page 105) is a colorful companion.   *4 to 6 servings.*

STEAK SUPPER IN FOIL

1½-pound chuck steak, 1 inch thick
1 can (10½ ounces) condensed cream of
  mushroom soup
1 envelope (about 1½ ounces)
  onion soup mix
3 medium carrots, quartered
2 stalks celery, cut into 2-inch pieces
3 medium potatoes, pared and quartered
2 tablespoons water

Heat oven to 450°. Place 24x18-inch piece of heavy-duty aluminum foil in baking pan; place meat on foil. Stir together mushroom soup and onion soup mix (dry); spread on meat. Top meat with vegetables;

sprinkle water on vegetables. Fold foil over and seal securely. Cook 1½ hours or until tender.

All this meal needs is the zing of Country-style Waldorf Salad (page 106). For dessert, serve ice cream and Sour Cream Brownies (page 162).   *4 servings.*

CUBE STEAK STROGANOFF

> 1 package (about 17½ ounces)
>   beef cubed steaks
> 1 package (5.5 ounces) noodles Stroganoff dinner
> ¼ teaspoon garlic salt
> ⅛ teaspoon pepper
>   Sliced pitted ripe olives
>   Pimiento strips

Cut meat into ½-inch strips. Brown meat over medium-high heat. Drain off fat; set meat aside.

Cook noodles and prepare sauce as directed on package except—omit ground beef and stir garlic salt and pepper into sauce. Stir meat into sauce; heat through. Serve on noodles and garnish with olive slices and pimiento strips.

Company fare with Asparagus à la Polonaise (page 108), Sweet and Sour Beets (page 111) and Orange-Cherry Pie (page 195).   *4 servings.*

LONDON BROIL

Score 1½- to 2-pound flank steak; place in shallow glass dish. Pour 1 bottle (8 ounces) Italian salad dressing on steak. Cover; refrigerate at least 8 hours, turning meat occasionally.

Set oven control at broil and/or 550°. Remove steak from dressing; reserve dressing. Broil steak 3 to 4 inches from heat about 5 minutes on each side, brushing several times with the reserved dressing. Cut meat across grain at a slanted angle into thin slices.

4 to 6 servings.

SWISS STEAK

¼ cup all-purpose flour
½ teaspoon salt
¼ teaspoon pepper
2-pound beef round steak, 1 inch thick
2 tablespoons shortening
1 can (8 ounces) tomatoes
½ cup minced onion
¼ cup minced green pepper
½ teaspoon salt
⅛ teaspon pepper

Mix flour, salt and pepper. Sprinkle one side of meat with half the flour mixture; pound in. Turn meat; pound in remaining flour mixture. Cut meat into 6 serving pieces. Melt shortening in large skillet; brown meat over medium heat, about 15 minutes.

Cover tightly; simmer 1 hour. Add small amount of water if necessary. Mix remaining ingredients; pour on meat. Cover tightly; simmer 30 minutes or until tender.

Broccoli 'n Chips (page 112), combining two family favorites, is a good choice for the vegetable. 6 *servings*.

BRAISED SHORT RIBS

2 pounds beef short ribs, cut into pieces
2 teaspoons salt
½ teaspoon pepper
2 tablespoons shortening
½ cup water
2 tablespoons horseradish
8 small carrots
4 medium onions
3 stalks celery, cut into eighths

Season meat with salt and pepper. Melt shortening in Dutch oven; brown meat over medium-high heat. Drain off fat. Pour water and horseradish on meat.

Cover tightly; simmer on top of range or in 325° oven about 2½ hours or until meat is tender. Add small amount of water if necessary. About 1 hour before end of cooking time, add vegetables.

Nice with fluffy mashed potatoes and Tossed Salad with Classic Dressing (page 96).   *4 servings.*

BEEF MUSHROOM

> 1 pound beef stew meat, cut into 1-inch cubes
> ½ teaspoon seasoned instant meat tenderizer
> 2 tablespoons salad oil
> 1 can (10½ ounces) mushroom gravy
> 5 ounces uncooked medium noodles

Sprinkle meat with tenderizer; pierce each piece with fork. Cover; refrigerate 2 to 24 hours.

In large skillet, brown meat in oil over medium heat. Reduce heat; stir in gravy. Cover tightly; simmer about 45 minutes, stirring occasionally. (Meat will not be fork-tender but it will be tender to eat.)

Cook noodles as directed on package; drain. Serve beef and gravy on noodles.

Complete the meal with Green and Gold Salad (page 97) and Biscuit Fan-tans (page 142). And for dessert, offer Caramel Peach Crisps (page 151).

3 or 4 servings.

Stew-pendous Substitutes

You're proud of your beef stew and you always buy foreshank or brisket beef. But why not branch out? Especially if you find a special on beef. From the chuck, use blade or arm pot-roast. From the round, use rump or round roast; the steaks, too. For a lighter stew, switch off to veal or lamb—just forego the browning.

GOOD BROWN STEW

2 pounds beef stew meat, cut into 1-inch cubes
1 to 2 tablespoons salad oil
¼ cup instant chopped onion
1 small bay leaf
2 teaspoons salt
1 teaspoon sugar
¼ teaspoon allspice
⅛ teaspoon instant minced garlic
1 teaspoon lemon juice
1 teaspoon Worcestershire sauce
1 can (16 ounces) whole carrots, drained
(reserve liquid)
1 can (15 ounces) whole potatoes, drained
(reserve liquid)
1 can (8 ounces) whole onions, drained
(reserve liquid)

In Dutch oven, brown meat in oil over medium heat. Sprinkle seasonings on meat. Add enough water to reserved vegetable liquids to measure 4 cups; pour on meat. Heat to boiling.

Reduce heat; simmer 2 hours or until meat is tender. Add small amount of water if necessary. Add vegetables; simmer 15 minutes longer or until vegetables are heated through.

Serve with a simple salad of lettuce wedges and a typical U.S.A. dessert—strawberry shortcake.

6 servings.

Substitutions

For instant onion: 1 large onion, chopped.
For instant garlic: 1 clove garlic, minced.
For canned vegetables: 6 carrots, quartered, 3 medium potatoes, pared and cut into eighths, 8 small onions; add 30 minutes before end of cooking time.

OVEN STEW

2 pounds beef round steak, cut into 1-inch cubes
2 cups sliced carrots
1 cup sliced celery
2 medium onions, sliced
1 can (5 ounces) water chestnuts, drained and sliced
1 can (6 ounces) sliced mushrooms, drained
3 tablespoons flour
1 tablespoon sugar
1 tablespoon salt
1 can (16 ounces) tomatoes
1 cup red Burgundy

Mix meat, carrots, celery, onions, water chestnuts and mushrooms in Dutch oven. Mix flour, sugar and salt; stir into meat mixture. Stir in tomatoes and wine. Cover tightly; cook in 325° oven or on top of range 4 hours.

Bread in the Round (page 143) goes well with this easy but elegant stew.   6 *servings.*

Substitution

For Burgundy: 1 cup water and 1 teaspoon instant beef bouillon.

PICCALILLI STEW

1 can (24 ounces) beef stew
½ cup pickle relish

Stir together stew and pickle relish in saucepan. Simmer about 10 minutes or until heated through.

Quick meal plan: sliced tomatoes, bread sticks and a fixed-up frozen apple pie (page 193).   4 *servings.*

VARIATION

■ *Stroganoff Stew:* Stir ½ cup dairy sour cream into heated stew, or serve sour cream as a garnish. Nice to serve on toast.

SAVORY BEEF PIE

>   2 tablespoons shortening
>   ¼ cup chopped onion
>   2 tablespoons chopped green pepper
>   2 cups cut-up cooked beef
>   2 cups cooked vegetables
>   1¼ cups gravy
>   Drop Biscuits

Melt shortening in large skillet; cook and stir onion and green pepper until tender. Stir in meat, vegetables and gravy; heat about 5 minutes.

Heat oven to 450°. Prepare 10 to 12 Drop Biscuits as directed on buttermilk baking mix package except— drop dough by spoonfuls onto hot meat mixture. Bake uncovered 15 to 20 minutes or until biscuits are brown.

Serve with individual tossed green salads and, for the finale, Triple Fudge Cake (page 180).

4 to 6 servings.

Substitutions

For gravy: 1 can (10¾ ounces) gravy or 1 envelope (⅞ ounce) gravy mix prepared as directed.

For cooked vegetables: 1 package (10 ounces) frozen mixed vegetables, broken apart.

VARIATIONS

■ *Savory Lamb or Veal Pie:* Substitute 2 cups cut-up cooked lamb or veal for the beef.

Spicing Up Yesterday's Beef

Sunday dinner's gone, but the pot-roast lingers on. Lucky you, you're a meal ahead. And here's your chance to experiment with spices. Accompany the second go-round with fluffy mashed potatoes and whip in a taste of horseradish and a pinch of dill weed. Delicious! Or how about beefing up the leftover gravy with a dash of allspice or nutmeg?

If cold beef sandwiches are a specialty of the house, spice up the spread for the bread—just a sprinkling of chili powder or ginger mixed into the butter.

For a salad supper, try this: diced cold beef and rice, mixed with mayonnaise and spiced with dill weed, mace or soy sauce.

However and whatever you spice, sprinkle softly. You know what they say about too much of a good thing.

DRIED BEEF CASSEROLE

1 cup uncooked elbow macaroni
    (about 4 ounces)
1 can (10½ ounces) condensed cream
    of mushroom soup
½ cup milk
1 cup shredded Cheddar cheese
    (about 4 ounces)
3 tablespoons finely chopped onion
¼ pound dried beef,* cut into bite-size pieces
2 hard-cooked eggs, sliced

Heat oven to 350°. Cook macaroni as directed on package; drain. Blend soup and milk in large bowl. Stir in cheese, onion, macaroni and dried beef; fold in eggs.

Pour mixture into ungreased 1½-quart casserole. Cover tightly; bake 30 minutes or until heated through.

4 to 6 servings.

---

* *If dried beef is very salty, pour boiling water over it and drain.*

Substitution

For fresh onion: 1 tablespoon instant minced onion.

CORNED BEEF STEW

  1 can (12 ounces) corned beef
  1 can (15 ounces) sliced white potatoes, drained
  1 can (16 ounces) tomatoes, cut up
  1 can (16 ounces) whole onions
  1 package (10 ounces) frozen peas and carrots
  1 teaspoon salt
  ½ teaspoon marjoram
  ½ teaspoon thyme
  2 cups shredded Cheddar cheese (8 ounces)

Break apart corned beef in Dutch oven. Stir in potatoes, tomatoes (with liquid), onions (with liquid), frozen peas and carrots, salt, marjoram and thyme. Heat to boiling, stirring occasionally. Reduce heat. Cover tightly; simmer 30 minutes. Serve topped with cheese.

6 servings.

LIVER

To Panfry: Have liver sliced ½ to ¾ inch thick. Coat with flour. Melt ¼ cup shortening in skillet; brown liver over medium-high heat, 2 to 3 minutes on each side. Season to taste.

To Broil: Have baby beef, veal (calf) or lamb liver sliced ½ to ¾ inch thick. Dip into melted bacon drippings, butter or margarine. Set oven control at broil and/or 550°. Broil liver 3 to 5 inches from heat just long enough for meat to change color and become light brown, about 3 minutes on each side.

To Braise: Have beef or pork liver sliced ½ to ¾ inch thick. Coat with flour. Brown in small amount of fat. Add ¼ cup liquid. Cover tightly; cook on top of range or in 350° oven 20 to 30 minutes. For a large piece, increase liquid to ½ cup; cook about 30 minutes per pound.

LIVER AND ONIONS

Have 1 pound liver sliced ½ to ¾ inch thick. In large skillet, cook and stir 2 cups thinly sliced onion in 3 tablespoons butter or margarine until tender. Remove from skillet; keep warm. Panfry liver as directed, page 18. Add onions for the last minute of cooking.

4 servings.

LIVER CREOLE

4 slices bacon
1 pound sliced beef liver
3 tablespoons flour
⅓ cup chopped green pepper
1 can (16 ounces) tomatoes
1½ teaspoons salt
½ teaspoon chili powder
⅛ teaspoon cayenne red pepper

Fry bacon until crisp; remove bacon and drain. Drain off all but 3 tablespoons fat. Coat liver with flour; brown in bacon fat. Stir in remaining ingredients except bacon. Cover tightly; simmer 20 minutes. Garnish with bacon. *4 servings.*

BAKED MEATBALLS

2 pounds ground beef
1 cup dry bread crumbs
½ cup milk
2 eggs
¼ cup instant minced onion
2 teaspoons salt
¼ teaspoon pepper

Mix all ingredients. Shape mixture by ¼ cupfuls into balls (do not pack). Place in ungreased jelly roll pan, 15½x10½x1 inch. Bake uncovered in 350° oven 30 to 40 minutes or until brown. *6 servings (18 meatballs).*

Substitutions

For dry bread crumbs: 3 slices bread, cubed.
For instant onion: ¾ cup minced onion.

MEATBALL STEW

1 pound ground beef
1 egg
½ cup dry bread crumbs
¼ cup milk
2 tablespoons instant minced onion
1 teaspoon salt
⅛ teaspoon pepper
1 can (16 ounces) stewed tomatoes
1 package (24 ounces) frozen vegetables for stew
2 teaspoons salt

Mix ground beef, egg, bread crumbs, milk, onion, 1 teaspoon salt and the pepper. Shape mixture by ¼ cupfuls into balls (do not pack); brown in Dutch oven over medium-high heat. Drain off fat.

Stir in stewed tomatoes, frozen vegetables and 2 teaspoons salt; heat to boiling. Reduce heat. Cover tightly; simmer on top of range or in 325° oven until vegetables are tender, 1¼ to 1½ hours.

Serve with Garlic French Bread Sticks (page 140) and, for dessert, Spice Cake with Browned Butter Icing (page 187).   *4 or 5 servings.*

Substitution

For instant onion: ⅓ cup minced onion.

BAKED MEAT LOAF

2 pounds ground beef
1 cup seasoned bread crumbs
¾ cup milk
2 eggs
2 tablespoons instant minced onion
2 teaspoons salt
¼ teaspoon pepper

Mix all ingredients. Spread mixture in ungreased loaf pan, 9x5x3 inches. Bake uncovered in 350° oven about 1½ hours or until done.   *8 to 10 servings.*

CORN HAMBURGER BAKE

    1 pound ground beef
    1 large onion, sliced
    ¼ cup sliced celery
    2 cans (16 ounces each) cream-style corn
    1 teaspoon salt
    ¼ teaspoon pepper
    1 teaspoon instant beef bouillon
    1 cup buttermilk baking mix
    2 tablespoons butter or margarine, melted
    ¼ teaspoon garlic salt

Heat oven to 450°. Cook and stir ground beef, onion and celery in large skillet until meat is brown. Drain off fat.

Reserve ½ cup of the corn. Stir remaining corn, the salt, pepper and bouillon into meat mixture; heat to boiling. Pour into ungreased 2½-quart casserole.

Stir baking mix and reserved corn with fork to a soft dough. Drop dough by tablespoonfuls onto hot meat mixture. Mix butter and garlic salt; drizzle half the butter on biscuit dough. Bake 20 to 25 minutes. Brush biscuits with remaining butter.

For the salad, offer lettuce with a simple dressing of mayonnaise laced with chili sauce or turn to your favorite combination of mixed greens.   *6 servings.*

Substitution

    For instant bouillon: 1 beef bouillon cube.

COMPLETE HAMBURGER CASSEROLE

> 1 pound ground beef
> 1 tablespoon instant minced onion
> ½ teaspoon salt
> ½ teaspoon pepper
> 1 package (10 ounces) frozen mixed vegetables,
>   broken apart
> 1 can (10¾ ounces) condensed Cheddar cheese soup
> 1 package (16 ounces) frozen fried shredded
>   potato rounds

Heat oven to 375°. Mix beef, onion, salt and pepper in ungreased 2-quart casserole. Arrange vegetables on meat; pour cheese soup on vegetables. Cover with frozen potato rounds. Bake uncovered 1 hour or until potatoes are golden brown.

Add crunch to this dinner in a dish with celery and carrot sticks. Try Raspberry-Raspberry (page 156) and Almond Shortbreads (page 166) for dessert.

4 or 5 servings.

Substitutions

For instant onion: 3 tablespoons minced onion.

For frozen mixed vegetables: 1 package (10 ounces) frozen peas and carrots, corn or chopped broccoli.

For cheese soup: 1 cup cheese sauce.

HEARTY HAMBURGER BAKE

1 pound ground beef
1 small onion, chopped (about ⅓ cup)
1 teaspoon salt
¼ teaspoon pepper
1 can (16 ounces) cut green beans, drained
1 can (10¾ ounces) condensed tomato soup
Instant mashed potato puffs
(enough for 4 servings)

Heat oven to 350°. Cook and stir meat and onion in large skillet until meat is brown. Drain off fat. Stir in seasonings, beans and soup. Pour into ungreased 2-quart casserole.

Prepare potato puffs as directed on package. Spoon potatoes onto meat mixture in 4 mounds. Bake uncovered 30 minutes or until hot and bubbly. *4 servings.*

COUNTRY-STYLE HOMINY

1 pound ground beef
¼ cup instant chopped onion
⅛ teaspoon instant minced garlic
⅓ cup chopped ripe or pimiento-stuffed olives
1 can (28 ounces) tomatoes
1 teaspoon salt
1 teaspoon oregano
⅛ teaspoon red pepper sauce
¼ cup butter or margarine
2 cans (20 ounces each) hominy, drained

Cook and stir ground beef, onion and garlic until meat is brown. Drain off fat. Stir in remaining ingredients except butter and hominy. Simmer uncovered 1 hour.

Melt butter in medium saucepan. Stir hominy into butter; heat through. Serve sauce on hominy.

4 to 6 servings.

Substitutions

For instant onion: 1 large onion, chopped.
For instant garlic: 1 clove garlic, minced.
For hominy: 3 to 4 cups hot cooked rice, macaroni or noodles.

HAMBURGER STROGANOFF

1 pound ground beef
½ cup minced onion
1 clove garlic, minced
1 can (10½ ounces) condensed cream of
  mushroom soup
1 teaspoon salt
1 cup dairy sour cream
2 to 3 cups hot cooked noodles

Cook and stir ground beef, onion and garlic until meat is brown. Stir in mushroom soup and salt; simmer uncovered 10 minutes. Mix in sour cream; heat through. Serve on noodles.   *4 servings.*

Substitutions

For fresh onion: 3 tablespoons instant minced onion.
For garlic clove: ⅛ teaspoon instant minced garlic.

CHILI CON CARNE

1 pound ground beef
½ pound bulk pork sausage
1 can (16 ounces) tomatoes
1 can (15½ ounces) chili beans
4 medium onions, chopped (about 2 cups)

In large skillet, cook and stir ground beef and pork sausage until brown. Drain off fat. Stir in remaining ingredients; simmer uncovered 1 hour.

Nice with Molded Waldorf Salad (page 100) and crackers or quick-from-a-mix corn muffins. *4 servings.*

Substitution

For chili beans: 1 can (15½ ounces) kidney beans and 1 to 2 tablespoons chili powder.

GIANT BURGER

1½ pounds ground beef
1½ teaspoons salt
1 package (3 ounces) cream cheese, softened
1 tablespoon prepared mustard
1 tablespoon horseradish, drained
1 can (3½ ounces) French fried onion rings,
   if desired

Heat oven to 350°. Mix ground beef and salt; divide in half. Pat one half evenly in 8-inch pie pan. Mix cream cheese, mustard and horseradish; spread to within 1 inch of edge of meat in pan.

Shape remaining meat into 8-inch circle. Place on cheese mixture; pinch edge to seal securely. Bake uncovered 45 minutes for medium, 55 minutes for well.

Heat onion rings in oven 5 minutes. Remove meat to large serving plate; arrange onion rings around meat. Cut into wedges.

Complete menu plan: Mushroom Italian Green Beans (page 111), Cucumber Relish Mold (page 99), potatoes and Caramel Peach Crisps (page 151).

4 to 6 servings.

VARIATION

■ *Gourmet Burger:* Add 2 tablespoons crumbled blue cheese to cream cheese mixture.

Pork

TO ROAST FRESH PORK

Select roast from those listed in chart at right. Allow
about ½ pound per person—less for boneless roasts,
more for roasts with a bone. If desired, season with
salt and pepper.

Place meat fat side up on rack in open shallow
roasting pan. The rack keeps the meat out of the drippings. (In some roasts, the ribs form a natural rack.)
It is not necessary to baste.

Insert meat thermometer so tip is in center of thickest
part of meat and does not touch bone or rest in fat. Do
not add water. Do not cover.

Roast meat in 325° oven. (It is not necessary to preheat oven.) Roast to desired degree of doneness (see
Timetable), using thermometer reading as final guide.
Roasts are easier to carve if allowed to set 15 to 20
minutes after removing from oven. Since meat continues to cook after removal from oven, if roast is to
"set," it should be removed from oven when thermometer registers 5° lower than the desired doneness.

You'll find some guidelines for carving a pork loin
roast on page 296.

MUSTARD-TOMATO SAUCE

    2 egg yolks
    ½ cup sugar
    ½ cup undiluted condensed tomato soup
    ½ cup prepared mustard
    ½ cup butter or margarine
    ¼ cup vinegar

Mix all ingredients in saucepan. Cook over low heat,
stirring constantly, until sauce thickens. This is one of
our favorite accompaniments for pork roasts.   *2 cups.*

TIMETABLE

Cut	Approximate Weight	Meat Thermometer Reading	Approximate Cooking Time (Minutes per Pound)
Loin			
Center	3 to 5 pounds	170°	30 to 35
Half	5 to 7 pounds	170°	35 to 40
Blade or Sirloin	3 to 4 pounds	170°	40 to 45
Boneless Top (double)	3 to 5 pounds	170°	35 to 45
Boneless Top	2 to 4 pounds	170°	30 to 35
Picnic Shoulder			
Arm Picnic	5 to 8 pounds	170°	30 to 35
Rolled	3 to 5 pounds	170°	35 to 40
Blade Boston	4 to 6 pounds	170°	40 to 45
Leg (fresh ham)			
Whole (bone in)	12 to 14 pounds	170°	22 to 26
Boneless	10 to 14 pounds	170°	24 to 28
Half (bone in)	5 to 8 pounds	170°	35 to 40
Tenderloin	½ to 1 pound		¾ to 1 hour (total)
Spareribs, Back Ribs, Country-style Ribs*			1½ to 2½ hours (total)

* All three are always cooked until well done.

TO BROIL FRESH PORK

For each serving, allow about ½ to ¾ pound of chops and steaks with bone in, about ⅓ pound for boneless cuts.

Diagonally slash outer edge of fat on chops or steaks at 1-inch intervals to prevent curling (do not cut into lean). Set oven control at broil and/or 550°. Place meat on rack in broiler so top of meat is 3 to 5 inches from heat. Broil until light brown. The meat should be about half done by this time (see Timetable).

If desired, season brown side with salt and pepper. (Always season after browning as salt tends to draw moisture to surface and delay browning.) Turn meat; broil until brown.

TIMETABLE

Cut	Approximate Cooking Time per Side
Chops (¾ to 1 inch)	10 to 12 minutes
Shoulder Steaks (½ to ¾ inch)	10 to 12 minutes
Patties (1 inch)	10 to 12 minutes
Kabobs (1½x1½x¾ inch)	11 to 12 minutes

PORK CHOP DINNER

    4 pork loin or rib chops, 1 inch thick
    ¼ cup water
    4 medium potatoes, pared
    4 small carrots
    4 medium onions
    1 teaspoon salt
    ¼ teaspoon pepper

Brown meat in large skillet over medium heat. Drain off fat. Add water and vegetables. Season with salt and pepper. Cover tightly; simmer 1 hour or until done.

4 servings.

MEXICAN PORK CHOPS

    4 pork loin or rib chops, 1 inch thick
    1 teaspoon salt
    ⅛ teaspoon pepper
    1 medium green pepper, cut into 4 rings
    4 tablespoons uncooked instant rice
    1 can (about 16 ounces) stewed tomatoes

Brown meat over medium heat. Season with salt and pepper. Top each chop with a green pepper ring; fill each ring with 1 tablespoon rice. Carefully pour ¼ cup stewed tomatoes on rice in each ring. Pour remaining tomatoes into skillet. Cover tightly; simmer 1 hour or until done. Add a small amount of water if necessary.

Menu mates: lettuce wedges, Perky Lima Beans (page 110) and Graham Cracker Torte (page 184).

4 servings.

STUFFING-TOPPED PORK CHOPS

    6 pork loin or rib chops, 1 inch thick
    ½ cup water
    ¼ cup chopped celery
    2 tablespoons finely chopped onion
    2 tablespoons butter or margarine
    2 cups herb-seasoned stuffing
    1 can (8 ounces) cream-style corn

Heat oven to 350°. Arrange meat in ungreased baking dish, 13½x9x2 inches. Add the water and bake uncovered 45 minutes.

Cook and stir celery and onion in butter until tender; stir in stuffing and corn. Spoon ⅓ cup stuffing onto each chop. Bake uncovered 30 minutes longer.

Accompany with buttered spinach and Okra and Tomato Salad (page 98).

6 servings.

BRAISED PORK CHOPS

> 4 pork loin or rib chops, ½ to 1 inch thick
> 1 teaspoon salt
> ¼ teaspoon pepper
> ¼ cup pineapple juice
> Pan Gravy (below)

Brown meat over medium heat. Season with salt and pepper. Reduce heat; pour pineapple juice on meat. Cover tightly; simmer ½-inch chops 20 to 25 minutes, 1-inch chops 30 to 35 minutes or until done. Serve with Pan Gravy.

Sprouts Sauté (page 112), an apple salad and mashed potatoes are nice serve-alongs for the braised chops. For dessert try Coconut Pudding (page 154).

4 servings.

PAN GRAVY

Place meat on warm platter; keep warm while making gravy. Pour drippings (fat and juices) into bowl, leaving brown particles in pan. Let fat rise to top of drippings; skim off fat, reserving ¼ cup. Place the ¼ cup reserved fat in pan. Blend in ¼ cup all-purpose flour. Cook over low heat, stirring until mixture is smooth and bubbly. Remove from heat. Stir in 2 cups water. Heat to boiling, stirring constantly. Boil and stir 1 minute. Season with salt and pepper.

2 cups.

Substitution

For pineapple juice: ¼ cup apple juice or ¼ cup water.

For Perfect Pan Gravy

Pan gravy is really very simple. Just follow the instructions carefully and rely on three little secrets to success:

☐ Be exact with the fat—too little makes the gravy lumpy.

☐ Be just as exact with the flour—too little makes the gravy greasy. And when you blend it into the fat, scrape the pan often as you go.

☐ Then boil for just a minute, stirring until smooth. You can even deepen the color with a few drops of bottled brown bouquet sauce.

BARBECUED RIBS

4½ pounds pork back ribs, cut into pieces
¼ cup soy sauce
1 tablespoon plus 2 teaspoons cornstarch
1 bottle (18 ounces) barbecue sauce

Arrange ribs meaty side up in open shallow roasting pan. Do not add water. Do not cover. Roast in 325° oven 1¾ hours.

Mix remaining ingredients; pour on meat. Bake uncovered about 45 minutes longer or until meat is done.

Team up with Best Tossed Salad (page 94) and Hopping John (page 137), a zesty combo of blackeye peas and rice.   *5 or 6 servings.*

Substitution

For back ribs: 4½ pounds spareribs.

BAKED SPARERIBS

Arrange 3 to 4 pounds spareribs meaty side up in open shallow roasting pan. Do not add water. Do not cover. Roast in 325° oven 1½ to 2½ hours or until meat is done.   *4 servings.*

GLAZED BARBECUED SPARERIBS

>   4 servings ready-to-eat barbecued spareribs
>   ¼ cup orange marmalade, melted
>   2 tablespoons lemon juice

Heat oven to 300°. Arrange spareribs meaty side up in ungreased baking pan, 13x9x2 inches. Mix marmalade and lemon juice; spoon onto ribs. Heat uncovered 25 minutes or until heated through.

While you're at the deli, pick up some coleslaw and potato salad. Garnish them prettily and no one will guess you didn't do it *all* yourself.   *4 servings.*

Substitution

For orange marmalade: ¼ cup lime marmalade.

PINEAPPLE-STUFFED SPARERIBS

>   1 rack spareribs (about 3 pounds)
>   ¼ cup chopped celery
>   2 tablespoons chopped onion
>   2 tablespoons butter or margarine
>   1 can (13¼ ounces) pineapple tidbits,
>   drained (reserve syrup)
>   ½ teaspoon cloves
>   2 cups packaged seasoned stuffing

Tie spareribs in circle; place bone tips up on rack in open shallow roasting pan. Do not add water. Do not cover. Roast in 325° oven 2 hours.

Cook and stir celery and onion in butter until tender. Mix with pineapple, cloves, stuffing and enough reserved pineapple syrup to moisten. Spoon dressing into circle of ribs; bake uncovered 30 minutes longer or until meat is done.   *4 servings.*

GLAZED RIBS

    4 pounds spareribs
    1 can (15 ounces) tomato sauce
    1 envelope (.7 ounce) onion salad
       dressing mix
    ¼ cup vinegar
    ¼ cup light molasses
    2 tablespoons salad oil
    1 teaspoon dry mustard
    1 cup water

Heat oven to 350°. Arrange spareribs meaty side up in open shallow roasting pan. Heat remaining ingredients to boiling, stirring constantly. Boil and stir 3 minutes. Pour sauce on meat. Bake uncovered about 1½ hours, basting 4 or 5 times.

Buttered Brussels sprouts and Green Rice (page 137) are nice accompaniments.   *4 servings.*

Substitution

For spareribs: 4 pounds pork back ribs or country-style ribs.

TENDERLOIN PATTIES SUPREME

    6 pork tenderloin patties, 1 inch thick
      Salt
    6 onion slices, ¼ inch thick
    ¼ cup catsup
    ⅓ cup lemon-lime carbonated beverage
    1 teaspoon Worcestershire sauce
    ⅛ teaspoon chili powder

Season patties with salt; arrange in ungreased baking pan, 9x9x2 inches. Top each patty with an onion slice. Bake patties uncovered in 325° oven 30 minutes.

Mix remaining ingredients; pour on patties. Bake uncovered 30 minutes longer. Serve patties with sauce.

Pork patties for a party? Sure! Dress them up with Green Beans and Bacon (page 109) and Poppy Seed Noodles (page 131). For dessert, Lemon Pudding Shells (page 155).   *4 servings.*

PORK AND FRUIT SKILLET

Uncooked instant rice (enough for 6 servings)
1 can (13¼ ounces) pineapple chunks, drained
  (reserve syrup)
1 package (about 17½ ounces) frozen breaded
  pork patties (10)
1 cup bottled sweet and sour sauce
½ cup dried or canned apricot halves
½ cup water

Cook rice as directed on package except—substitute reserved pineapple syrup for part of the water. Cook pork patties as directed on package.

While meat cooks, heat pineapple chunks, sweet and sour sauce, apricot halves and water to boiling. Reduce heat; simmer uncovered 10 minutes. Spoon sauce on pork patties. Serve with rice.

For a quick-as-can-be meal, serve with buttered peas and Pudding-Pie Dessert (page 154), a speedy but smashingly attractive combination of canned pudding and pie filling.   *5 or 6 servings.*

CHEESE-TOPPED PORK CUTLETS

Pound 1½ pounds pork cutlets to flatten. Season with salt and pepper. Dip into beaten egg, then coat with dry bread crumbs. Melt shortening in large skillet; brown meat over medium heat. Pour in small amount of water. Cover tightly; simmer 30 minutes.

Arrange cutlets in lightly oiled baking pan; sprinkle 1 package (4 ounces) shredded Cheddar cheese on meat. Set oven control at broil and/or 550°. Broil until cheese is bubbly.   *6 servings.*

CHINESE PORK AND RICE

⅔ cup uncooked regular rice
1 medium onion, chopped
2 stalks celery, cut into diagonal slices
2 tablespoons salad oil
1½ cups boiling water
1 teaspoon instant chicken or beef bouillon
2 tablespoons soy sauce
2 cups cut-up cooked pork (¾- to 1-inch pieces)
1 medium green pepper, chopped

In large skillet, cook and stir rice, onion and celery in oil over medium heat until rice is golden brown and onion is tender. Stir in remaining ingredients except green pepper and heat to boiling. Reduce heat.

Cover tightly; simmer 18 to 20 minutes or until rice is tender and liquid absorbed. Stir in green pepper. Cover tightly; simmer 10 minutes longer.

Serve with a salad of tossed greens sparked with watermelon pickles.   *4 servings.*

Note: Be sure to use regular rice—not converted or instant.

Substitution

For instant bouillon: 1 chicken or beef bouillon cube.

SUBGUM

1 can (4 ounces) sliced mushrooms
2 cups diced cooked pork
4 stalks celery, sliced (about 2 cups)
1 tablespoon butter or margarine
1½ cups gravy
1 can (20 ounces) bean sprouts, drained
Chow mein noodles or hot cooked rice

Cook and stir mushrooms (with liquid), pork and celery in butter until celery is tender, about 10 minutes. Stir in gravy; reduce heat. Cover tightly; simmer 15 minutes. Stir in bean sprouts; heat through. Serve on chow mein noodles.   *4 servings.*

BAKED MEAT SANDWICH

>   1 pound ground lean pork
>   ½ cup chopped onion
>   ½ cup shredded Swiss cheese
>   ¼ cup grated Parmesan cheese
>   1 egg, slightly beaten
>   2 tablespoons snipped parsley
>   1½ teaspoons salt
>   ¼ teaspoon red pepper sauce
>   Rolled Biscuit dough
>   2 tablespoons mayonnaise or salad dressing

Heat oven to 400°. Grease baking pan, 8x8x2 inches, or
4 individual casseroles. In large skillet, cook and stir
pork and onion until pork is light brown. Drain off
fat. Stir in cheeses, egg, parsley, salt and pepper sauce.
Remove from heat.

Prepare Biscuit dough for 10 to 12 biscuits as directed on buttermilk baking mix package except—add
mayonnaise with the water. With floured fingers, pat
half the dough into pan. Spread meat mixture on
dough. Turn remaining dough onto meat mixture;
with floured fingers, pat on meat. Bake uncovered 25
to 30 minutes. Especially delicious with cheese or
mushroom sauce.   *4 to 6 servings.*

Substitution

For pork: 1 pound ground beef.

BAKED HAM

Select ham or other cut from those listed in chart on
page 38. Allow about ½ pound per person—less for
boneless roasts, more for a roast with a bone. Place ham
fat side up on rack in open shallow roasting pan. The
rack keeps the meat out of the drippings. It is not
necessary to baste.

Insert meat thermometer so tip is in center of
thickest part of meat and does not touch bone or rest in
fat. Do not add water. Do not cover.

Roast meat in 325° oven. (It is not necessary to preheat oven.) Roast to desired degree of doneness (see Timetable), using thermometer reading as final guide.

Ham is easier to carve if allowed to set 15 to 20 minutes after removing from oven. Since meat continues to cook after removal from oven, if ham is to "set," it should be removed when thermometer registers 5° lower than desired doneness.

You'll find some guidelines for carving a whole ham on page 296.

GLAZED BAKED HAM

For a glazed ham, remove ham 30 minutes before it is done. Pour drippings from pan. Score fat surface of ham lightly, cutting uniform diamond shapes. A whole clove can be inserted in each. Pour on Orange Glaze (below); continue baking 30 minutes, basting as directed. Or use any of the commercial glazes now available in supermarkets, but be sure to follow the directions on the label.

ORANGE GLAZE

> 1 can (6 ounces) frozen orange
>   juice concentrate (thawed)
> ¼ cup brown sugar (packed)
> ¼ teaspoon cloves
> ¼ teaspoon cinnamon

Mix all ingredients. Pour half the glaze on ham. Baste ham occasionally with remaining glaze during the last 30 minutes of baking time. *Enough for a 4-pound ham.*

TIMETABLE

Cut	Approximate Weight	Meat Thermometer Reading	Approximate Cooking Time (Minutes per Pound)
Ham (cook before eating)			
Whole	10 to 14 pounds	160°	18 to 20
Half	5 to 7 pounds	160°	22 to 25
Shank Portion	3 to 4 pounds	160°	35 to 40
Rump Portion	3 to 4 pounds	160°	35 to 40
Ham (fully cooked)			
Whole	10 to 15 pounds	140°	15 to 18
Half	5 to 7 pounds	140°	18 to 24
Loin	3 to 5 pounds	160°	25 to 30
	5 to 8 pounds	170°	35
Arm Picnic (cook before eating)	5 to 8 pounds	140°	25 to 30
Arm Picnic (fully cooked)	2 to 3 pounds	170°	35 to 40
Shoulder Roll	2 to 4 pounds	160°	35 to 40
Canadian-style Bacon	2 pounds	160°	1½ hours (total)
Ham Loaf	1 inch thick		¾ to 1 hour (total)
Ham Patties			

SMOKED HAM SLICE

Allow about ½ to ¾ pound for each serving. Diagonally slash outer edge of fat at 1-inch intervals to prevent curling. Then proceed with your favorite method of cooking.

To Bake: Place 1-inch-thick ham slice in ungreased baking dish. If desired, spread with ¼ cup favorite jelly, slightly beaten, or Brown Sugar Glaze: Mix ½ cup brown sugar (packed), ¼ teaspoon dry mustard and 1½ teaspoons vinegar. Bake uncovered in 325° oven 30 minutes.

To Panfry: Rub skillet with small piece of fat cut from slice. Cook ½-inch-thick ham slice over medium heat about 3 minutes or until light brown. Turn ham slice; cook about 3 minutes longer.

To Broil: Set oven control at broil and/or 550°. Place 1-inch-thick ham slice on rack in broiler pan so top of ham slice is 3 inches from heat. Broil about 10 minutes or until light brown. Turn ham slice; broil about 6 minutes longer. If desired, after turning and during last 2 minutes of broiling, brush with 3 tablespoons jelly, slightly beaten.

HAM 'N LIMAS

 1 package (10 ounces) frozen baby lima beans
 1 fully cooked smoked ham slice, 1 inch thick
 1 cup shredded Cheddar cheese (4 ounces)

Cook lima beans as directed on package; drain. Diagonally slash outer edge of fat on ham slice at 1-inch intervals to prevent curling.

Set oven control at broil and/or 550°. Broil ham 3 inches from heat about 10 minutes or until light brown. Turn meat; broil 6 minutes longer. Top with lima beans and sprinkle with cheese. Broil about 2 minutes or until cheese is melted and bubbly.

For family or company, serve with Cinnamon-Applesauce Salad (page 102), Tangy Noodles (page 130) and Perfect Pineapple Pie (page 196).

4 to 6 servings.

TAHITIAN HAM DINNER

> 1 fully cooked smoked ham slice, ¾ inch thick
>   (about 1½ pounds)
> 2 packages (10 ounces each) frozen
>   Brussels sprouts
> 2 tablespoons water
> 1 or 2 bananas
>   Sauce (below)

Place 30x18-inch piece of heavy-duty aluminum foil in jelly roll pan, 15½x10½x1 inch. Place ham slice on foil; arrange Brussels sprouts around ham. Sprinkle water on Brussels sprouts. Fold foil over meat and seal securely. Cook in 400° oven 40 minutes.

Open foil packet; fold edges back, keeping Brussels sprouts covered. Diagonally slice bananas onto meat. Pour Sauce on bananas.

Set oven control at broil and/or 550°. Broil 4 to 5 inches from heat 5 minutes or until Sauce is bubbly and brown.   *6 or 7 servings.*

SAUCE

Heat 12 large marshmallows (or 1 cup miniature marshmallows), 3 tablespoons milk and 2 tablespoons butter or margarine over medium heat, stirring constantly, just until marshmallows are melted.

SCALLOPED POTATOES "AND"

Prepare 1 package (5.5 ounces) scalloped potatoes as directed except—try one of the additions below:

■ *Canadian-style Bacon:* Before baking, top with four ½-inch-thick slices Canadian-style bacon. Bake 30 to 35 minutes.

■ *Ham Cubes:* Omit butter; stir in 1½ cups cubed cooked ham. Bake 35 to 40 minutes.

■ *Sausage:* Omit butter; top with 1 package (8 ounces) fully cooked brown and serve link sausage. Bake 35 to 40 minutes.   *4 servings.*

HAM CASSEROLE

>   1 cup shredded sharp Cheddar cheese (4 ounces)
>   ½ cup light cream
>   2 cups diced cooked potatoes
>   1½ to 2 cups cubed cooked ham
>   2 tablespoons chopped pimiento

Heat oven to 350°. In medium saucepan, heat cheese and cream, stirring constantly, until cheese melts and sauce is creamy. Remove from heat. Stir in remaining ingredients. Pour into ungreased 1½-quart casserole. Cover tightly; bake 45 minutes.

Brussels and Carrots Salad (page 98) is a colorful salad that's perfect with this family favorite.

4 servings.

Substitution

For ham: 1½ to 2 cups cubed pork luncheon meat.

RAVIOLI-SAUSAGE CASSEROLE

>   1 can (4 ounces) mushroom stems
>   and pieces, drained
>   1 can (15½ ounces) ravioli in tomato sauce
>   ¼ cup catsup
>   1 green pepper, finely chopped
>   1 cup shredded mozzarella cheese (4 ounces)
>   1 package (8 ounces) fully cooked brown and
>   serve link sausage

Heat oven to 350°. Mix mushrooms, ravioli in tomato sauce and catsup.

In ungreased 1-quart casserole, alternate layers of ⅓ of the ravioli mixture and ½ each green pepper and cheese. Arrange sausage spoke-fashion on top. Bake uncovered 45 minutes or until bubbly.

Best Tossed Salad (page 94) and hot French bread are the simple but perfect asides for this double-quick casserole.   *6 to 8 servings.*

LAYERED HAM DINNER

    1 package (9 ounces) frozen cut green beans
    1 can (10½ ounces) condensed cream of celery soup
  ¼ cup mayonnaise
    1 tablespoon prepared mustard
    2 packages (3 or 4 ounces each) thinly sliced
      cooked ham
    1 cup shredded Cheddar cheese (4 ounces)
  ¼ cup dry bread crumbs

Heat oven to 350°. Rinse beans with small amount of running cold water to separate and remove ice crystals; drain. Place beans in ungreased 1½-quart casserole.

Mix soup, mayonnaise and mustard; spoon half the mixture on beans. Top with ham and spoon remaining soup mixture on meat. Sprinkle with cheese and bread crumbs. Bake uncovered 20 minutes.

To accompany this hearty casserole, we suggest Pineapple-Banana Salad (page 106) and parsley buttered potatoes.   *4 to 6 servings.*

Substitution

For packaged ham: ½ pound fully cooked ham, cut into julienne strips.

SAUSAGE AND KRAUT ROMANOFF

    1 package (8 ounces) fully cooked brown
      and serve link sausage
    1 package (5.5 ounces) noodles Romanoff
  ½ teaspoon caraway seed
    1 can (8 ounces) sauerkraut, drained

Heat oven to 350°. Brown meat as directed on package. Drain off fat. Prepare noodles Romanoff as directed on package except—increase milk to ½ cup and stir in caraway seed and sauerkraut.

Pour into ungreased 1½-quart casserole; arrange sausage spoke-fashion on top. Cover tightly; bake 25 minutes.   *4 servings.*

PINEAPPLE-CHERRY BOLOGNA

    1-pound ring bologna
    Pineapple-Cherry Glaze (below)
    Instant mashed potato puffs
    (enough for 4 servings)

If necessary, remove casing from bologna; arrange in ungreased 9-inch pie pan. Cut ring diagonally at 2-inch intervals, not cutting completely through. Separate cuts and spoon in part of glaze. Spread remaining glaze on top of bologna.

Heat oven to 400°. Prepare potato puffs as directed on package. Mound potatoes in center of ring. Bake 20 minutes or until potatoes are light brown. *4 servings.*

PINEAPPLE-CHERRY GLAZE

    ½ cup crushed pineapple
    ¼ cup coarsely chopped maraschino cherries
    ¼ cup light corn syrup
    2 tablespoons white vinegar
    ¼ teaspoon cloves
    2 drops red food color
    1½ teaspoons water
    1½ teaspoons cornstarch

Heat pineapple, cherries, corn syrup, vinegar, cloves and food color to boiling, stirring occasionally. Reduce heat; simmer 15 minutes. Blend water and cornstarch; stir into fruit. Cook, stirring constantly, until mixture thickens and boils. Boil and stir 1 minute.

POLISH SAUSAGE BOIL

>　1 pound fully cooked Polish sausage
>　½ to ¾ cup beer

In covered skillet, simmer Polish sausage in beer 10 minutes. (If using uncooked Polish sausage, increase cooking time to 20 minutes.)

Sauerkraut or Scalloped Potato Salad (page 127) and dark pumpernickel buns are perfect go-withs.

4 servings.

Substitution

For beer: ½ to ¾ cup water.

PEASANTS' FEAST

>　1 can (16 ounces) sauerkraut
>　1 can (16 ounces) tomatoes
>　1 medium onion, thinly sliced
>　2 tablespoons brown sugar, if desired
>　½ teaspoon salt
>　4 medium baking potatoes
>　1 package (12 ounces) smoked small sausage links
>　Butter
>　Snipped parsley

Heat oven to 350°. Mix sauerkraut, tomatoes, onion, sugar and salt in ungreased baking dish, 11½ x 7½ x 1½ inches. Rub potatoes with shortening and prick with fork; arrange on sauerkraut mixture. Bake uncovered 1 hour.

Add sausages, covering each with sauerkraut mixture. Bake uncovered 30 minutes longer or until potatoes are done. Make crosswise slits on potatoes; squeeze until some potato pops up through opening. Slip butter into opening and sprinkle with parsley.

All this meal-in-one needs is a simple green salad.

4 servings.

Substitution

For sausage links: About 1 pound Polish sausage or 2-pound piece large bologna (if necessary, remove casing; score top of piece and place on sauerkraut mixture).

FRANKFURTER CASSEROLE

6 frankfurters, cut into 1-inch pieces
1 package (9 ounces) frozen cut green beans,
    broken apart
1 can (10¾ ounces) condensed Cheddar
        cheese soup
1 cup unseasoned croutons

Heat oven to 375°. Mix frankfurters, green beans and
soup. Pour into greased 1½-quart casserole. Sprinkle
with croutons. Bake uncovered 30 minutes or until
sauce is bubbly.   *6 servings.*

Substitution

For cheese soup: 1 cup cheese sauce.

CREOLE WIENERS

8 slices bacon, diced
3 cups minced onion
1 can (16 ounces) tomatoes
¾ teaspoon salt
⅛ teaspoon pepper
1 pound frankfurters

Fry bacon and onion in large skillet until bacon is
crisp and onion is tender. Drain off all but 2 tablespoons fat. Stir in tomatoes, salt and pepper.

Heat to boiling. Reduce heat; simmer 15 minutes,
stirring occasionally. Stir in frankfurters. Cover tightly;
simmer 15 minutes.

Menu plan: rice, green beans, Perfection Salad
(page 101) and Chocolate-Cherry Parfait (page 153).
                        5 or 6 servings.

CHILI DOGS

12 frankfurters
1 slice American cheese, 3½x3½ inches
2 cans (15 ounces each) chili hot beans
1 can (8 ounces) tomato sauce
¼ teaspoon chili powder
¼ teaspoon cumin
⅛ teaspoon cayenne red pepper, if desired

Heat oven to 400°. Make three ½-inch-deep diagonal cuts at regular intervals in each frankfurter. Cut cheese slice into 36 strips, about 1x¼ inch. Insert cheese strip in each frankfurter cut.

Mix beans, tomato sauce and seasonings in ungreased baking dish, 11½x7½x1½ inches. Arrange franks on beans. Bake 20 to 25 minutes.

Superstar supper plan for a teenage bash: Fresh Vegetable Relishes (page 281) and Bun Sticks (page 140) for the crunch; Chocolate Fondue (page 152) for sweet swirling.   *4 or 5 servings.*

Substitutions

For frankfurters: 1 package (12 ounces) smoked small sausage links.

For chili hot beans: 2 cans (15½ ounces each) kidney beans.

For seasonings: 1 envelope (1¼ ounces) chili seasoning mix.

Lamb

TO ROAST LAMB

Select roast, allowing about ½ to ¾ pound per person. Do not remove "fell" (the paperlike covering). Roasts keep their shape better, cook in less time and are juicier when the "fell" is left on.

If desired, season meat with salt and pepper. For a quick seasoning, 4 or 5 slivers of garlic can be inserted in roast. Remove garlic before serving.

Place meat fat side up on rack in open shallow roasting pan. It is not necessary to baste; the meat does its own basting.

Insert meat thermometer so tip is in center of thickest part of meat and does not touch bone or rest in fat. Do not add water. Do not cover.

Roast meat in 325° oven. Roast to desired degree of doneness (see Timetable), using thermometer reading as final guide. Lamb is done when meat thermometer registers 175 to 180°.

Roasts are easier to carve if allowed to set 15 minutes. If roast is to "set," it should be removed from oven when thermometer registers 5 to 10° lower than the desired doneness.

See page 297 for carving tips.

TIMETABLE

Cut	Approximate Weight	Approximate Cooking Time (Minutes per Pound)
Shoulder		
Square	4 to 6 pounds	30 to 35
Boneless	3 to 5 pounds	40 to 45
Cushion	3 to 5 pounds	30 to 35
Crown Roast	4 to 6 pounds	40 to 45
Rib*	1½ to 3 pounds	35 to 45
Leg	5 to 8 pounds	30 to 35
Rolled Leg	3 to 5 pounds	35 to 40

*Roast at 375°

CUCUMBER SAUCE

1 cup finely chopped unpared cucumber
(about 1 medium cucumber)
½ teaspoon finely chopped onion
1 tablespoon prepared mustard
½ cup mayonnaise or salad dressing
½ teaspoon salt
¼ teaspoon pepper

Mix all ingredients. Cover and refrigerate. A delicious sauce for lamb—try it with veal and fish, too. *1¼ cups.*

SWEDISH LEG OF LAMB

> 5-pound leg of lamb roast
> 1 tablespoon salt
> 1 teaspoon pepper
> 5 carrots, sliced
> 3 onions, sliced
> 1 teaspoon instant beef bouillon
> 1 cup hot water
> 1½ cups hot strong coffee
> ½ cup milk
> 1 tablespoon sugar

Place meat fat side up on rack in open shallow roasting pan. Season with salt and pepper. Insert meat thermometer so tip is in center of thickest part of meat and does not touch bone or rest in fat. Do not add water. Do not cover. Roast in 325° oven 1½ hours. Drain off fat.

Mix remaining ingredients; pour on meat. Continue baking about 1 hour, basting meat every 15 minutes with liquid. Meat thermometer should register 175°. If desired, prepare gravy using liquid.

Need menu help? Serve the roast with a spinach salad, boiled potatoes, Minted Grapefruit (page 147) and Creamy Vanilla Fondant (page 175).

8 to 10 servings.

Substitution

For instant bouillon and water: 1 cup canned condensed beef broth (bouillon).

BEST BROILED LAMB PATTIES

1 pound ground lamb
2 tablespoons dry bread crumbs
1 tablespoon parsley flakes
½ teaspoon salt
¼ teaspoon dill weed
1 egg
⅛ teaspoon instant minced garlic
4 slices bacon

Mix meat, bread crumbs, parsley, salt, dill weed, egg and garlic. Shape mixture into 4 patties, 1 inch thick and about 3 inches in diameter. Wrap slice of bacon around edge of each patty and secure with wooden picks.

Set oven control at broil and/or 550°. Broil patties 3 inches from heat about 15 minutes, turning once.

4 servings.

TO BROIL LAMB CHOPS

Remove "fell" (the paperlike covering) if it is on chops. Diagonally slash outer edge of fat on meat at 1-inch intervals to prevent curling. Set oven control at broil and/or 550°. Place chops on rack in broiler pan so tops of ¾ - to 1-inch chops are 2 to 3 inches from heat, 1- to 2-inch chops are 3 to 5 inches from heat. Broil until brown. The chops should be about half done (see Timetable).

If desired, season *brown* side with salt and pepper. Turn chops; broil until brown.

TIMETABLE

Thickness	Approximate Cooking Time per Side*
1 inch	6 to 7 minutes
1½ inches	9 to 10 minutes
2 inches	10 to 11 minutes

* *Time given is for medium doneness; lamb chops are not usually served rare.*

PRINCESS LAMB CHOPS

4 lamb shoulder chops, 1 inch thick
½ cup red wine
½ cup salad oil
1 tablespoon vinegar
2 tablespoons chopped green onion
1 teaspoon grated lemon peel
1½ teaspoons salt
½ teaspoon pepper
¼ teaspoon dry mustard
⅛ teaspoon thyme
⅛ teaspoon basil
⅛ teaspoon instant minced garlic

Place meat in shallow glass dish. Mix remaining ingredients; pour on meat. Cover; refrigerate at least 2 hours, turning meat occasionally.

Set oven control at broil and/or 550°. Brush some of the marinade on meat. Broil 3 inches from heat 7 minutes. Brush meat with marinade; turn and brush again. Broil 5 minutes longer. *4 servings.*

Substitutions

For wine: ½ cup apple juice.
For instant garlic: 1 clove garlic, minced.

Charcoal-grilled Lamb Chops

Beautifully juicy and slightly pink—that's how charcoal-grilled lamb chops should be. And are, with a little know-how. Choose loin, rib or shoulder chops, one or two to a person. Trim off the excess fat and place the chops on grill 4 inches from medium coals. Grill ¾-inch chops 10 to 12 minutes on each side; for 1-inch chops, make it 14 to 16 minutes. Test for doneness by making a knife slit along the bone. Perfect!

MIXED GRILL

6 lamb kidneys
6 lamb loin or rib chops, 1 inch thick
6 pork sausage links
1 teaspoon salt
6 tomato slices, ½ inch thick
½ teaspoon salt
¼ teaspoon pepper
¼ teaspoon basil leaves
6 large fresh mushroom caps, washed and trimmed
1 tablespoon butter or margarine, melted

Wash kidneys; split each in half. Remove membrane, hard parts and white veins. Arrange kidneys, lamb chops and sausages on rack in broiler pan. Set oven control at broil and/or 550°. Broil 3 inches from heat 7 minutes. Season chops and kidneys with 1 teaspoon salt; turn meats.

Place tomato slices on rack. Mix ½ teaspoon salt, the pepper and basil leaves; sprinkle on tomatoes. Place mushroom caps rounded side up on rack; brush with butter.

Broil 5 minutes, brushing mushrooms with butter once during broiling. Season chops and kidneys with salt. To serve, arrange a chop, kidney, sausage link, mushroom cap and tomato slice on each plate.

Carrots Bouillon (page 113) and Best Tossed Salad (page 94) add just the right color accents.   *6 servings.*

Substitutions

For kidneys: 6 chicken livers or 6 small pieces of calf liver.

For sausage: 6 slices bacon.

LAMB OSSOBUCO

 ¼ cup all-purpose flour
 1 teaspoon salt
 ¼ teaspoon pepper
 4 lamb shanks (about ¾ pound each)
 ⅓ cup shortening
 ½ cup tomato sauce
 ½ cup white wine
 ½ cup water
 ½ teaspoon instant beef bouillon
 2 carrots, chopped
 3 stalks celery, chopped
 ⅛ teaspoon each oregano, thyme, rosemary
    and basil

Mix flour, salt and pepper; coat meat with flour mixture. Melt shortening in large skillet or Dutch oven;
brown meat over medium heat, turning occasionally.
Drain off fat.

Reduce heat; stir in remaining ingredients. Cover
tightly; simmer 2 hours or until meat is tender. If you
like, thicken broth.   *4 to 6 servings.*

CURRIED LAMB AND BARLEY CASSEROLE

 1 pound boneless lamb, cut into 1-inch cubes
 ¾ cup uncooked barley
 2 cups water
 1 can (16 ounces) whole tomatoes
 1 tablespoon plus 1 teaspoon instant chopped onion
 1 tablespoon parsley flakes
 2 teaspoons salt
 ½ teaspoon curry powder

Heat oven to 350°. Mix all ingredients in ungreased
2½-quart casserole. Cover tightly; bake 2 hours or
until barley is tender and liquid is absorbed.
                                            4 servings.

Substitutions

   For instant onion: 4 tablespoons chopped onion.
   For parsley flakes: 1 tablespoon snipped parsley.

SHEPHERDS' PIE

  Instant mashed potato puffs (enough for
  8 servings)
  2 tablespoons parsley flakes
  2 cups cubed cooked lamb or beef
¼ cup chopped onion
  2 cups cooked vegetables (peas, carrots, corn)
  2 cups gravy
½ teaspoon salt

Heat oven to 350°. Prepare potato puffs as directed on package except—stir in parsley flakes; set potatoes aside.

Mix remaining ingredients in ungreased 2½-quart casserole. Mound potatoes on meat mixture. Bake uncovered 30 minutes or until potatoes brown slightly.

4 to 6 servings.

Substitutions

For parsley flakes: 2 tablespoons snipped parsley.

For cooked vegetables: 1 package (10 ounces) frozen mixed vegetables, broken apart.

For gravy: 2 cans (10¾ ounces each) gravy or 2 envelopes (⅞ ounce each) gravy mix prepared as directed.

Veal

TO ROAST VEAL

Select roast, allowing about ½ pound per person—
less for boneless roasts, more for roasts with a bone.
If desired, season with salt and pepper before, during
or after roasting.

Place meat fat side up on rack in open shallow
roasting pan. The rack keeps the meat out of the
drippings. (In roasts such as rib roasts or racks, the ribs
form a natural rack.) If roast has little or no fat, place
2 or 3 slices bacon or salt pork on top.

Insert meat thermometer so tip is in center of thickest
part of meat and does not touch bone or rest in fat.
Do not add water. Do not cover.

Roast meat in 325° oven. (It is not necessary to pre-
heat oven.) Roast to desired degree of doneness (see
Timetable), using thermometer reading as final guide.
Veal is done when meat thermometer registers 170°.

Roasts are easier to carve if allowed to set 15 to 20
minutes after removing from oven. If roast is to "set,"
remove from oven when thermometer registers 5 to 10°
lower than the desired doneness.

TIMETABLE

Cut	Approximate Weight	Approximate Cooking Time (Minutes per Pound)
Round or Sirloin	5 to 8 pounds	25 to 35
Loin	4 to 6 pounds	30 to 35
Rib	3 to 5 pounds	35 to 40
Boneless Rump	3 to 5 pounds	40 to 45
Boneless Shoulder	4 to 6 pounds	40 to 45

SAVORY VEAL ROAST

4-pound veal boneless rump or sirloin roast
1 teaspoon salt
¼ teaspoon pepper
¼ cup soy sauce
¼ teaspoon garlic powder

Place meat fat side up on rack in open shallow roasting pan. Season with salt and pepper. If roast has little or no fat, place 2 or 3 slices bacon on top. Insert meat thermometer so tip is in center of thickest part of meat. Do not add water. Do not cover.

Roast in 325° oven 2½ to 3 hours or until thermometer registers 170°. During last hour of baking, baste often with mixture of soy sauce and garlic powder.

Wondering what to serve with the roast? We like Green Rice (page 137) and Perfection Salad (page 101.)

6 to 8 servings.

VEAL PAPRIKA

⅓ cup all-purpose flour
3 teaspoons salt
2 teaspoons paprika
⅛ teaspoon pepper
2 pounds boneless veal, cut into 1-inch cubes
3 tablespoons shortening
⅛ teaspoon instant minced garlic
2 cups dairy sour cream
Poppy Seed Noodles (page 131)

Heat oven to 350°. Mix flour, salt, paprika and pepper; coat meat with flour mixture. Melt shortening in large skillet. Add garlic and meat; brown meat thoroughly. Remove from heat; stir in sour cream. Cover tightly; bake 1 hour. Serve on Poppy Seed Noodles.

Marinated Cucumber Salad (page 97) adds just the right degree of contrast—in flavor and texture.

6 servings.

SEASONED CITY CHICKEN

    1 egg
    ¼ cup water
    1 envelope (about .6 ounce) blue cheese salad
        dressing mix
    6 city chicken* (about 1½ pounds)
    ¼ cup shortening
    ½ to ¾ cup dry bread crumbs
    ¼ cup shortening
    1 teaspoon salt

Beat egg and water slightly; stir in salad dressing mix.
Dip meat into egg, then coat with bread crumbs. Melt
shortening in large skillet; brown meat quickly. Season
with salt and pepper. Reduce heat.

    Cover tightly; simmer 1 hour or until meat is done.
Add small amount of water if necessary.

    Turn city chicken into company fare with broiled
tomatoes, French-style green beans and noodles
Romanoff.   *4 servings.*

---

  * *Equal parts pork and veal cubes placed on skewers.*

VEAL WITH TOMATO SAUCE

    6 veal cutlets (about 4 ounces each)
    ¼ cup salad oil
    2 cloves garlic, crushed
    1 cup thinly sliced onion
    1 jar (3 ounces) sliced mushrooms, drained
    2 tablespoons flour
    1 teaspoon salt
    ¼ teaspoon salt
    1 can (8 ounces) tomato sauce
    ⅔ cup water

Pound meat until ¼ inch thick. In large skillet, heat
oil and garlic over medium-high heat. Brown meat
quickly, about 5 minutes. Remove meat from skillet.

    Reduce heat to medium. Add onion and mushrooms;
cook and stir until onion is tender. Stir in flour, salt

and pepper; pour in tomato sauce and water. Heat to boiling, stirring constantly. Boil and stir 1 minute. Return meat to skillet. Cover tightly; simmer about 30 minutes or until tender.

Theme your whole menu Italian with Green and White Salad (page 95), buttered spaghetti and Parmesan Supper Bread (page 144). Fruit Dessert Freeze (page 157) is a refreshing finish.   *6 servings.*

Substitution

For canned mushrooms: 2 cups sliced fresh mushrooms (¼ pound).

SCHNITZEL SURPRISE

> 5 thin slices Swiss cheese (each about
>   3¾ x 2½ inches)
> 5 thin slices boiled ham (each about
>   3¾ x 2½ inches)
> 1 package (about 20 ounces)
>   frozen breaded veal patties (10)
> ½ teaspoon salt

Heat oven to 450°. Place Swiss cheese and ham on 5 frozen veal patties; top with remaining patties. Season with ¼ teaspoon salt.

Bake on ungreased baking sheet 10 minutes. Turn patties; season with ¼ teaspoon salt. Bake 10 minutes longer.   *4 or 5 servings.*

Substitution

For frozen breaded veal patties: 1 pound veal round steak, cut into 8 serving pieces and pounded until ¼ inch thick. Dip into beaten egg, then coat with 1 cup dry bread crumbs.

Coping with Cutlets

Most veal cutlet recipes call for meat that's ¼ inch thick. Sometimes you can buy the cutlets that way; sometimes you have to do the pounding yourself. You can even buy veal round steak and do both the cutting *and* the pounding. It's up to you—and your budget.

If you're a do-it-yourselfer, start with ½-inch-thick cutlets or steaks. To pound down to ¼ inch, use a metal or wooden mallet—or even the dull edge of a knife or cleaver. Or do as grandma did and use the edge of a saucer. However you get them pounded, do make sure they're ¼ inch thick so you'll have no problem with the cooking time in the recipes.

BREADED VEAL CUTLETS

    ½ cup all-purpose flour°
    1 teaspoon salt
    ½ teaspoon paprika
    ¼ teaspoon pepper
    4 veal cutlets (about 4 ounces each)
    1 egg
    2 tablespoons water
    1 cup dry bread crumbs
    ¼ cup shortening
    1 lemon, cut into wedges

Mix flour, salt, paprika and pepper; coat meat with flour mixture. Pound until ¼ inch thick. Beat egg and water slightly. Dip meat into egg, then coat with bread crumbs.

Melt shortening in large skillet; brown meat quickly. Reduce heat. Cover tightly; cook about 45 minutes or until done. Serve with lemon wedges.   *4 servings.*

° *If using self-rising flour, decrease salt to ½ teaspoon.*

VEAL MUSTARD

    4 veal rib or loin chops, ¾ inch thick
    1 teaspoon salt
    ½ teaspoon pepper
    3 tablespoons prepared mustard
    ½ cup diced bacon
    ¾ cup light cream (20%)
    2 tablespoons drained capers

Heat oven to 350°. Season meat with salt and pepper; spread mustard on both sides. Arrange meat in ungreased baking pan, 9x9x2 inches. Sprinkle bacon on and around meat. Bake uncovered 1 hour 15 minutes. Place meat on warm platter; keep warm while making sauce.

Drain off all but 1 tablespoon fat, leaving bacon and mustard in pan. Stir in cream and capers. Heat to boiling, stirring constantly. Reduce heat; simmer about 10 minutes or until sauce is consistency of thin white sauce. Pour sauce on chops.   *4 servings.*

Substitution

For veal chops: 2 veal sirloin chops, cut in half.

Chicken

ROAST CHICKEN

Young chickens of any weight can be roasted, stuffed or unstuffed. A plump chicken, at least 2½ pounds, is particularly desirable. Allow about ¾ pound per serving. If desired, season cavity of chicken lightly with salt. Do not salt cavity if bird is to be stuffed.

Stuff chicken just before roasting—not ahead of time. (See Sausage Stuffing, below.) Fill wishbone area with stuffing first. Fasten neck skin to back with skewer. Fold wings across back with tips touching. Fill body cavity lightly. (Do not pack—stuffing will expand while cooking.) Tie drumsticks to tail.

Heat oven (see Timetable). Brush chicken with melted butter or margarine. Place breast side up on rack in open shallow roasting pan. Do not add water. Do not cover.

Follow Timetable for approximate total cooking time. Chicken is done when drumstick meat feels very soft when pressed between fingers.

You'll find some guidelines for carving a roast chicken on page 297.

TIMETABLE

Ready-to-Cook Weight	Oven Temperature	Approximate Total Cooking Time
Broiler-fryer		
1½ to 2 pounds	400°	¾ to 1 hour
2 to 2½ pounds	400°	1 to 1¼ hours
2½ to 3 pounds	375°	1¼ to 1¾ hours
3 to 4 pounds	375°	1¾ to 2¼ hours
Capon (stuffed)		
5 to 8 pounds	325°	2½ to 3½ hours

GIBLETS

Wash gizzard, heart, liver and neck. Cover all except liver with water; season with ½ teaspoon salt, 2 peppercorns, 2 cloves, a small bay leaf and a little onion. Heat to boiling. Reduce heat; cover and simmer 1 to 2 hours or until gizzard is tender. Liver is very tender and can be fried, broiled or simmered in water, 5 to 10 minutes.

Giblet broth can be used in stuffing, gravy and recipes where chicken broth is specified. Cooked giblets can be cut up and added to gravy or stuffing. Refrigerate giblets and broth separately.

SAUSAGE STUFFING

Prepare 1 package (7 ounces) dry herbed stuffing mix as directed on package except—add ½ pound bulk pork sausage, crumbled and browned.

About 5 cups (enough for 5- to 8-pound chicken).

VARIATIONS

■ *Apple-Raisin Stuffing:* Omit sausage; add 1 medium apple, finely chopped, and ⅓ cup raisins.

■ *Pecan Stuffing:* Omit sausage; add 1 cup coarsely chopped pecans.

CHICKEN IN A POT

    1 apple, quartered
2½- to 3-pound broiler-fryer chicken
    2 tablespoons lemon juice
    2 teaspoons onion salt
    ½ teaspoon rosemary
    ⅛ teaspoon instant minced garlic

Heat oven to 375°. Place apple in cavity of chicken. Fold wings across back with tips touching. Place chicken breast side up in small Dutch oven or clay pot. (If using clay pot, line with parchment.) Brush chicken with lemon juice; season with remaining ingredients. Cover and bake about 1½ hours or until done.   *4 servings.*

Substitution

For instant garlic: 1 clove garlic, minced.

FRIED CHICKEN

> ½ cup all-purpose flour*
> 1 teaspoon salt
> ½ teaspoon paprika
> ¼ teaspoon pepper
> Salad oil
> 2- to 3-pound broiler-fryer, cut up

Mix flour, salt, paprika and pepper. Heat salad oil (¼ inch) in large skillet. Coat chicken with flour mixture. Brown chicken lightly in oil over medium heat, 15 to 20 minutes.

Reduce heat. Cover tightly; simmer 30 to 40 minutes or until done. (If skillet cannot be covered tightly, add 1 to 2 tablespoons water.) Turn chicken once or twice to assure even browning. Uncover for the last 5 minutes of cooking to crisp chicken.

Team this traditional favorite with something unexpected—perhaps Okra and Tomato Salad (page 98) and Curried Rice (page 135).   *4 servings.*

If using self-rising flour, decrease salt to ½ teaspoon.

VARIATION

■ *Maryland Fried Chicken:* Beat 2 eggs and 2 tablespoons water. After coating chicken with flour, dip into egg, then coat with 2 cups cracker crumbs or dry bread crumbs.

OVEN-FRIED CHICKEN

    ¼ cup shortening
    ¼ cup butter or margarine
    ½ cup all-purpose flour*
     1 teaspoon salt
     1 teaspoon paprika
    ¼ teaspoon pepper
  2½- to 3-pound broiler-fryer chicken, cut up

Heat oven to 425°. In oven, melt shortening and butter in baking pan, 13x9x2 inches. Mix flour, salt, paprika and pepper; coat chicken with flour mixture.

Arrange chicken skin side down in shortening. Bake uncovered 30 minutes. Turn chicken; bake uncovered 30 minutes longer or until done.

For an easy, everything-in-the-oven meal, accompany with baked squash, Oven-fried Eggplant (page 115) and even Raspberry Pie (page 194).   *4 servings.*

---

  * *If using self-rising flour, omit salt.*

VARIATIONS

■ *Crusty-Curried Chicken:* Omit flour mixture; coat chicken with mixture of 1 cup buttermilk baking mix, 2 tablespoons curry powder, 1½ teaspoons salt and ¼ teaspoon pepper.

■ *Garlic Chip Chicken:* Omit flour mixture for coating chicken. In large skillet, melt ¼ cup butter or margarine with 1 teaspoon garlic salt, 1 teaspoon salt and ⅛ teaspoon pepper. Remove from heat. Finely crush 1 bag (5½ ounces) potato chips. Dip chicken into garlic butter, then coat with crushed chips.

CHICKEN BAKE

2½-pound broiler-fryer chicken, cut up
1 can (10½ ounces) condensed cream of
   mushroom soup
½ envelope (about 1½-ounce size) onion soup mix

Heat oven to 375°. Arrange chicken skin side up in un-greased baking pan, 13x9x2 inches. Mix mushroom soup and onion soup mix (dry); pour on chicken. Cover tightly; bake 30 minutes. Uncover; bake 45 minutes longer or until done.

Need some menu help? We suggest Celery Seed Mashed Potatoes (page 124), Peas and Almonds (page 117) and Chocolate Chip Bars (page 166) with ice cream.   *4 to 6 servings.*

GOLDEN PARMESAN CHICKEN

1¼ cups grated Parmesan cheese
1 teaspoon salt
¼ teaspoon pepper
3-pound broiler-fryer chicken, cut up
⅓ cup butter or margarine, melted

Heat oven to 425°. Grease baking pan, 13x9x2 inches. Mix cheese, salt and pepper. Dip chicken into butter, then coat with cheese mixture.

Arrange chicken skin side down in pan. Pour re-maining butter on chicken. Bake uncovered 30 minutes. Turn chicken; bake uncovered 20 minutes longer or until done.

Chilled Asparagus (page 108) and potato salad play up to the Parmesan.   *4 servings.*

Note: This is delicious served cold. After baking, cool, cover and refrigerate.

BARBECUED CHICKEN

    ¼ cup butter or margarine
    2½- to 3-pound broiler-fryer chicken, cut up
    ½ cup barbecue sauce
    ¼ cup frozen lemonade concentrate
       (thawed)
    ¼ cup water
    2 tablespoons instant minced onion

Heat oven to 425°. In oven, melt butter in baking pan,
13x9x2 inches. Place chicken in butter, turning to coat.
Arrange skin side down in pan. Bake uncovered 30
minutes. Drain off fat; turn chicken.

Mix remaining ingredients; pour on chicken. Bake
uncovered 30 minutes longer or until done, basting
occasionally with sauce.   *4 servings.*

Substitution

For instant onion: ⅓ cup minced onion.

ISLANDER CHICKEN

    4 servings ready-to-eat fried chicken
       (about 12 pieces)
    1 cup bottled sweet and sour sauce
    8 large twist pretzels, if desired

Heat oven to 300°. Brush chicken with sauce. Arrange
in ungreased baking pan, 13x9x2 inches. Bake uncovered 30 minutes or until heated through. Heat
pretzels during the last 5 minutes.

With Snow Peas and Carrot Nuggets (page 117)
and Mashed Potatoes flecked with green pepper (page
124), who would guess this meal started at the deli?
                                      4 servings.

BARBECUED CHICKEN FIX-UP

1 ready-to-eat barbecued chicken, split in half
¼ cup honey
¼ cup lemon juice
¼ teaspoon tarragon

Heat oven to 300°. Place chicken skin side up in ungreased baking pan, 13x9x2 inches. Mix remaining
ingredients; pour on chicken. Bake uncovered about
25 minutes or until heated through.

Pick up a three-bean salad at the deli.   *2 servings.*

STEWED CHICKEN

3- to 4-pound broiler-fryer chicken, cut up
1 sprig parsley
1 celery stalk with leaves, cut up
1 carrot, sliced
1 small onion, sliced
2 teaspoons salt
½ teaspoon pepper

Place chicken with giblets and neck in kettle or Dutch
oven. Add water to cover chicken. Add remaining ingredients; heat to boiling. Reduce heat. Cover tightly;
simmer about 45 minutes or until done. Allow chicken
to cool slightly in broth; refrigerate just until cool.

When cool, remove meat from bones and skin in
pieces as large as possible. Skim fat from broth. Refrigerate broth and chicken pieces separately in covered containers; use within several days. For longer
storage, package chicken and broth together and
freeze.
*3 to 4 cups cubed cooked chicken and 2 to 3½ cups
broth.*

Note: To cook a stewing chicken, select 4- to 5- pound
stewing chicken. Simmer 2½ to 3½ hours or until
tender.
*About 5 cups cubed cooked chicken and 5 to 6 cups
broth.*

BROILED CHICKEN

Young chickens, weighing 2½ pounds or less, can be broiled. They should be halved, quartered or cut into pieces. If using chicken halves or quarters, turn wing tips onto back side.

Set oven control at broil and/or 550°. Brush chicken with melted butter or margarine. Place skin side down on rack in broiler pan; place broiler pan so top of chicken is 7 to 9 inches from heat. (If it is not possible to place the broiler pan this far from heat, reduce temperature to 450°.)

Broil chicken 30 minutes. Season brown side with salt and pepper. Turn chicken; if desired, brush again with butter or margarine. Broil 20 to 30 minutes longer or until brown, crisp and done.

Concocting a Casserole?

Improvising, stretching or changing just for the sake of change? Whatever your reason for wanting to ad lib a bit, you can do so if you know how to figure.

To Equal:	Use:
2 cups cooked chicken or turkey	half of a 3- to 4-pound broiler-fryer or stewing chicken *or* 1½ to 2 pounds turkey pieces
1 cup cleaned cooked shrimp	¾ pound raw shrimp in the shell *or* 1 package (7 ounces) frozen peeled shrimp *or* 1 can (4½ to 5 ounces) shrimp
1 cup cooked rice	⅓ cup regular rice *or* ¼ cup converted rice *or* ½ cup instant (precooked) rice
2 cups cooked macaroni, spaghetti or noodles	3½ ounces macaroni or spaghetti *or* 4 ounces noodles

---

CAN-OPENER COMBO

> 1 can (16 ounces) French-style green beans, drained
> 1 can (10½ ounces) condensed cream of mushroom
> soup
> 2 jars (5½ ounces each) boned chicken
> ½ teaspoon sage
> Chow mein noodles

Heat green beans, soup, chicken and sage, stirring occasionally. Serve on noodles.

A simple salad of lettuce wedges and your favorite dressing is just enough.   *4 servings.*

Substitution

For chicken: 1½ cups cubed cooked chicken or turkey.

CHICKEN AND MACARONI CASSEROLE

> 1½ cups uncooked elbow macaroni (about 5 ounces)
> 1 cup shredded Cheddar cheese (4 ounces)
> 1½ cups cut-up cooked chicken
> 1 can (4 ounces) mushroom stems and
> pieces, drained
> ¼ cup chopped pimiento
> 1 can (10½ ounces) condensed cream of
> chicken soup
> 1 cup milk
> ½ teaspoon salt
> ½ teaspoon curry powder

Heat oven to 350°. Mix all ingredients in ungreased 1½-quart casserole. Cover tightly; bake 1 hour.

Complete the menu with broccoli, Cucumber Relish Mold (page 99) and Date or Mocha Brownies (page 162).   *4 to 6 servings.*

VARIATIONS

■ *Ham or Turkey and Macaroni Casserole:* Substitute 1½ cups cubed cooked ham or 1½ cups cubed cooked turkey for the chicken.

Turkey

ROAST TURKEY

Allow ¾ to 1 pound per serving when roasting turkeys under 12 pounds. For heavier birds, 12 pounds and over, allow ½ to ¾ pound per serving. If desired, season cavity of turkey lightly with salt. Do not salt cavity if turkey is to be stuffed.

Stuff turkey just before roasting. Fill wishbone area with stuffing first. Fasten neck skin to back with skewer. Fold wings across back with tips touching. Fill body cavity lightly. (Stuffing will expand.) Tuck drumsticks under band of skin or tie together with heavy string, then tie to tail.

Heat oven to 325°. Place turkey breast side up on rack in open shallow roasting pan. Brush with shortening, oil or butter. Insert meat thermometer so tip is in thickest part of inside thigh muscle or thickest part of breast meat and does not touch bone. Do not add water. Do not cover.

Follow Timetable. Place a tent of aluminum foil loosely over turkey when it starts to turn golden. When ⅔ done, cut band or string holding legs.

There is no substitute for a meat thermometer. It should register 185°. If the bird is stuffed, the point of the thermometer can be placed in the center of the stuffing and will register 165°. If a thermometer is not used, test for doneness about 30 minutes before Timetable so indicates. Move drumstick up and down —if done, the joint should give readily.

When turkey is done, remove from oven and allow to stand about 20 minutes for easiest carving. As soon as possible after serving, remove every bit of stuffing from turkey. Cool stuffing, meat and any gravy promptly; refrigerate separately. Use gravy or stuffing within 1 or 2 days; heat them thoroughly before serving. Serve cooked turkey meat within 2 or 3 days after roasting. If frozen, it can be kept up to 1 month.

See page 297 for carving tips.

TIMETABLE

Ready-to-Cook Weight	Approximate Total Cooking Time	Internal Temperature
6 to 8 pounds	3 to 3½ hours	185°
8 to 12 pounds	3½ to 4½ hours	185°
12 to 16 pounds	4½ to 5½ hours	185°
16 to 20 pounds	5½ to 6½ hours	185°
20 to 24 pounds	6½ to 7 hours	185°

This timetable is based on chilled or completely thawed turkeys at a temperature of about 40° and placed in preheated ovens. Time will be slightly less for unstuffed turkeys. Differences in the shape and tenderness of individual turkeys can also necessitate increasing or decreasing the cooking time slightly. For best results, use a meat thermometer. For prestuffed turkeys, follow package directions carefully; do not use timetable.

COOKING TURKEY IN FOIL

Prepare turkey as directed for Roast Turkey (at left). To wrap, place turkey breast side up in middle of large sheet of heavy-duty aluminum foil. (For larger birds, join two widths of foil.)

Brush with shortening, oil or butter. Place small pieces of aluminum foil over the ends of legs, tail and wing tips to prevent puncturing. Bring long ends of aluminum foil up over the breast of turkey and overlap 3 inches. Close open ends by folding up foil so drippings will not run into pan. Wrap loosely and do not seal airtight.

Heat oven to 450°. Place wrapped turkey, breast up, in open shallow roasting pan. Follow Timetable for approximate cooking time. Open foil once or twice during cooking to judge doneness. When thigh joint and breast meat begin to soften, fold back foil completely to brown turkey and crisp skin. Insert meat thermometer at this time.

TIMETABLE

Ready-to-Cook Weight	Approximate Total Cooking Time	Internal Temperature
7 to 9 pounds	2¼ to 2½ hours	185°
10 ot 13 pounds	2¾ to 3 hours	185°
14 to 17 pounds	3½ to 4 hours	185°
18 to 21 pounds	4½ to 5 hours	185°
22 to 24 pounds	5½ to 6 hours	185°

TURKEY ROAST ORANGE

Bake 2-pound frozen turkey roast as directed on package except—20 minutes before end of roasting time, remove roast to ovenproof platter. Spread ½ cup orange marmalade on roast; bake uncovered 20 minutes longer.

We like this with Green and White Salad (page 95) and Frozen Rice in Combination (page 134). *6 servings.*

ROAST HALF TURKEY

Prepare half turkey as directed for Roast Turkey (page 70) except—skewer skin to meat along cut edges to prevent shrinking from meat during roasting. Prepare 1 package (7 ounces) dry herbed stuffing as directed. On aluminum foil-covered rack in shallow roasting pan, mound stuffing on foil in shape of cavity. Place turkey skin side up on stuffing. Press foil up around base of turkey. Insert meat thermometer in thickest part of breast. Be sure it does not touch bone. Roast until meat thermometer registers 185°—approximately 3 to 3½ hours for an 8- to 10-pound half turkey, approximately 3½ to 4 hours for a 10- to 12-pound half turkey.

HERBED TURKEY ROAST

3½- to 4-pound turkey roast
1 cup white wine
2 tablespoons butter or margarine, melted
½ teaspoon salt
⅛ teaspoon pepper
⅛ teaspoon sage
⅛ teaspoon thyme
¼ cup water
2 tablespoons flour

Bake turkey roast as directed on package except—
before roasting, mix wine, butter, salt, pepper, sage and
thyme and pour on roast.

Remove roast from pan; keep warm. Skim fat from
broth. Measure broth; return 1 cup to roasting pan. In
tightly covered jar, shake water and flour; stir slowly
into broth in pan. Heat to boiling, stirring constantly.
Boil and stir 1 minute. Serve gravy with turkey.

Serve this elegant roast with elegant accompaniments: Honey-Chili Squash (page 120), Creamed
Onions and Broccoli (page 116), Molded Waldorf
Salad (page 100) and Hot Fruit Compote (page 151).
6 to 8 servings.

Note: If turkey roast is in cello-bag and directions call
for cooking in bag, do not remove. With kitchen
scissors, snip a small X in top of bag; pour wine mixture through funnel into bag.

Substitution

For wine: 1 cup apple juice.

PINEAPPLE BRAISED DRUMSTICKS

> 1 package (about 2½ pounds) frozen
>   turkey drumsticks, thawed
> 2 tablespoons shortening
>   Salt and pepper
> 1 cup pineapple juice
> ½ cup pineapple juice
> 2 tablespoons flour

In large skillet, brown drumsticks slowly in shortening. Drain off fat. Season with salt and pepper and pour on 1 cup pineapple juice. Cover tightly; simmer 2 to 2½ hours or until tender, turning occasionally. Remove drumsticks and keep warm.

In tightly covered jar, shake ½ cup pineapple juice and flour; stir slowly into hot liquid. Heat to boiling, stirring constantly. Boil and stir 1 minute. Serve gravy with drumsticks.

Menu suggestions: spinach, Cucumber Relish Mold (page 99) and Coconut Rice (page 134).   *4 servings.*

VARIATION

■ *Deluxe Turkey Drumsticks:* Stir in 1 can (13½ ounces) pineapple chunks, drained, and 1 green pepper, thinly sliced, 15 minutes before end of cooking time.

WILD RICE AND TURKEY CASSEROLE

> 2 cups cut-up cooked turkey
> 1 package (6 ounces) seasoned long grained
>   and wild rice
> 1 can (10½ ounces) condensed cream of
>   mushroom soup
> ⅓ cup milk
> ¼ cup chopped onion
> ½ teaspoon salt
> 2¼ cups boiling water

Heat oven to 350°. Mix all ingredients in ungreased 2-quart casserole. Cover tightly; bake about 50 minutes or until rice is tender. Uncover; bake 10 to 15 minutes longer.

We like Green and White Salad (page 95) with this easy oven casserole.   6 *servings.*

VARIATION

■ *Wild Rice and Chicken Casserole:* Substitute 2 cups cut-up cooked chicken for the turkey.

TURKEY DIVAN

> 2 packages (10 ounces each) frozen broccoli spears
> 6 slices turkey, about ¼ inch thick
> 6 slices process American cheese
> 1 can (10½ ounces) condensed cream of
>   mushroom soup
> ⅓ cup milk
> 1 can (3½ ounces) French fried onion rings

Heat oven to 350°. Rinse broccoli with small amount of running cold water to separate and remove ice crystals; drain. Arrange broccoli in ungreased baking dish, 11½x7½x1½ inches. (If broccoli stems are more than ½ inch in diameter, cut lengthwise in half.)

Top with turkey and cheese slices. Cover with mixture of soup and milk. Bake uncovered 25 minutes. Sprinkle with onion rings; bake 5 minutes longer.

                                          4 *to 6 servings.*

Substitutions

For broccoli: 2 packages (10 ounces each) frozen asparagus spears.

For sliced turkey: 1½ to 2 cups cut-up cooked turkey.

VARIATION

■ *Chicken Divan:* Substitute 1½ to 2 cups cut-up cooked chicken for the turkey slices.

FRUITED TURKEY SALAD

   1½ cups cut-up cooked turkey
    1 can (8¼ ounces) green grapes, drained
    1 can (5 ounces) water chestnuts, drained
      and chopped
    1 can (11 ounces) mandarin orange
      segments, drained
   ½ cup mayonnaise or salad dressing
   ½ teaspoon salt
   ¼ teaspoon curry powder

Combine turkey, grapes, water chestnuts and orange
segments. Mix remaining ingredients; toss with turkey
mixture.

So pretty when served in a bowl lined with greens
and garnished with toasted almonds.   *3 or 4 servings.*

Substitution

For canned grapes: 1 cup fresh seedless green grapes.

VARIATION

■ *Fruited Chicken Salad:* Substitute 1½ cups cut-up
cooked chicken for the turkey.

SLICED TURKEY AND DRESSING BAKE

   1 package (7 ounces) dry herbed stuffing mix
   1 package (28 ounces) frozen turkey slices in gravy

Heat oven to 400°. Prepare stuffing as directed on
package; pat into greased baking dish, 11½x7½x1½
inches. Remove frozen turkey and gravy from foil;
place on stuffing. Bake uncovered 1 hour.   *6 servings.*

VARIATION

■ *Sliced Beef and Dressing Bake:* Substitute 1 package
(24 ounces) frozen beef slices in gravy for the turkey
slices in gravy.

Fish and Seafood

BAKED FISH

2 pounds fish fillets or steaks
Salt and pepper
2 tablespoons lemon juice
1 teaspoon grated onion
¼ cup butter or margarine, melted

Heat oven to 350°. If fillets are large, cut into serving pieces. Season with salt and pepper. Mix lemon juice, onion and butter; dip fish into butter mixture.

Arrange fish in greased baking pan, 9x9x2 inches. Pour remaining butter mixture on fish. Bake uncovered 25 to 30 minutes or until fish flakes easily with fork. Sprinkle with paprika if you like.   *About 6 servings.*

GOLDEN SOLE

1 package (16 ounces) frozen sole fillets
Salt and pepper
1 tablespoon butter or margarine
1 package (1¾ ounces) hollandaise sauce mix
1 can (19 ounces) asparagus spears, drained

Thaw fillets just until they can be separated. Heat oven to 475°. Arrange fish in ungreased baking dish, 11½x7½x1½ inches, leaving space in center of dish. Season fish with salt and pepper and dot with butter. Bake uncovered 15 minutes.

While fish bakes, prepare hollandaise sauce as directed on package. Remove fish from oven; arrange asparagus in center of dish. Pour hollandaise sauce on asparagus. Bake 5 minutes or until heated through.

Serve with Country-style Waldorf Salad (page 106), a green vegetable and Dill Mashed Potatoes (page 124). Strawberry Cream (page 207) is the beverage-dessert.
3 or 4 servings.

HALIBUT WITH VEGETABLES

1½ to 2 pounds halibut fillets
1 teaspoon salt
¼ teaspoon pepper
¼ teaspoon paprika
2 carrots
3 stalks celery
6 green onions
1 teaspoon salt
¼ cup butter or margarine
1 tablespoon lemon juice

Heat oven to 350°. Arrange fish in ungreased baking pan, 13x9x2 inches. Season with 1 teaspoon salt, the pepper and paprika.

Cut carrots, celery and onions (with tops) into 1-inch lengths. Place in blender; add water to cover. Chop, watching carefully. Drain thoroughly. (Or carrots can be shredded and celery and onions finely chopped by hand.)

Spread vegetables on fish; season with 1 teaspoon salt. Dot with butter and sprinkle with lemon juice. Cover tightly; bake 30 minutes or until fish flakes easily with fork.

Herbed Zucchini (page 120) and Creamy Blackeye Peas (page 118) round out the main dish.   *6 servings.*

Note: This dish can be prepared ahead of time, refrigerated and baked later. Increase the baking time 15 minutes.

PARSLEYED FISH BROIL

1½ to 2 pounds fish fillets or steaks, ¾ to 1 inch thick
1 teaspoon salt
⅛ teaspoon pepper
½ cup butter or margarine, melted
¼ cup lemon juice
2 tablespoons snipped parsley

Set oven control at broil and/or 550°. Grease rack in broiler pan and place in oven to heat. Season fish with salt and pepper. Mix remaining ingredients; brush some of the butter mixture on fish.

Broil fish 2 to 3 inches from heat 3 to 5 minutes or until brown. Brush with butter mixture; turn carefully and brush again. Broil 3 to 5 minutes longer or until fish flakes easily with fork. Serve with remaining butter mixture.

Suggested go-withs: Sautéed Spinach (page 119). Perfection Salad (page 101) and Potatoes O'Brien (page 125).

POACHED FISH

1 medium onion, sliced
3 slices lemon
3 sprigs parsley
1 bay leaf
1 teaspoon salt
2 peppercorns
1 pound fish fillets

Pour water (1½ inches) into large skillet; add onion, lemon slices, parsley, bay leaf, salt and peppercorns and heat to boiling.

Arrange fish in single layer in skillet. Cover tightly; simmer 4 to 6 minutes or until fish flakes easily.

2 or 3 servings.

BROILED FISH

2 pounds fish fillets or steaks, about
1 inch thick
1 teaspoon salt
⅛ teaspoon pepper
¼ cup butter or margarine, melted

Set oven control at broil and/or 550°. Grease broiler pan and place in oven to heat. If fillets are large, cut into serving pieces. Season with salt and pepper. If fish has not been skinned, arrange skin side up in broiler pan; brush with some of the butter.

Broil fish 2 to 3 inches from heat 5 to 8 minutes or until light brown. Brush with butter; turn carefully and brush again. Broil 5 to 8 minutes longer or until fish flakes easily with fork.   *6 servings.*

VARIATION

■ *Broiled Fish Italiano:* Omit salt, pepper and butter; brush fish with ¼ cup Italian salad dressing during broiling.

CRISPY FISH STICKS

    1 package (16 ounces) frozen fish sticks
    ¼ cup tomato French salad dressing
    ½ to ¾ teaspoon barbecue spice
    1 tablespoon lemon juice
    ½ teaspoon prepared mustard

Arrange frozen fish sticks on ungreased baking sheet. Mix remaining ingredients; brush on fish. Bake or broil as directed on package.

Serve with Dilled Peas and Cauliflower (page 117) and an orange and grapefruit salad.   *4 or 5 servings.*

LIME-GLAZED FISH STICKS

    1 package (8 ounces) frozen fish sticks
    ¼ cup lime marmalade, melted
    2 tablespoons lime juice

Bake fish sticks as directed on package for oven method except—blend marmalade and juice; spoon onto fish sticks for the last 5 minutes of baking.   *3 servings.*

VARIATION

■ *Orange-glazed Fish Sticks:* Substitute ¼ cup orange marmalade, melted, for the lime marmalade and 2 tablespoons lemon juice for the lime juice.

FISH STICKS
WITH MUSHROOMS AND PECANS

> 1 package (8 ounces) frozen fish sticks
> 1 can (4 ounces) mushrooms stems and
>   pieces, drained
> ¼ cup chopped onion
> ¼ cup butter or margarine, melted
> ¼ cup chopped pecans

Arrange frozen fish sticks in jelly roll pan, 15½ x 10½ x 1 inch. Mix remaining ingredients and spoon onto fish sticks. Bake as directed on package.

Nice with our colorful Pineapple-Cheese Mold (page 102).   *3 servings.*

PANFRIED FISH

> 2 pounds fish fillets, steaks or pan-dressed fish
> 1 teaspoon salt
> ⅛ teaspoon pepper
> 1 egg
> 1 tablespoon water
> 1 cup all-purpose flour
>   Shortening (part butter)

If fillets are large, cut into serving pieces. Season with salt and pepper. Beat egg and water slightly. Dip fish into egg, then coat with flour. Melt shortening (⅛ inch) in skillet; fry fish over medium heat, about 10 minutes.   *4 to 6 servings.*

Substitution

For flour: 1 cup buttermilk baking mix, cornmeal or grated Parmesan cheese.

VARIATION

■ *Fish Almondine:* Brown ¼ cup butter or margarine in small skillet; stir in ¼ cup toasted slivered blanched almonds, ¼ teaspoon salt and 2 teaspoons lemon juice. Just before serving, top fish with almond butter.

OVEN-FRIED FILLETS

    2 pounds fish fillets or steaks
    1 tablespoon salt
    ½ cup milk
    1 cup dry bread crumbs
    ¼ cup butter or margarine, melted

Heat oven to 500°. If fillets are large, cut into serving pieces. Stir salt into milk. Dip fish into milk, then coat with bread crumbs. Arrange in well-greased baking pan, 13x9x2 inches.

Pour butter on fish. Place pan on rack slightly above middle of oven; bake uncovered 10 to 12 minutes or until fish flakes easily with fork.   *6 servings.*

HERBED SALMON STEAKS

    3 packages (12 ounces each) frozen salmon steaks
    ¼ cup lemon juice
    2 tablespoons butter or margarine, melted
    2 teaspoons marjoram leaves
    2 teaspoons onion salt
    ½ teaspoon seasoned pepper
      Paprika
      Lemon wedges
      Snipped parsley

Heat oven to 450°. Arrange frozen salmon steaks in greased baking pan, 13x9x2 inches. Mix lemon juice, butter, marjoram leaves, onion salt and seasoned pepper; brush on fish. Bake uncovered 35 minutes or until fish flakes easily with a fork. Sprinkle with paprika; garnish with lemon wedges and parsley.

Menu mates: Crunchy Creamy Spinach (page 118), sliced tomatoes and potato salad.   *6 servings.*

SCALLOP CASSEROLE

>1 package (12 ounces) frozen scallops, thawed
>¾ cup light cream (20%)
>1 cup dry bread crumbs
>½ cup butter or margarine, melted
>2 teaspoons celery seed
>1 teaspoon salt
>¼ teaspoon pepper
>Paprika

Heat oven to 375°. If scallops are large, cut into 1½-inch pieces. Remove any shell particles and wash scallops. Arrange in greased baking dish, 11½x7½x1½ inches.

Pour about half the cream on scallops. Mix bread crumbs, butter and seasonings; sprinkle on scallops. Pour on remaining cream (liquid should come about ¾ of the way up on scallops). Sprinkle with paprika. Bake uncovered 25 to 30 minutes.   *4 servings.*

Substitution

For frozen scallops: ¾ pound fresh scallops.

JIFFY LOBSTER NEWBURG

>1 can (5½ ounces) lobster, drained
>1 can (10¾ ounces) condensed cream of shrimp soup
>¼ cup milk
>3 tablespoons sherry
>2 or 3 slices toast

Break lobster meat into pieces. Heat soup and milk, stirring occasionally. Add lobster; cook over low heat until heated through. Stir in wine. Serve on hot toast.
     2 or 3 servings.

VARIATION

■ *Shrimp Newburg:* Substitute 1 can (4½ or 5 ounces) shrimp, rinsed and drained, for the lobster.

SKILLET PAELLA

1 package (12 ounces) frozen peeled shrimp
1 can (7 to 8 ounces) minced clams
1 can (5 ounces) boned chicken
1 can (16 ounces) tomatoes
1 package (10 ounces) frozen green peas,
   broken apart
2 cups uncooked instant rice
2 tablespoons instant minced onion
1 teaspoon paprika
1 teaspoon instant chicken bouillon
¼ teaspoon cayenne red pepper
⅛ teaspoon saffron

Rinse frozen shrimp under running cold water to remove ice crystals. Stir together all ingredients in large skillet. Heat to boiling, stirring occasionally. Reduce heat; simmer 5 minutes. Remove skillet from heat. Cover tightly; let stand about 10 minutes.

4 or 5 servings.

Substitutions

For frozen shrimp: 2 cans (4½ ounces each) jumbo shrimp, drained.
For canned chicken: ½ cup cubed cooked chicken.
For tomatoes: 1 can (16 ounces) stewed tomatoes.
For instant onion: ⅓ cup minced onion.
For instant bouillon: 1 chicken bouillon cube.

CREAMY SHRIMP AND PEAS

1 package (7 ounces) frozen peeled shrimp
1 can (10½ ounces) condensed cream of shrimp soup
1 package (10 ounces) frozen green peas
2 tablespoons pasteurized process cheese spread
2 tablespoons sherry
4 baked patty shells

Rinse frozen shrimp under running cold water to remove ice crystals. Heat shrimp, soup and peas to boiling. Boil and stir 5 minutes. Stir in cheese spread and sherry; cook, stirring until cheese is melted. Serve in patty shells.

Molded Waldorf Salad (page 100) adds color to the meal.   *4 servings.*

Substitutions

For sherry: 1 tablespoon plus 1 teaspoon sherry flavoring.
For patty shells: Toast points.

SALMON PUFF

> 2 cans (16 ounces each) salmon, drained
> (reserve liquid)
> About ¾ cup milk
> 2 eggs, slightly beaten
> 3 cups coarse cracker crumbs
> ¼ cup frozen chopped onion
> 1 teaspoon lemon pepper
> ¼ teaspoon salt

Heat oven to 350°. Flake salmon, removing bone and skin. Add enough milk to reserved salmon liquid to measure 1½ cups. Mix all ingredients. Pour into greased 2-quart casserole. Bake uncovered 45 minutes. Garnish with lemon twists or wedges.

We like this light, fluffy casserole with Best Tossed Salad (page 94) and Classic Bean Casserole (page 109)—baked in the same oven. Blender Orange-Raisin Cake (page 185) is the dessert choice. *6 to 8 servings.*

Substitutions

For frozen onion: ¼ cup chopped onion.
For lemon pepper: 1 teaspoon lemon juice and ¼ teaspoon seasoned pepper.

TUNA AND RICE MELANGE

1 small onion, thinly sliced
1 tablespoon salad oil
1 package (10 ounces) frozen mixed vegetables
½ cup water
3 cups cooked rice (without salt)
2 cans (6½ ounces each) tuna, drained
1 cup thinly sliced celery
¼ cup soy sauce

In large skillet, cook and stir onion in oil until tender. Add frozen vegetables and water; heat to boiling. Reduce heat. Cover tightly; simmer 5 to 10 minutes or until vegetables are tender. Stir in remaining ingredients; heat through.   *6 to 8 servings.*

TUNA-NOODLE DINNER

1 package (6 ounces) noodles almondine
1 can (6½ ounces) tuna, drained
1 package (10 ounces) frozen mixed vegetables,
   broken apart

Heat oven to 350°. Prepare noodles almondine as directed on package for oven method except—use 2 cups boiling water; stir in tuna and vegetables. Bake uncovered about 25 minutes or until liquid is absorbed. Stir before serving; garnish with packet of almonds.

This complete meal-in-a-dish needs only the crunch of celery sticks.   *4 servings.*

Substitution

For frozen vegetables: 1 cup cooked mixed vegetables.

Cheese, Eggs and Beans

JIFFY CHEESE FONDUE

> 1 clove garlic
> 2 cans (10¾ ounces each) condensed
>   Cheddar cheese soup
> ½ cup dry white wine
>   French bread

Rub cut clove of garlic around the inside of an earthenware fondue pot. Heat cheese soup and wine. Pour into fondue pot and keep hot over low heat. Use long-handled forks to spear 1-inch cubes of French bread, then dip and swirl in fondue.

Try other dippers for the fondue—cubes of cooked ham, cherry tomatoes, avocado chunks.   *4 servings.*

PIZZA RICE

> 12 slices bacon, diced
>   Cooked instant rice (enough for 4 servings)
> 1½ cups shredded Cheddar cheese (6 ounces)
> ¼ cup instant minced onion
> 2 tablespoons dried green pepper
> 1 can (10½ ounces) pizza sauce

Fry bacon until crisp; drain off fat. Stir in rice and cheese; sprinkle with onion and green pepper. Pour sauce on rice. Cover tightly; cook over low heat until cheese melts, about 10 minutes.   *4 to 6 servings.*

Substitutions

For instant rice: 2 cups cooked rice.
For instant onion: 1 large onion, chopped.
For dried green pepper: ⅓ cup chopped green pepper.

CHEESE-SPINACH SOUFFLÉ

1 package (12 ounces) frozen spinach
  soufflé, thawed
2 packages (12 ounces each) frozen cheese
  soufflé, thawed

Heat oven to 350°. Butter 8-cup soufflé dish or 2-quart casserole. (If using soufflé dish, make a 4-inch band of triple thickness aluminum foil 2 inches longer than circumference of dish; butter one side. Extend depth of dish by securing foil band, buttered side in, around outside top of dish.)

Pour spinach soufflé into soufflé dish. Top with cheese soufflés. Bake 1 hour or until knife inserted halfway between edge and center comes out clean. Serve immediately. Carefully remove foil band and divide soufflé into sections with 2 forks.

Let the soufflé star for company. Lead off with Guacamole Dip with Tacos (page 282), then serve the soufflé with Artichokes and Peas (page 107) and Sesame Rye Fingers (page 140). Offer Cookie Refrigerator Dessert (page 157) for dessert.   *5 or 6 servings.*

EGGS CONTINENTAL

¼ cup dry bread crumbs
1 tablespoon butter or margarine, melted
4 hard-cooked eggs, sliced
3 slices bacon, diced
1 cup dairy sour cream
1 tablespoon milk
1 tablespoon instant minced onion
½ teaspoon salt
¼ teaspoon paprika
⅛ teaspoon pepper
½ cup shredded Cheddar cheese

Heat oven to 350°. Toss bread crumbs in melted butter; divide among 4 buttered 10-ounce casseroles or baking dishes. Layer egg slices on crumbs.

Fry bacon until crisp; remove bacon and drain. Stir together bacon, sour cream, milk, onion and seasonings; spoon onto eggs. Top with cheese. Bake uncovered 10 to 15 minutes or until cheese is melted.

Buttered Brussels sprouts and rye toast make good go-withs.   *4 servings.*

Substitution

For instant onion: 3 tablespoons minced onion.

EGG FOO YONG

> 2 tablespoons salad oil
> 3 eggs
> 1 cup bean sprouts, drained
> ½ cup chopped cooked pork
> 2 tablespoons chopped onion
> 1 tablespoon soy sauce
> Sauce (below)

Heat oil in large skillet. Beat eggs until thick; stir in bean sprouts, pork, onion and soy sauce.

Pour ¼ cup mixture at a time into skillet; with broad spatula, push cooked egg up over meat to form a patty. When patties are set, turn to brown other side. Serve hot with Sauce.   *5 servings.*

SAUCE

> 1 teaspoon cornstarch
> 1 teaspoon sugar
> 1 teaspoon vinegar
> 2½ tablespoons soy sauce
> ½ cup water

Mix all ingredients in small saucepan. Cook, stirring constantly, until mixture thickens and boils. Boil and stir 1 minute.

CREAMED HAM AND EGGS

3 tablespoons butter or margarine
3 tablespoons flour
½ teaspoon dry mustard
¼ teaspoon salt
⅛ teaspoon pepper
2¼ cups milk
1 cup diced cooked ham
4 hard-cooked eggs, quartered
Buttered toast

Melt butter in large saucepan over low heat. Blend in flour and seasonings. Cook over low heat, stirring until mixture is smooth and bubbly. Remove from heat. Stir in milk. Heat to boiling, stirring constantly. Boil and stir 1 minute. Gently stir in ham and eggs; heat through. Serve hot on toast.   *6 servings.*

Substitution

For toast: Toast cups, biscuits or hot fluffy rice.

CHEDDAR EGG BAKE

6 eggs, slightly beaten
1 cup shredded Cheddar cheese (4 ounces)
½ cup milk
2 tablespoons soft butter or margarine
1 teaspoon prepared mustard
½ teaspoon salt
¼ teaspoon pepper

Heat oven to 325°. Mix all ingredients. Pour into ungreased baking pan, 8x8x2 inches. Bake 25 to 30 minutes or until eggs are set.   *6 servings.*

COUNTRY CASSOULET

    1 pound bulk pork sausage
    1 cup sliced celery
    ½ cup chopped onion
    ½ cup chopped green pepper
    ⅛ teaspoon instant minced garlic
    1 teaspoon salt
    1 can (16 ounces) pork and beans
    1 can (16 ounces) lima beans
    1 can (6 ounces) tomato paste

Cook and stir sausage, celery, onion, green pepper, garlic and salt until meat is brown. Drain off fat. Stir in pork and beans (with sauce), lima beans (with liquid) and tomato paste. Simmer uncovered 10 minutes.

A tossed green salad—and lots of it—is all you need with this dinner in a dish.   *5 or 6 servings.*

LAZY MAN'S CHILI BEANS

    4 slices bacon, diced
    2 large onions, thinly sliced
    2 cans (16 ounces each) kidney beans
    1 can (15 ounces) chili without beans
    ¼ cup sugar
    2 teaspoons salt
    ¼ teaspoon instant minced garlic

Fry bacon in large skillet until golden. Stir in onions; cook and stir until onion is tender. Stir in remaining ingredients. Simmer uncovered 25 to 30 minutes.

                            6 to 8 servings.

Substitution

For instant garlic: 2 cloves garlic, minced.

SPEEDY BAKED BEANS

>   2 cans (20 ounces each) baked beans (with pork)
>   ¼ cup bacon-flavored vegetable protein chips
>   ¼ cup chili sauce
>   1 tablespoon instant minced onion
>   1 teaspoon prepared mustard

Heat oven to 350°. Combine all ingredients in greased 1½-quart casserole. Bake uncovered 45 minutes or until bubbly.   *6 servings.*

Substitution

For instant onion: 3 tablespoons minced onion.

SERVE-WITHS AND SIDE DISHES

■

Salads

BOTTLED SALAD DRESSING FIX-UPS

Add the homemade touch to bottled dressing ease with any of the following combinations:

For vegetable salads:

¼ cup oil and vinegar salad dressing and ¼ teaspoon savory leaves, crushed

¼ cup oil and vinegar salad dressing and ¼ teaspoon oregano leaves, crushed

¼ cup oil and vinegar salad dressing and ¼ teaspoon thyme leaves, crushed

¼ cup oil and vinegar salad dressing and ¼ teaspoon chili powder

For cottage cheese salads:

¼ cup creamy French salad dressing and 1 tablespoon pickle sandwich spread

¼ cup creamy sour cream salad dressing and 1 teaspoon horseradish

¼ cup creamy blue cheese salad dressing and 1 tablespoon catsup or chili sauce

¼ cup creamy blue cheese salad dressing and ⅛ teaspoon curry powder (also good on fruit)

For fruit salads:

¼ cup creamy blue cheese salad dressing and 1 tablespoon apricot preserves

¼ cup creamy blue cheese salad dressing and 2 tablespoons creamy French salad dressing

¼ cup fruit salad dressing and ¼ teaspoon sesame seed

RUBY-RED FRUIT SALAD DRESSING

Beat ½ cup currant jelly and ¼ cup oil and vinegar salad dressing with rotary beater.   *¾ cup.*

Substitution

For currant jelly: ½ cup cranberry jelly.

VEGETABLE SALAD DRESSINGS

Catsup Mayonnaise: Blend ½ cup mayonnaise and ¼ cup catsup.

Chili Mayonnaise: Blend ½ cup mayonnaise, ¼ cup chili sauce, 1 drop red pepper sauce and dash chili powder.

Fluffy Mayonnaise: Blend ½ cup mayonnaise and ¼ cup frozen whipped topping (thawed).   *¾ cup.*

CREAMY LEMON DRESSING

⅓ cup frozen lemonade concentrate (thawed)
⅓ cup honey
⅓ cup dairy sour cream
1 teaspoon celery seed

Beat all ingredients with rotary beater. Perfect for fruit salads.   *¾ cup.*

Substitution

For dairy sour cream: ⅓ cup salad oil.

BEST TOSSED SALAD

1 small head lettuce
1 small bunch leaf lettuce
½ small bunch endive
½ bag (10-ounce size) spinach
¼ cup oil and vinegar salad dressing

Into large salad bowl or plastic bag, tear greens into bite-size pieces (12 cups). Toss with salad dressing until greens are well coated. If you like, toss in 1 cup herb-seasoned croutons.   *6 to 8 servings.*

For Gorgeous Greens

A little TLC please. The beautiful greens deserve it. Buy them crisp and fresh, of course; store them, covered, in the refrigerator. And think twice about tossing away the outer leaves; that's where the vitamins are at their best.

Wash greens only as you need them. And do put aside that knife. Greens were meant to be torn, not cut—unless you're serving wedges, or want shredded leaves for slaw.

Avoid the head lettuce rut. Make friends with the whole family of leafy greens: romaine, endive, escarole, watercress. Use them together—the dark and the light, the crisp and the tender—and create your own splendid setting for vegetable sparkers and your favorite dressing.

But before you add these final fillips, make sure the greens are cold and dry. Then pour on the dressing at the very last moment—just enough to coat the leaves lightly—and toss. But ever so gently; that's all they need.

GREEN AND WHITE SALAD

> 1 small head lettuce
> ½ small bunch endive
> ½ small cauliflower
> 1 jar (6 ounces) marinated artichoke hearts, drained (reserve marinade)
> 12 pitted ripe olives
> 2 tablespoons tarragon vinegar
> 1 teaspoon salt
> 1 teaspoon instant minced garlic

Into large salad bowl, tear greens into bite-size pieces (about 8 cups). Break cauliflower into flowerets, cut artichoke hearts in half and slice olives; add to greens.

Sprinkle with reserved artichoke marinade; toss until greens glisten. Sprinkle with vinegar, salt and garlic; toss until greens are well coated.   *6 to 8 servings.*

Substitutions

For endive: 4 cups bite-size pieces spinach (4 ounces).
For instant garlic: 1 clove garlic, minced.

TOSSED SALAD WITH CLASSIC DRESSING

> 1 medium head lettuce
> 1 medium cucumber, cut into thin slices
> 8 cherry tomatoes, cut into halves
> 1 tablespoon plus 1 teaspoon salad oil
> ½ teaspoon salt
>   Dash garlic powder
>   Dash pepper
> 2 teaspoons wine vinegar

Into salad bowl, tear lettuce into bite-size pieces. Add cucumber slices and tomato halves to salad bowl.

Sprinkle with oil; toss until lettuce glistens. Season with salt, garlic powder and pepper. Sprinkle with vinegar; toss until lettuce is well coated.   *4 servings.*

BLENDER COLESLAW

> ½ medium cabbage
> 1 small onion
> ⅔ cup dairy sour cream
> ¼ cup mayonnaise or salad dressing
> ½ teaspoon salt
> ½ teaspoon dry mustard
>   Dash pepper

Cut cabbage into 2-inch pieces. Quarter onion. Place half the cabbage in blender; add water to cover. Chop, watching carefully. Drain thoroughly. Repeat with remaining cabbage and the onion. (Or vegetables can be shredded or finely chopped by hand.) Mix vegetables, sour cream, mayonnaise, salt, mustard and pepper. Chill.   *6 to 8 servings.*

VARIATIONS

■ *Dill Slaw:* Add ½ teaspoon dill weed.

■ *Herbed Slaw:* Omit mustard and pepper; add 1 teaspoon celery seed and ½ teaspoon chervil leaves.

■ *Pineapple-Marshmallow Slaw:* Omit onion; stir in 1 can (13½ ounces) pineapple tidbits, drained, 1 cup miniature marshmallows and 1 tablespoon lemon juice.

GREEN AND GOLD SALAD

   1 package (10 ounces) frozen green peas
   ½ cup shredded natural Cheddar cheese
   2 tablespoons chopped onion
   2 tablespoons mayonnaise or salad dressing
   1½ teaspoons prepared mustard
   ¼ teaspoon salt
     Crisp salad greens

Rinse peas with small amount of running cold water to separate and remove ice crystals; drain. Mix all ingredients except salad greens. Serve salad on greens.
4 or 5 servings.

Substitution

For frozen green peas: 1 can (8 ounces) green peas, drained.

MARINATED CUCUMBER SALAD

   1 medium cucumber
   1 small onion
   ½ cup vinegar
   ½ cup water
   2 tablespoons sugar
   ¼ teaspoon salt
     Crisp salad greens

Run tines of fork lengthwise down side of unpared cucumber. Thinly slice cucumber and onions. Mix vinegar, water, sugar and salt; pour on cucumber and onion in glass bowl. Cover; refrigerate at least 2 hours. Drain and serve on salad greens.   *4 to 6 servings.*

BRUSSELS AND CARROTS SALAD

    ½ cup oil and vinegar salad dressing
    1 package (10 ounces) frozen Brussels sprouts
    1 can (16 ounces) sliced carrots, drained

In covered saucepan, heat salad dressing and Brussels sprouts to boiling. Reduce heat; cover and simmer 8 minutes. Add carrots; cook until Brussels sprouts are tender. Turn into serving dish. Cover; refrigerate at least 6 hours, stirring occasionally.   *6 to 8 servings.*

OKRA AND TOMATO SALAD

    1 package (10 ounces) frozen whole okra
    1 tomato, chopped
    ½ cup sliced celery
    1 teaspoon cream-style horseradish
    3 tablespoons oil and vinegar salad dressing
    Crisp salad greens

Cook okra as directed on package; drain and cut into ½-inch pieces. Mix all ingredients except salad greens. Cover; refrigerate at least 4 hours. Serve on salad greens.   *4 or 5 servings.*

Yesterday's Vegetables—Today's Salads

You cooked too many peas yesterday? Great! You've got a headstart on a new salad: marinate them in oil and vinegar, with chopped green pepper, onion and celery for added flavor. Then garnish with pimiento to serve. Or if you have cooked cauliflowerets around, combine them with tomato wedges and cucumber slices. Let the flavors mingle in French dressing; serve in lettuce cups. And don't let leftover cooked potatoes throw you. Soak them in the liquid of marinated artichoke hearts—along with the hearts, of course—for a very fancy salad. The marinating time for each leftover vegetable, and its new-found friends, should be about 4 hours, in the refrigerator.

BRIGHT BEAN SALAD

> 1 medium carrot
> 1 can (15½ ounces) French-style green beans,
>   drained
> 2 tablespoons chopped onion
> ⅛ teaspoon salt
> 3 tablespoons oil and vinegar salad dressing

Cut carrot into 1-inch lengths; chop in blender, watching carefully. (Or carrot can be finely chopped by hand.) Mix all ingredients. Cover; refrigerate at least 4 hours.   *4 servings.*

Substitutions

For canned green beans: 1 package (9 ounces) frozen French-style green beans, cooked and drained.

For fresh onion: 1 tablespoon instant minced onion.

CUCUMBER RELISH MOLD

> 1 package (3 ounces) lime-flavored gelatin
> 1 medium cucumber
> 2 celery stalks
> 5 green onions
> ½ teaspoon salt

Prepare gelatin as directed on package except—decrease water to 1½ cups and chill until slightly thickened but not set.

Cut unpared cucumber lengthwise into quarters, then into 1½-inch lengths. Cut celery and onions into 1½-inch lengths. Place vegetables in blender; add water to cover. Chop, watching carefully. Drain thoroughly. (Or vegetables can be finely chopped by hand. Be sure to drain cucumber thoroughly.)

Stir vegetables and salt into gelatin. Pour into 4-cup mold or 6 individual molds. Chill until firm, at least 6 hours. For a festive touch, unmold on salad greens. A sour cream salad dressing offers an interesting contrast.
                                      6 servings.

MOLDED WALDORF SALAD

> 1 cup boiling water
> 1 package (3 ounces) lemon-flavored gelatin
> 1 can (11 ounces) mandarin orange segments
> 1 can (8½ ounces) pineapple tidbits
> 1 medium apple, diced
> 1 medium banana, sliced
> ¼ cup nuts, coarsely chopped

Pour boiling water on gelatin in large bowl, stirring until gelatin is dissolved. Stir in orange segments (with syrup), pineapple tidbits (with syrup), apple, banana and nuts.

Pour into 5-cup mold or 8 to 10 individual molds. Chill until firm. Serve with your favorite fruit salad dressing.   *6 to 8 servings.*

To Keep That Perfect Shape

There's no mystique to unmolding a salad. Use the method that's easiest for you.

The warm water way: Dip mold in warm (not hot) water up to the depth of contents; loosen around edge with tip of knife. Place plate on mold and invert both. Jiggle the mold gently; lift off.

The hot towel treatment: Press hot, damp towel around mold and into any depressions. Shake mold gently; lift off. Repeat if necessary.

PERFECTION SALAD

    1 cup boiling water
    1 package (3 ounces) lemon-flavored gelatin
    1 can (8½ ounces) crushed pineapple,
       drained (reserve syrup)
    2 tablespoons lemon juice or vinegar
    1 teaspoon salt
  ¼ medium cabbage
    2 celery stalks
    3 tablespoons chopped pimiento

Pour boiling water on gelatin in large bowl, stirring until gelatin is dissolved. Add enough water to reserved pineapple syrup to measure 1 cup; stir into gelatin with lemon juice and salt.

Cut cabbage into 2-inch pieces. Cut celery into 1½-inch lengths. Place half the cabbage in blender; add water to cover. Chop, watching carefully. Drain thoroughly. Repeat with remaining cabbage and the celery. (Or vegetables can be finely chopped by hand.)

Stir pineapple, vegetables and pimiento into gelatin. Pour into 4-cup mold or 10 to 12 individual molds. Chill until firm. If you like, garnish with curly endive and serve with mayonnaise or salad dressing.

6 to 8 servings.

PINEAPPLE-CHEESE MOLD

1 cup boiling water
1 package (3 ounces) lemon-flavored gelatin
1 can (8½ ounces) crushed pineapple, drained
(reserve syrup)
2 tablespoons lemon juice or vinegar
1 cup shredded Cheddar cheese (4 ounces)
1 cup whipping cream, whipped

Pour boiling water on gelatin in large bowl, stirring until gelatin is dissolved. Add lemon juice and enough water to reserved pineapple syrup to measure 1 cup; stir into gelatin. Chill until slightly thickened but not set.

Stir in pineapple and cheese; fold in whipped cream. Pour into 4-cup mold or 8 individual molds. Chill until firm.   *8 servings.*

Substitution

For whipped cream: 1 envelope (about 2 ounces) dessert topping mix prepared as directed.

CINNAMON-APPLESAUCE SALAD

¼ to ½ cup red cinnamon candies
½ cup water
1 package (3 ounces) lemon-flavored gelatin
1½ cups applesauce

Heat cinnamon candies and water, stirring frequently, until candies are melted. Pour on gelatin in bowl, stirring until gelatin is dissolved. Stir in applesauce.

Pour into 3- or 4-cup mold or into baking pan, 8x8x2 inches. Chill until firm. Try a garnish of cream cheese balls rolled in chopped nuts.   *6 servings.*

Note: For 12 servings, double amounts and pour into 6-cup mold or into baking pan, 13x9x2 inches.

FROZEN COCKTAIL SALAD

 2 cups dairy sour cream
¾ cup sugar
 1 tablespoon plus 1 teaspoon lemon juice
 1 can (30 ounces) fruit cocktail, drained
 2 medium bananas, cut into ¼-inch slices
½ cup coarsely chopped walnuts
 1 jar (10 ounces) maraschino cherries
  (¾ cup), halved

Mix sour cream, sugar and lemon juice. Stir in fruit cocktail, bananas, nuts and cherries. Pour into 2 refrigerator trays. Freeze 24 hours or until firm. (Upright or chest freezers will freeze salad in about 2 hours.)

About 15 minutes before serving, remove trays from freezer and place in refrigerator. Cut each salad into 8 pieces, 2x2¼ inches. Stemmed red cherries make a bright garnish. *16 servings.*

Note: This salad can be kept covered in freezer 3 to 4 weeks.

SEEDLESS GRAPE SALAD

 1 can (8¼ ounces) seedless grapes, drained
 1 cup diced celery
½ cup maraschino cherries, halved
¼ cup coarsely chopped nuts
 2 tablespoons fruit salad dressing
  Lettuce cups

Toss grapes, celery, cherries, nuts and fruit salad dressing. Serve in lettuce cups. *2 or 3 servings.*

Substitution

For canned grapes: 1 cup fresh seedless green grapes.

ORANGE-CAULIFLOWER SALAD

2 cans (11 ounces each) mandarin orange
  segments, drained
2 cup uncooked cauliflowerets
¼ cup chopped green pepper
2 cups bite-size pieces spinach (about 2 ounces)
¼ cup French salad dressing
  Lettuce cups

Toss orange segments, cauliflowerets, green pepper,
spinach and salad dressing. Serve in lettuce cups.

5 or 6 servings.

Substitution

For French salad dressing: Fruit salad dressing.

AMBROSIA SALAD

1 can (11 ounces) mandarin orange segments,
  drained
1 medium unpared apple, chopped
2 medium bananas, sliced
¼ cup chopped dates (sugar rolled)
2 tablespoons fruit salad dressing
  Lettuce cups
  Plain or toasted coconut

Toss orange segments, apple, bananas, dates and fruit
salad dressing. Serve in lettuce cups. Sprinkle salads
with coconut.

4 or 5 servings.

ORANGE AND ONION SALAD

        2 cans (11 ounces each) mandarin orange
          segments, drained
        3 tablespoons finely chopped onion
          Crisp salad greens

Toss orange segments and onion. Serve on salad greens.
Nice with Roquefort dressing.   *4 servings.*

MACARONI FRUIT SALAD

        1½ cups uncooked macaroni rings
        1 tablespoon cornstarch
        1 tablespoon sugar
        1 can (30 ounces) fruit cocktail, drained
          (reserve ½ cup syrup)
        2 tablespoons lemon juice
        ½ cup chilled whipping cream
        1 tablespoon sugar
        ¼ cup maraschino cherries, halved

Cook macaroni rings as directed on package; drain.
Blend cornstarch and 1 tablespoon sugar in saucepan.
Gradually stir in reserved fruit cocktail syrup and the
lemon juice. Cook over medium heat, stirring constantly, until mixture thickens and boils. Boil and stir
1 minute. Mix with hot macaroni rings. Cover; chill
at least 4 hours.

Just before serving, beat cream and 1 tablespoon
sugar in chilled bowl until stiff. Fold cream, fruit
cocktail and cherries into macaroni rings.
                                        4 to 6 servings.

Substitution

For whipping cream and 1 tablespoon sugar: 1 tablespoon sugar mixed into ½ cup dairy sour cream or unflavored yogurt, or ½ envelope (2-ounce size) dessert
topping mix prepared as directed on package except—
decrease milk to ¼ cup and mix in 1 tablespoon sugar.

PINEAPPLE-BANANA SALAD

> 2 small bananas
> 1 can (15¼ ounces) pineapple spears, drained
>   Crisp salad greens
> 2 cups strawberries
> ⅓ cup mayonnaise or salad dressing
> 2 tablespoons chopped nuts

Cut bananas crosswise in half, then cut into length-wise slices. On each salad plate, alternate banana slices and pineapple spears on greens. Divide strawberries among salads.

Top each salad with about 1 tablespoon mayonnaise; sprinkle with nuts.   *5 or 6 servings.*

COUNTRY-STYLE WALDORF SALAD

> 2 cups diced unpared apple
> 1 cup diced celery
> 1 can (8¼ ounces) seedless grapes, drained
> ⅓ cup coarsely chopped nuts
> 4 cups bite-size pieces lettuce
> ½ cup mayonnaise or salad dressing

Toss all ingredients. Garnish with slices of red apple for added color.   *4 to 6 servings.*

Substitution

For canned grapes: 1 cup fresh seedless green grapes.

Vegetables

BUTTERS FOR VEGETABLES

Almond Butter: Melt 1 tablespoon butter or margarine; stir in 2 or 3 drops almond extract.

Almondine Butter: Melt 1 tablespoon butter or margarine; add 1 tablespoon toasted slivered almonds.

Lemon Butter: Melt 1 tablespoon butter or margarine; stir in 1 teaspoon lemon juice.

Mustard-Dill Butter: Melt 1 tablespoon butter or margarine; add ⅛ teaspoon dry mustard and ¼ teaspoon dill weed.

Olive Butter: Melt 1 tablespoon butter or margarine; add 1 tablespoon sliced or chopped ripe olives.

Oriental Butter: Melt 1 tablespoon butter or margarine; stir in 1 teaspoon soy sauce.

Seasoned Butter: Melt 1 tablespoon butter or margarine; add ¼ teaspoon seasoned salt and dash pepper.

Enough for 1 package (9 or 10 ounces) frozen vegetables or 1 can (16 ounces) vegetables.

ARTICHOKES AND PEAS

1 package (10 ounces) frozen artichoke hearts
1 package (10 ounces) frozen green peas
¾ cup water
1 teaspoon salt
1 tablespoon butter or margarine, melted
1 tablespoon lemon juice

In covered saucepan, heat frozen vegetables, water and salt to boiling. Reduce heat and cook until peas and artichoke hearts are tender, 5 to 8 minutes; drain. Turn into serving dish; pour butter and lemon juice on vegetables.   *4 or 5 servings.*

ASPARAGUS WITH CHEESE SAUCE

      1 package (10 ounces) frozen cut asparagus
      ½ can (11-ounce size) condensed Cheddar
        cheese soup (⅔ cup)
      ½ cup canned French fried onion rings

Cook asparagus as directed on package; drain. Return
to saucepan. Stir in cheese soup; heat through. Turn
into serving dish; top with onion rings.   *4 servings.*

Substitution

    For French fried onion rings: ½ cup slivered almonds.

ASPARAGUS À LA POLONAISE

      ¼ cup seasoned croutons
      1 tablespoon butter or margarine
      2 cans (15 ounces each) cut asparagus
      1 tablespoon butter or margarine, melted
      1 hard-cooked egg, chopped

Cook and stir croutons in 1 tablespoon butter until
brown. Heat asparagus; drain. Turn asparagus into
serving dish; drizzle with melted butter and sprinkle
with croutons and egg.   *4 or 5 servings.*

Substitution

    For canned asparagus: 2 packages (9 ounces each)
frozen cut asparagus, cooked as directed on package.

CHILLED ASPARAGUS

Cook 2 packages (10 ounces each) frozen asparagus
spears as directed on package; drain. Season with ½
teaspoon seasoned salt and ⅛ teaspoon pepper. Cover;
chill several hours. Serve as either the vegetable or
the salad.   *8 to 10 servings.*

DELUXE BEAN CASSEROLE

        2 packages (9 ounces each) frozen
            French-style green beans
        1 can (15 ounces) bean sprouts, rinsed
            and drained
        1 can (10½ ounces) condensed cream of
            mushroom soup
        1 tablespoon soy sauce
        1 teaspoon salt
        1 cup canned French fried onion rings

Heat oven to 350°. Rinse beans with small amount of running cold water to separate and remove ice crystals; drain. Mix all ingredients except onion rings in ungreased 2-quart casserole. Bake uncovered 25 minutes. Top with onion rings; bake 5 minutes longer.

6 to 8 servings.

VARIATION

■ *Classic Bean Casserole:* Omit bean sprouts and soy sauce.

GREEN BEANS AND BACON

        3 slices bacon
        1 tablespoon chopped onion
    ⅛ teaspoon instant minced garlic
        1 tablespoon soy sauce
        1 can (16 ounces) French-style green beans,
            drained

Fry bacon until crisp; remove bacon and drain. Drain off all but 2 teaspoons fat. Cook and stir onion in fat until tender. Stir in remaining ingredients; heat through. Turn beans into serving dish; crumble bacon on beans.

4 servings.

Substitutions

For instant garlic: 1 clove garlic, minced.

For French-style green beans: 1 can (16 ounces) cut green beans, drained.

PERKY LIMA BEANS

1 package (10 ounces) frozen lima beans
2 tablespoons soft butter or margarine
1 teaspoon sugar
1 teaspoon dry mustard
1 teaspoon lemon juice
¼ teaspoon salt

Cook lima beans as directed on package; drain. Stir in remaining ingredients.   *4 servings.*

Substitution

For frozen lima beans: 1 can (15 ounces) lima beans, heated and drained.

HICKORY LIMAS

1 package (10 ounces) frozen lima beans
¼ cup pasteurized process cheese spread with hickory smoke flavor
2 tablespoons milk

Cook lima beans as directed on package; drain. Return to saucepan. Stir in cheese spread and milk; heat, stirring constantly, until cheese spread is melted and smooth.   *4 servings.*

Substitutions

For frozen lima beans: 1 can (15 ounces) lima beans, heated and drained.

For cheese spread: ¼ cup pasteurized process cheese spread with bacon or garlic.

MUSHROOM ITALIAN GREEN BEANS

> 1 can (4 ounces) mushroom stems and pieces,
>   drained (reserve liquid)
> 1 package (9 ounces) frozen Italian green beans
> 1 tablespoon butter or margarine
> ½ teaspoon salt

Add enough water to reserved mushroom liquid to measure ½ cup; pour into medium saucepan. Add beans, butter and salt; cook as directed on package or until beans are tender.   *4 servings.*

SAVORY BEETS

> 1 can (16 ounces) whole or sliced beets
> 2 tablespoons butter or margarine
> 1 teaspoon salt
> ½ teaspoon savory
> ½ teaspoon basil

In covered saucepan, heat all ingredients to boiling. Reduce heat; simmer 10 minutes.   *4 servings.*

SWEET AND SOUR BEETS

> 1 jar (16 ounces) pickled beets, drained
>   (reserve syrup)
> 1 tablespoon cornstarch
> 1 can (11 ounces) mandarin orange segments, drained

Blend reserved beet syrup and the cornstarch in medium saucepan. Cook, stirring constantly, until mixture thickens and boils. Boil and stir 1 minute. Stir in beets and orange segments; heat through.   *4 servings.*

Substitutions

For pickled beets and cornstarch: 1 jar (16 ounces) Harvard beets.

For mandarin orange segments: 1 can (8½ ounces) pineapple tidbits.

BROCCOLI ELEGANT

1 package (10 ounces) frozen broccoli spears
½ can (11-ounce size) condensed Cheddar
   cheese soup (⅔ cup)
3 tablespoons milk
2 tablespoons sliced ripe olives

Cook broccoli as directed on package; drain. Mix
cheese soup and milk in saucepan. Stir in broccoli and
olives; heat through.   *4 servings.*

BROCCOLI 'N CHIPS

1 package (10 ounces) frozen chopped broccoli
¼ cup canned shoestring potatoes
2 teaspoons lemon juice

Cook broccoli as directed on package; drain. Turn into
serving dish; top with shoestring potatoes and sprinkle
with lemon juice.   *4 servings.*

SPROUTS SAUTÉ

1 package (10 ounces) frozen Brussels sprouts
½ cup water
1 teaspoon instant chicken bouillon
½ medium onion, sliced and separated into rings
2 tablespoons butter or margarine

In covered saucepan, heat Brussels sprouts, water and
bouillon to boiling. Reduce heat; cook 5 minutes. Stir
in onion and butter; cook uncovered until onion is
tender, about 5 minutes.   *3 servings.*

Substitution

For instant bouillon: 1 chicken bouillon cube.

BOHEMIAN CABBAGE

1 medium cabbage (about 1½ pounds),
    shredded (about 5 cups)
¼ cup water
1 tablespoon instant minced onion
1 teaspoon salt
½ teaspoon caraway seed
¼ teaspoon pepper
½ cup dairy sour cream

Mix all ingredients except sour cream in skillet. Cover tightly; cook 5 minutes or until cabbage is crisp-tender. Stir in sour cream; heat through.   *6 servings.*

Substitution

For instant onion: 3 tablespoons minced onion.

HOT VEGETABLE RELISHES

1 can (16 ounces) whole carrots
2 stalks celery, cut into ¼-inch diagonal
    slices (about 1 cup)
½ cup sweet pickle sticks
½ teaspoon salt

Mix carrots (with liquid), celery, pickle sticks and salt in saucepan; heat through.   *4 servings.*

Substitution

For sweet pickle sticks: ½ cup drained watermelon pickles.

CARROTS BOUILLON

1 can (16 ounces) carrot slices
2 teaspoons instant minced onion
1 teaspoon instant beef bouillon
1 bay leaf

In covered saucepan, heat carrot slices (with liquid), onion, bouillon and bay leaf to boiling. Reduce heat; simmer 5 minutes.   *4 servings.*

CAULIFLOWER AND BRUSSELS SPROUTS

1 package (10 ounces) cauliflower frozen in
cheese sauce in cooking pouch
1 package (10 ounces) frozen Brussels sprouts
2 tablespoons crumble herb stuffing, if desired

Cook each vegetable as directed on package. Drain
Brussels sprouts and turn into serving dish. Pour cauliflower on sprouts; toss to mix. Sprinkle with stuffing.

5 or 6 servings.

Substitution

For Brussels sprouts: 1 package (10 ounces) frozen
lima beans.

CREAMY CORN AND CUCUMBER

1 package (1½ ounces) white sauce mix
1 teaspoon instant chicken bouillon
1 medium cucumber
1 can (17 ounces) whole kernel corn, drained

Prepare white sauce as directed on package except—
stir instant chicken bouillon into white sauce mix
before adding milk.

Cut unpared cucumber lengthwise into quarters,
then crosswise into 1-inch pieces. Stir cucumber and
corn into white sauce; heat through.   *5 servings.*

CORN SESAME SAUTÉ

    1 tablespoon butter or margarine
    1 clove garlic, crushed
    2 tablespoons sesame seed
    ½ teaspoon salt
    ¼ teaspoon basil leaves
    ⅛ teaspoon pepper
    1 can (12 ounces) vacuum-pack whole kernel corn

In medium skillet, cook and stir all ingredients except
corn over medium heat until sesame seed is toasted.
Stir in corn; heat through.   *4 servings.*

OVEN-FRIED EGGPLANT

    ½ cup seasoned crumbs
    1 teaspoon salt
    1 small eggplant (about 1 pound), pared
    1 egg, slightly beaten

Heat oven to 375°. Grease jelly roll pan, 15½x10½x1
inch. Mix seasoned crumbs and salt. Cut eggplant into
½-inch slices. Dip slices into egg, then coat with
crumbs. Arrange in pan. Bake uncovered 15 minutes;
turn and bake 15 minutes longer.   *4 servings.*

Substitution

    For seasoned crumbs: ½ cup dry bread crumbs and
¼ teaspoon pepper.

HOLLANDAISE ONIONS

Prepare 1 package (about 1½ ounces) hollandaise
sauce mix as directed. Stir in 2 cups frozen whole
onions. Heat over medium heat, stirring frequently,
until tender, about 7 minutes.   *4 servings.*

CREAMED ONIONS AND BROCCOLI

1 package (10 ounces) frozen small onions
    in cream sauce
1 package (10 ounces) frozen broccoli spears
1 tablespoon creamy peanut butter

Cook each vegetable as directed on package except—stir peanut butter into onions until sauce is smooth. Drain broccoli and turn into serving dish; pour onions over broccoli.   *4 or 5 servings.*

VARIATION

■ *Nutmeg Creamed Onions and Broccoli:* Omit peanut butter and stir in ⅛ teaspoon nutmeg.

BROILED ONIONS AND POTATOES

Shape aluminum foil into a broiler pan, 10x7x1½ inches. Drain 1 can (16 ounces) whole onions and 1 can (16 ounces) whole potatoes. Place onions and potatoes in foil pan; dot with 1 or 2 tablespoons soft butter or margarine.

Set oven control at broil and/or 550°. Place pan on rack in broiler pan. Broil 3 inches from heat 4 minutes. Turn onions and potatoes; sprinkle with seasoned salt and paprika. Broil 3 minutes longer.   *4 servings.*

PEAS WITH CELERY AND ONION

1 package (10 ounces) frozen green peas
1 stalk celery, sliced (about ½ cup)
1 small onion, thinly sliced

Cook peas, celery and onion as directed on package for peas; drain. If desired, toss vegetables with 1 tablespoon soft butter or margarine.   *3 or 4 servings.*

PEAS AND ALMONDS

¼ cup slivered almonds
1 tablespoon butter or margarine
1 package (10 ounces) frozen green peas,
  broken apart
½ teaspoon salt

Cook and stir almonds in butter until light brown, 2 to 3 minutes. Stir in peas and salt. Cook, stirring frequently, until peas are tender, 5 to 7 minutes.

3 servings.

DILLED PEAS AND CAULIFLOWER

1 package (8 ounces) frozen green peas with
  cream sauce
1 package (10 ounces) frozen cauliflower
⅔ cup water
1 tablespoon butter or margarine
½ teaspoon dill weed

In covered saucepan, heat all ingredients to boiling. Reduce heat; cook 5 to 8 minutes or until cauliflower is tender. Remove from heat; stir until sauce is smooth.

4 servings.

SNOW PEAS AND CARROT NUGGETS

1 package (7 ounces) frozen Chinese pea pods
1 package (10 ounces) carrot nuggets frozen in
  butter sauce in cooking pouch
2 teaspoons lemon juice

Cook each vegetable as directed on package. Drain pea pods and turn into serving dish. Pour carrots and lemon juice on pea pods; toss.   *4 servings.*

Substitution

For pea pods: 1 package (9 ounces) frozen Italian green beans.

CREAMY BLACKEYE PEAS

> 1 package (10 ounces) frozen blackeye peas
> 4 slices bacon, diced
> 1 can (10½ ounces) condensed cream
>   of chicken soup
> ¼ teaspoon Worcestershire sauce
> Dash pepper

Cook peas and bacon as directed on package for peas; drain. Return to saucepan. Stir in remaining ingredients; heat through.   *4 servings.*

SPINACH AND BROCCOLI

> 1 package (10 ounces) frozen chopped spinach
> 1 package (10 ounces) frozen chopped broccoli
> ⅔ cup water
> 1 teaspoon salt
> 1 tablespoon butter or margarine, melted
> 1 tablespoon lemon juice

In covered saucepan, heat spinach, broccoli, water and salt to boiling, breaking vegetables apart with a fork. Reduce heat and cook 5 to 10 minutes or until vegetables are tender; drain. Turn into serving dish; toss with mixture of butter and lemon juice. *6 or 7 servings.*

CRUNCHY CREAMY SPINACH

> 1 package (10 ounces) frozen chopped spinach
> ½ cup dairy sour cream
> 1 can (3½ ounces) French fried onion rings

Cook spinach as directed on package; drain. Stir in sour cream. Turn into serving dish; top with onion rings.   *4 servings.*

SAUTÉED SPINACH

2 slices bacon, diced
1 small onion, thinly sliced
1 package (10 ounces) frozen chopped spinach,
  broken apart
½ teaspoon salt
Dash pepper

In medium skillet, cook and stir bacon and onion until bacon is crisp. Stir in spinach, salt and pepper.
Cover tightly; cook until spinach is tender, 5 to 8
minutes.   *4 servings.*

NUTTY BAKED SQUASH

2 acorn squash (1 pound each)
⅔ cup graham cracker crumbs
⅓ cup coarsely chopped pecans
⅓ cup soft butter or margarine
3 tablespoons brown sugar
¼ teaspoon salt
¼ teaspoon nutmeg

Heat oven to 400°. Cut each squash in half; remove
seeds and fibers. Stir together remaining ingredients.
Spoon ¼ of the crumb mixture into each squash half.
  Arrange squash halves in ungreased baking dish,
11½x7½x1½ inches. Pour water (¼ inch) into baking dish. Cover; bake 35 to 40 minutes or until squash
is tender.   *4 servings.*

Substitution
  For graham cracker crumbs: ⅔ cup soda cracker crumbs.

HONEY-CHILI SQUASH

    ¼ cup honey
    2 tablespoons butter or margarine
    ½ to 1 teaspoon chili powder
    ½ teaspoon salt
    1 can (15 ounces) squash
    ½ cup crumble herb stuffing

Heat oven to 350°. In small skillet, heat honey, butter, chili powder and salt just to boiling, stirring occasionally. Reserve 2 tablespoons of the honey mixture; pour remainder into ungreased 1-quart casserole.

Blend squash into honey mixture in casserole. Toss stuffing with reserved honey mixture; sprinkle on squash. Bake uncovered 25 minutes or until topping is brown.   *4 or 5 servings.*

Substitutions

For honey and butter: ⅓ cup honey butter.

For canned squash: 1 package (12 ounces) frozen squash, thawed.

VARIATIONS

■ *Crusty Pecan Squash Bake:* Omit chili powder and stir in ⅛ teaspoon nutmeg. Substitute ½ cup coarsely chopped pecans for the herb stuffing.

■ *Marshmallow Puff Squash Bake:* Blend all the honey mixture into squash. Omit herb stuffing and sprinkle ½ cup miniature marshmallows on squash. Bake 30 minutes or until marshmallows are puffed and golden brown.

HERBED ZUCCHINI

Cut 2 pounds unpared zucchini into 1-inch slices. Heat 1 inch salted water (½ teaspoon salt to 1 cup water) to boiling. Add zucchini. Cover tightly; heat to boiling. Reduce heat and cook until tender, 5 minutes; drain. Sprinkle with oregano.   *4 servings.*

ITALIAN-STYLE ZUCCHINI

1½ pounds zucchini (about 6 small)
1 tablespoon Italian salad dressing mix
¼ cup salad oil
Grated Parmesan cheese

Cut unpared zucchini lengthwise into ½-inch slices.
Place slices in skillet; sprinkle with salad dressing mix
and pour oil on zucchini. Cover tightly; cook until
zucchini is tender, 12 to 16 minutes. Turn into serving
dish; sprinkle with Parmesan cheese. *4 or 5 servings.*

TOMATO-CABBAGE SKILLET

1 teaspoon instant beef bouillon
1 can (16 ounces) tomato wedges in tomato juice,
    drained (reserve liquid)
1 small cabbage (about 1 pound), shredded
    (about 3 cups)

In medium skillet, heat bouillon and reserved tomato
liquid until bouillon is dissolved. Stir in cabbage.
Cover tightly; cook 3 minutes, stirring occasionally.
  Stir in tomatoes. Cover; cook 3 to 5 minutes longer or
until cabbage is crisp-tender and tomatoes are heated
through.   *4 servings.*

Substitution
  For instant bouillon: 1 beef bouillon cube.

BAKED STUFFED TOMATOES

6 medium tomatoes (about 2 pounds)
⅔ cup crumble herb stuffing
¼ cup grated Parmesan cheese
Parsley

Heat oven to 350°. Remove stem ends of tomatoes. Remove pulp, leaving ½-inch wall. Chop pulp; mix with stuffing and cheese.

Fill tomatoes with stuffing; arrange in ungreased baking dish, 8x8x2 inches. Bake 20 to 25 minutes or until tomatoes are heated through. Garnish with parsley.   *6 servings.*

BROILED TOMATOES

Wash 4 medium tomatoes (about 1½ pounds). Remove stem end from each; cut tomatoes crosswise in half.

Set oven control at broil and/or 550°. Dot each half with ½ teaspoon butter or margarine. Season with salt, pepper, basil leaves, oregano leaves or ground savory. Broil tomato halves cut side up 3 to 5 inches from heat 5 minutes or until tops are golden brown.
                                           4 servings.

Potatoes

CHEESE POTATOES

Prepare instant mashed potato puffs as directed on package for 8 servings except—omit butter; after stirring in potato puffs, stir in 1 jar (5 ounces) pasteurized process sharp American cheese spread or flavored pasteurized Neufchâtel cheese spread (the latter is now available with a wide variety of added flavor sparkers).

Note: To prepare in oven, turn potato mixture into 1½-quart casserole. Bake uncovered in 350° oven 15 to 20 minutes or until heated through.

CHEESE POTATO CASSEROLE

        Instant mashed potato puffs
        (enough for 8 servings)
    ½ teaspoon garlic salt
    1 tablespoon snipped parsley
    1 cup shredded sharp Cheddar cheese
        (4 ounces)
  1½ cups cornflakes, crushed
    2 tablespoons soft butter
    ½ teaspoon dry mustard
    ½ teaspoon paprika
    ¼ teaspoon salt

Heat oven to 325°. Prepare potato puffs as directed on package except—decrease salt to ½ teaspoon and add garlic salt. Stir in parsley and cheese. Turn into 1½-quart casserole. Stir remaining ingredients together; sprinkle on potatoes. Bake 20 minutes.   8 *servings.*

Starting with a mix . . .
MASHED POTATO STIR-INS

Prepare instant mashed potato puffs as directed on package for 4 servings. Just before serving, try one of the following additions:

■ *Bacon:* Stir in 1 to 2 slices bacon, crisply fried and crumbled.

■ *Blue Cheese:* Stir in 1 to 1½ tablespoons crumbled blue cheese.

■ *Celery Seed:* Stir in ½ teaspoon celery seed.

■ *Chives:* Stir in 1 tablespoon snipped chives.

■ *Dill:* Stir in ¼ teaspoon dill weed.

■ *Green Peppers:* Stir in 1 tablespoon chopped green pepper.

■ *Mushroom:* Stir in 1 can (2 ounces) mushroom stems and pieces, drained.

■ *Mustard:* Stir in 1½ teaspoons prepared mustard.

■ *Olive:* Stir in 1½ tablespoons sliced pitted ripe olives or 1½ tablespoons sliced pimiento-stuffed olives.

■ *Pimiento:* Stir in 1 tablespoon chopped drained pimiento.

GOLDEN POTATO BAKE

> ½ cup cornflake crumbs
> 1 teaspoon salt
> 4 to 6 medium potatoes, pared
> 2 tablespoons butter or margarine, melted

Heat oven to 375°. Mix cornflake crumbs and salt. Brush potatoes with butter; coat with crumbs. Arrange in ungreased baking pan, 9x9x2 inches. Bake uncovered 1 to 1¼ hours or until potatoes are tender.

4 to 6 servings.

Starting with a mix . . .
AU GRATIN POTATO STIR-INS

Prepare 1 package (5.5 ounces) au gratin potatoes as directed except—before baking, try one of the following additions:

- *Bacon:* Stir in 3 slices bacon, crisply fried and crumbled.
- *Blue Cheese:* Stir in 2 tablespoons crumbled blue cheese.
- *Dill:* Stir in ½ teaspoon dill weed.
- *Green Onion:* Stir in 2 tablespoons thinly sliced green onion.
- *Green Pepper:* Stir in ½ cup chopped green pepper.
- *Mushroom:* Stir in 1 can (3 ounces) sliced mushrooms, drained.
- *Mustard:* Stir in 1 tablespoon prepared mustard.
- *Olive:* Stir in ¼ cup sliced pitted ripe olives or ½ cup sliced pimiento-stuffed olives.
- *Pimiento:* Stir in 1 jar (2 ounces) sliced pimiento, drained.

POTATOES O'BRIEN

⅓ cup chopped green pepper
2 tablespoons chopped pimiento
1 medium onion, chopped
¼ cup butter or margarine
1 package (16 ounces) frozen French fried potatoes, diced
1 teaspoon salt
⅛ teaspoon pepper

In large skillet, cook and stir green pepper, pimiento and onion in butter until onion is tender. Stir in potatoes, salt and pepper. Cook, stirring occasionally, until potatoes are brown and heated.   *4 servings.*

Starting with a mix . . .
SCALLOPED POTATO VARIATIONS

Prepare 1 package (5.5 ounces) scalloped potatoes as directed except—try one of the following variations:

■ *Blue Cheese:* Stir in 2 tablespoons crumbled blue cheese with the butter.

■ *Mushrooms:* Stir in 1 can (3 ounces) sliced mushrooms, drained, or ½ cup sautéed sliced mushrooms.

■ *Sour Cream:* Substitute ⅔ cup dairy sour cream for the milk.

4 to 6 servings.

CREAMY SCALLOPED POTATOES

1 package (5.5 ounces) scalloped potatoes
2 cups boiling water
1 can (10½ ounces) condensed cream of celery soup
2 tablespoons butter or margarine

Heat oven to 400°. Empty potato slices into ungreased 1½-quart casserole; sprinkle with sauce mix. Stir in water, soup and butter. Bake uncovered 35 to 40 minutes.   *4 to 6 servings.*

Substitution

For cream of celery soup: 1 can (10½ ounces) condensed cream of chicken soup or cream of mushroom soup.

SCALLOPED POTATO SALAD

1 package (5.5 ounces) scalloped potatoes
3 cups water
2 tablespoons salad oil
⅔ cup water
2 tablespoons white wine tarragon
  vinegar
½ cup mayonnaise or salad dressing
¼ teaspoon prepared mustard
½ cup diced celery
½ cup finely chopped onion
4 hard-cooked eggs, chopped
2 tablespoons snipped parsley

Heat potato slices and 3 cups water to boiling. Reduce heat; simmer until tender, 15 to 20 minutes. Rinse with cold water; drain. Place in large bowl; cover and chill.

In saucepan, blend sauce mix and oil; stir in ⅔ cup water and the vinegar. Heat to boiling over medium heat, stirring constantly. Cover and chill.

Blend mayonnaise and mustard; mix with potatoes, celery, onion, eggs and parsley.   *6 servings.*

SWEET POTATO CASSEROLE

1 can (18 ounces) vacuum-pack sweet potatoes
1 can (8½ ounces) crushed pineapple
¼ cup chopped dates (sugar rolled)
1 tablespoon brown sugar
1 tablespoon butter or margarine
1 teaspoon salt
½ teaspoon nutmeg
1 cup miniature marshmallows

Heat oven to 350°. In ungreased 1½-quart casserole, mash sweet potatoes. Stir in remaining ingredients except ½ cup of the marshmallows; sprinkle with remaining marshmallows. Bake uncovered 30 minutes or until marshmallows are puffed and golden brown.
4 servings.

CARAMEL-GLAZED SWEET POTATOES

      1 can (18 ounces) vacuum-pack sweet potatoes
      ½ teaspoon salt
      ⅓ cup caramel ice-cream topping

Heat oven to 350°. Arrange sweet potatoes in ungreased baking dish, 8x8x2 inches; season with salt. Spoon caramel topping on potatoes. Bake uncovered 25 to 30 minutes, basting occasionally with caramel topping in pan.   *4 servings.*

VARIATIONS

■ *Skillet-glazed Sweet Potatoes:* Arrange sweet potatoes in medium skillet; season with salt. Spoon ice-cream topping on potatoes. Heat just to boiling, stirring occasionally and carefully. (Don't cut or mash potatoes.) Reduce heat. Cook about 10 minutes longer, basting occasionally, until potatoes are heated through.

■ *Sweet Potatoes Orangé:* Substitute ⅓ cup orange marmalade for the caramel ice-cream topping.

Noodles and Spaghetti

CAULIFLOWER AND SPINACH NOODLES

1 small cauliflower (about 1 pound)
3 teaspoons salt
5 ounces uncooked spinach noodles (about 3 cups)
1 package (about 1½ ounces) hollandaise sauce mix
Pimiento strips

Heat 1 inch salted water (½ teaspoon salt to 1 cup water) to boiling; add cauliflower. Cover tightly; heat to boiling. Reduce heat. Cook 15 to 20 minutes or until tender; drain.

While cauliflower cooks, heat 6 cups water and the 3 teaspoons salt to boiling. Add noodles; heat to boiling. Boil uncovered, stirring occasionally, 7 to 10 minutes or until tender; drain.

Prepare hollandaise sauce as directed on package. Turn noodles onto platter; arrange cauliflower in center of noodles. Pour sauce on cauliflower and garnish with pimiento.   *4 servings.*

BACON AND ONION NOODLES

3 teaspoons salt
5 ounces uncooked noodles (about 3 cups)
4 slices bacon
1 small onion, chopped

Heat 6 cups water and the salt to boiling. Add noodles; heat to boiling. Boil uncovered, stirring occasionally, 7 to 10 minutes or until tender; drain.

While noodles cook, fry bacon until crisp; remove bacon and drain. Drain off all but 2 tablespoons fat. Cook and stir onion in fat until tender. Toss hot noodles with onion and fat; crumble bacon on noodles.
                    4 to 6 servings.

TANGY NOODLES

>   3 teaspoons salt
>   5 ounces uncooked noodles (about 3 cups)
>   ¼ cup Italian salad dressing

Heat 6 cups water and the salt to boiling. Add noodles; heat to boiling. Boil uncovered, stirring occasionally, 7 to 10 minutes or until tender; drain. Toss hot noodles with salad dressing.   *4 to 6 servings.*

Substitution

For Italian salad dressing: ¼ cup green goddess, creamy onion, blue cheese or oil and vinegar salad dressing.

NOODLE STIR-INS

Cook 8 ounces egg noodles as directed on package. Just before serving, try one of the following additions:

■ *Almonds:* Brown ¼ cup sliced almonds in 2 tablespoons melted butter; stir into noodles.

■ *Browned Crumbs:* Brown ½ cup fine bread crumbs in 2 tablespoons melted butter; stir into noodles.

■ *Herbs:* Stir ½ teaspoon each thyme leaves, basil leaves, snipped parsley and chopped chives or minced onion into 2 tablespoons melted butter; stir into noodles.

■ *Onion and Green Pepper:* Cook and stir ¼ cup chopped green pepper and 2 tablespoons chopped onion in 2 tablespoons melted butter until onion is tender; stir into noodles.

■ *Parmesan:* Stir in 2 tablespoons melted butter, then fold in ¼ cup grated Parmesan cheese.

■ *Poppy Seed:* Stir in 2 teaspoons poppy seed and 1 tablespoon soft butter.

NOODLES ROMA

Prepare 1 package (5.5 ounces) noodles Romanoff as directed except—toss with ⅓ to ½ cup shredded Parmesan cheese before serving.   *4 servings.*

Starting with a mix . . .
NOODLES ROMANOFF STIR-INS

Prepare 1 package (5.5 ounces) noodles Romanoff as directed except—try one of the following additions:

■ *Cheese-Chive:* Stir in ½ cup cottage cheese and 1 tablespoon snipped chives.

■ *Chive or Green Onion:* Stir in 1 tablespoon snipped chives or chopped green onion.

■ *Mushroom:* Stir in 1 can (4 ounces) mushroom stems and pieces, chopped and drained, and 2 tablespoons toasted chopped almonds.

■ *Poppy Seed:* Stir in 1 teaspoon poppy seed.

SPINACH AND NOODLE COMBO

1 package (5.5 ounces) noodles Romanoff
1 package (10 ounces) frozen chopped spinach
⅓ cup milk
2 tablespoons soft butter or margarine

Cook noodles as directed on package; drain. Cook spinach as directed on package; drain. Toss spinach, noodles, milk, butter and sour cream-cheese sauce mix.
        4 or 5 servings.

ITALIAN RICE AND SPAGHETTI

1 cup boiling water
1 cup tomato juice
½ envelope (2-ounce size) spaghetti sauce mix
   (about 2 tablespoons)
   About 2 ounces uncooked long spaghetti,
   broken into 3-inch lengths
⅓ cup uncooked converted rice
½ cup thinly sliced celery

Heat oven to 350°. Heat water, tomato juice and
spaghetti sauce mix to boiling, stirring occasionally.
Mix all ingredients in ungreased 1½-quart casserole.
Cover tightly; bake 35 to 40 minutes, stirring after
20 minutes of baking. Uncover; bake 5 minutes longer
or until rice and spaghetti are tender.   *5 servings.*

SAUCY SPAGHETTI AND SPROUTS

1 package (10 ounces) frozen Brussels sprouts
1 can (10¾ ounces) condensed Cheddar
   cheese soup
⅓ cup milk
3 teaspoons salt
   About 3½ ounces uncooked long spaghetti

Cook Brussels sprouts as directed on package except—
decrease cooking time by 5 minutes; drain. Mix cheese
soup and milk in saucepan. Return sprouts to saucepan. Cook over medium heat, stirring occasionally, 5
minutes or until sauce is heated through.

While Brussels sprouts cook, heat 6 cups water and
the salt to boiling. Add spaghetti; heat to boiling. Boil
uncovered, stirring occasionally, 7 to 10 minutes or
until tender; drain. Turn spaghetti onto platter; top
with Brussels sprouts and sauce.   *4 or 5 servings.*

TOMATOED MACARONI

1 can (16 ounces) tomatoes
2 tablespoons butter or margarine
1 teaspoon salt
¼ teaspoon oregano
3 teaspoons salt
2 cups uncooked elbow macaroni
Grated Parmesan cheese

Heat tomatoes, butter, 1 teaspoon salt and the oregano to boiling. Reduce heat; simmer 10 to 12 minutes, stirring occasionally.

While tomato sauce cooks, heat 6 cups water and the 3 teaspoons salt to boiling. Add macaroni; heat to boiling. Boil uncovered, stirring occasionally, 7 to 10 minutes or until tender; drain. Turn macaroni into serving dish; pour sauce on macaroni and sprinkle with cheese.   *6 servings.*

Rice

OVEN STEAMED RICE

> 1 cup uncooked regular rice
> 2 cups boiling water
> 1 teaspoon salt

Heat oven to 350°. Mix all ingredients in ungreased 1- or 1½-quart casserole or in baking dish, 10x6x1½ or 11½x7½x1½ inches. Cover tightly; bake until liquid is absorbed and rice is tender, 25 to 30 minutes.

4 to 6 servings.

VARIATIONS

■ *Coconut Rice:* Decrease water to 1 cup and heat 1 cup milk and the water to boiling. Stir in ½ cup flaked coconut and 1 medium onion, thinly sliced.

■ *Mushroom-Herb Rice:* Increase salt to 1½ teaspoons; stir in 1 can (4 ounces) mushroom stems and pieces, drained, 1 tablespoon instant chicken bouillon, 1 medium onion, thinly sliced, 1 tablespoon butter or margarine and ½ to 1 teaspoon chervil or 1 teaspoon parsley flakes.

■ *Orange Rice:* Decrease water to 1⅓ cups and heat ⅔ cup orange juice and the water to boiling. Stir in ¼ teaspoon allspice.

FROZEN RICE IN COMBINATION

Cook 1 package (12 ounces) frozen rice risotto in cooking pouch and 1 package (12 ounces) frozen Spanish rice in cooking pouch as directed on package. Empty each pouch into serving bowl; toss rices to mix.

6 to 8 servings (4 cups).

Note: Try a mixture of cooked rice verdi and rice pilaf or make your own combinations of flavored frozen rice.

RICE MEDLEY

> 1 can (17 ounces) peas and tiny onions,
>   drained (reserve liquid)
> 1½ cups uncooked instant rice
> 1 teaspoon butter or margarine
> ½ teaspoon salt
> 1 small carrot, shredded (about 3 tablespoons)

Add enough water to reserved liquid to measure 1½ cups; pour into 2-quart saucepan. Heat to boiling. Stir in peas, rice, butter, salt and shredded carrot; heat to boiling. Remove from heat. Cover tightly; let stand until liquid is absorbed and rice is tender, about 10 minutes.   *4 to 6 servings.*

CURRIED RICE

> Uncooked instant or converted rice
>   (enough for 6 servings)
> 1 tablespoon instant minced onion
> 2 teaspoons instant chicken bouillon
> 1 teaspoon curry powder
> ¼ teaspoon pepper
> ⅛ teaspoon instant minced garlic

Cook rice as directed on package except—decrease salt to ½ teaspoon and stir in remaining ingredients with the water. Cook until liquid is absorbed and rice is tender.   *6 servings.*

Substitutions

For uncooked instant or converted rice: 1 package (7 ounces) chicken-flavored rice; omit onion, chicken bouillon, pepper and garlic.

For instant onion: 3 tablespoons minced onion.

For instant bouillon: 2 chicken bouillon cubes.

For instant garlic: 1 clove garlic, minced.

SKILLET PILAF

>   3 tablespoons butter or margarine
>   Uncooked instant or converted rice
>   (enough for 6 servings)
>   1 small onion, chopped
>   2 teaspoons instant beef bouillon
>   ½ teaspoon salt
>   ½ teaspoon ground cardamom
>   ¼ teaspoon turmeric
>   ¼ teaspoon allspice
>   ⅛ teaspoon pepper

Melt butter in large skillet; cook and stir rice in butter until brown. Remove from heat. Stir in amount of water as directed on package for 6 servings and the remaining ingredients. Cook as directed on package or until liquid is absorbed and rice is tender. *6 servings.*

Substitutions

For uncooked instant or converted rice: 1 package (about 7 ounces) beef-flavored rice; omit beef bouillon, salt and pepper.

For instant bouillon: 2 beef bouillon cubes.

VARIATION

■ *Mushroom Pilaf:* Stir in 1 can (4 ounces) mushroom stems and pieces, drained, with the water and seasonings.

CARIBBEAN RICE AND BEANS

>   Uncooked instant rice (enough for 4 servings)
>   1 can (15½ ounces) kidney beans, drained
>   ½ teaspoon salt
>   ⅛ teaspoon pepper
>   ⅛ teaspoon instant minced garlic
>   2 tablespoons salad oil
>   1 tablespoon snipped chives

Cook rice as directed on package. While rice cooks, cook and stir beans, salt, pepper and garlic in oil until beans are heated through. Stir chives into rice. Turn rice onto platter; top with beans.   *4 servings.*

GREEN RICE

 ¾ cup uncooked regular rice
 1 package (10 ounces) frozen chopped spinach,
   thawed and drained
1½ cups boiling water
 1 tablespoon instant minced onion
 1 tablespoon butter or margarine
1½ teaspoons salt

Heat oven to 350°. Mix all ingredients in ungreased 1- or 1½-quart casserole or in baking dish, 10x6x1½ or 11½x7½x1½ inches. Cover tightly; bake until liquid is absorbed and rice is tender, 25 to 30 minutes.

4 to 6 servings.

Note: This easy method requires the use of regular rice for best results. Instant or converted rice should not be substituted.

Substitutions

For frozen spinach: 1 package (10 ounces) frozen chopped broccoli.

For instant onion: 3 tablespoons minced onion.

For boiling water: 1½ cups boiling chicken or beef bouillon.

HOPPING JOHN

 1 package (10 ounces) frozen blackeye peas
 4 slices bacon, diced
 2 cups water
1½ teaspoons salt
 ½ cup uncooked converted rice

In covered saucepan, heat all ingredients except rice to boiling. Reduce heat; cook 20 minutes. Stir in rice; cook 25 minutes longer or until liquid is absorbed and rice is tender.

4 or 5 servings.

MEXI-BARLEY

- ¾ cup uncooked barley
- 1 can (16 ounces) tomatoes
- 1 cup boiling water
- 1 medium onion, thinly sliced
- 1 tablespoon sugar
- 1 teaspoon salt
- ½ teaspoon basil
- ⅛ teaspoon instant minced garlic
- ⅛ teaspoon cayenne red pepper

Heat oven to 400°. Mix all ingredients in ungreased 1½-quart casserole. Cover tightly; bake 1 to 1¼ hours or until liquid is absorbed and barley is tender.

4 to 6 servings.

BARLEY PILAF

- 2 tablespoons butter or margarine
- 1 cup barley
- 3 tablespoons instant chopped onion
- 2 teaspoons celery salt
- 1 can (8 ounces) mushroom stems and pieces, drained
- ⅛ teaspoon pepper
- 2 teaspoons instant chicken bouillon
- 2 cups water

Heat oven to 350°. Melt butter in small skillet; cook and stir barley in butter 1 minute (do not allow barley to become brown). Pour into ungreased 1½-quart casserole. Stir in remaining ingredients. Cover tightly; bake about 1 hour or until barley is tender.

4 to 6 servings.

Substitutions

For instant onion: ½ cup chopped onion.

For instant bouillon: 2 chicken bouillon cubes dissolved in the water.

BULGUR PILAF

 2 tablespoons butter or margarine
 1 cup bulgur wheat
 1 teaspoon instant minced onion
 2 teaspoons instant chicken bouillon
 2 cups water
 ½ teaspoon salt
 ¼ teaspoon oregano
  Dash pepper

Melt butter in medium skillet; cook and stir bulgur wheat in butter until golden. Stir in remaining ingredients. Cover tightly; heat to boiling. Reduce heat; simmer 15 minutes.   *4 or 5 servings.*

Substitutions

 For instant onion: 1 tablespoon minced onion.
 For instant bouillon and water: 2 cups canned condensed chicken broth.

Dinner Breads

SESAME RYE FINGERS

Spread 4 to 6 slices of rye bread with soft butter or margarine and sprinkle with sesame seed. Cut each slice crosswise into 4 strips; arrange on ungreased baking sheet. Set oven control at broil and/or 550°. Broil 6 inches from heat 1½ to 2 minutes or until seeds are brown.   *4 to 6 servings.*

BUN STICKS

Heat oven to 425°. Cut split halves of 3 or 4 frankfurter buns into 1-inch strips. Spread both sides of each strip with soft butter or margarine; arrange on ungreased baking sheet. Bake 5 to 8 minutes or until light brown.
12 to 16 sticks.

GARLIC FRENCH BREAD STICKS

    ¾ cup butter or margarine, melted
    ⅛ teaspoon instant minced garlic
    1 loaf French bread, 19x3x2¼ inches

Heat oven to 425°. Mix butter and garlic. Cut bread into 5 pieces, each about 4 inches long; then cut each piece lengthwise into 6 sticks. Brush cut sides with garlic butter; arrange in ungreased jelly roll pan. Bake 8 minutes or until golden.   *30 sticks.*

VARIATIONS

■ *Dill French Sticks:* Omit garlic; sprinkle buttered sticks with 1 teaspoon dill weed.

■ *Parmesan French Sticks:* Omit garlic; sprinkle buttered sticks with ¼ cup Parmesan cheese.

ENGLISH MUFFIN DINNER ROUNDS

½ cup soft butter or margarine
½ teaspoon garlic salt
6 English muffins, split
1 to 2 tablespoons sesame, poppy, celery or
  caraway seed

Mix butter and garlic salt; spread on cut surfaces of muffins. Sprinkle each with ¼ to ½ teaspoon sesame seed.

Set oven control at broil and/or 550°. Broil muffins 4 inches from heat 5 to 6 minutes or until golden brown.   *12 rounds.*

VARIATION

■ *Parmesan Rounds*: Substitute grated Parmesan cheese for the sesame seed.

RICH DINNER BISCUITS

Heat oven to 450°. Mix 2 cups buttermilk baking mix and ⅔ cup light cream (20%) until soft dough forms. Gently smooth dough into a ball on floured cloth-covered board. Knead 5 times; roll ½ inch thick. Cut with floured 2-inch cutter. Bake on ungreased baking sheet 8 to 10 minutes.   *10 to 12 biscuits.*

Substitution

For light cream: ½ cup milk and ¼ cup soft butter.

HERB-TOPPED ROLLS

Heat oven to 400°. Brush tops of brown and serve rolls with melted butter or margarine. Sprinkle lightly with one of the following: parsley flakes or snipped chives, dill weed, onion salt or garlic salt or a mixture of 1 teaspoon each tarragon leaves, sweet basil leaves and thyme leaves and ½ teaspoon ground sage. Bake 10 to 12 minutes or until golden brown.

CHEESE PUFFS

    1 package brown and serve rolls
      (about 10 medium)
    2 cups shredded cheese (8 ounces)
    2 tablespoons soft butter or margarine
    ½ teaspoon dry mustard
    ½ teaspoon salt
    ⅛ teaspoon pepper

Slice rolls lengthwise in half. Mix remaining ingredients. Place about 1 tablespoon cheese mixture on each half; arrange on baking sheet. Bake as directed on package.   *20 puffs.*

CHIVE DINNER MUFFINS

    2 cups buttermilk baking mix
    2 tablespoons shortening
    1 egg
    ⅔ cup milk or water
    ¼ cup snipped chives

Heat oven to 400°. Grease 12 medium muffin cups (2¾ inches in diameter). Mix all ingredients with fork; beat vigorously ½ minute. Fill muffin cups ⅔ full. Bake 15 minutes.   *12 muffins.*

BISCUIT FAN-TANS

    2 cups buttermilk baking mix
    ½ cup cold water
    ¼ cup butter or margarine, softened

Heat oven to 450°. Mix baking mix and water with fork until a soft dough forms. Gently smooth dough into a ball on floured cloth-covered board. Knead 5 times. Roll dough ¼ inch thick.

    Spread half the butter on half of dough; fold over. Spread remaining butter on half of dough; fold in half again. Roll dough ½ inch thick. Cut with floured 2-

inch cutter. Place 2 biscuits on sides in each ungreased muffin cup. Bake about 10 minutes.   *8 or 9 fan-tans.*

VARIATION
■ *Bacon Fan-tans:* Stir ¼ cup crumbled crisply fried bacon into the dough.

TWIN PAN ROLLS

   2 loaves frozen bread dough
   ½ teaspoon dill weed
   ½ teaspoon salt
   2 tablespoons butter or margarine, melted
   1 tablespoon parsley flakes
   2 tablespoons butter or margarine, melted
      About ½ cup shredded Parmesan cheese

Let bread dough thaw and rise as directed on package except—grease 2 layer pans, 8 or 9x1½ inches. Shape each loaf into 18 equal balls. Arrange 18 balls in one pan.

Mix dill weed, salt and 2 tablespoons butter. Brush dill mixture on rolls in pan; sprinkle with parsley flakes. Dip remaining rolls into 2 tablespoons butter, then dip tops in cheese and arrange in other pan. Cover; let rise 20 minutes.

Heat oven to 375°. Bake 15 minutes or until golden.
3 dozen rolls.

BREAD IN THE ROUND

   4 cups buttermilk baking mix
   1 package (1½ ounces) sour cream sauce mix
1¾ cups milk
   2 eggs
   Poppy seed

Heat oven to 400°. Grease six 10-ounce custard cups. Mix all ingredients except poppy seed with fork until a soft dough forms; beat vigorously ½ minute. Spread in cups; sprinkle with poppy seed. Bake about 20 minutes.   *6 rounds.*

ALMOND FLATBREAD

    ¾ cup toasted almonds
    1 cup all-purpose flour*
  1½ teaspoons sugar
    ½ teaspoon salt
    ¼ teaspoon soda
    2 tablespoons butter or margarine, softened
    ¼ cup dairy sour cream
    3 tablespoons milk

Heat oven to 400°. Grind nuts in blender, watching carefully. (Or nuts can be finely chopped by hand.) Mix all ingredients with fork. Pinch off 1-inch balls. Roll each ball into 4-inch circle on floured board. Bake on ungreased baking sheet 6 to 8 minutes or until golden brown.   *About 2½ dozen rounds.*

---

* *Do not use self-rising flour in this recipe.*

PARMESAN SUPPER BREAD

  1½ cups buttermilk baking mix
    1 tablespoon sugar
    1 tablespoon instant minced onion
    1 egg
    ¼ cup milk
    ¼ cup white wine
    ½ teaspoon oregano
    ¼ cup grated Parmesan cheese

Heat oven to 400°. Grease layer pan, 8x1½ inches. Mix all ingredients except cheese with fork until a soft dough forms. Spread in pan; sprinkle with cheese. Bake 20 to 25 minutes. Cut into wedges.

    6 to 8 servings.

Substitutions

For instant onion: 3 tablespoons finely chopped onion.
For wine: ¼ cup apple juice.

BISCUIT QUICK BREAD

Heat oven to 450°. Prepare Biscuit dough (enough
for 10 to 12 biscuits) as directed on buttermilk baking
mix package except—do not knead. Spread or roll
dough on greased baking sheet into a rectangle, 10x8
inches. Spread dough with 1 tablespoon soft butter or
margarine. Bake 10 minutes. Serve hot, broken into
pieces or cut into squares.   *6 servings.*

VARIATION

■ *Caraway Quick Bread:* Stir 1 teaspoon caraway seed
into dough. Sprinkle salt and paprika on buttered dough.

CORN BREAD

> 2 eggs
> 1 cup buttermilk baking mix
> 1 cup white or yellow cornmeal
> 1½ cups buttermilk
> 2 tablespoons salad oil

Heat oven to 450°. Grease generously 12 medium
muffin cups (2¾ inches in diameter), corn stick pans
or baking pan, 9x9x2 inches. Heat in oven. Beat eggs
with rotary beater until fluffy. Beat in remaining ingredients *just* until smooth. (Do not overbeat corn
bread batter.)

Pour or spoon batter into hot pans until almost full.
Bake muffins or corn sticks 15 to 20 minutes; corn
bread 20 to 25 minutes. Serve piping hot. *12 servings.*

DESSERTS AND CONFECTIONS

■

Fruit Desserts

FRUIT AND CHEESE TRAY

Arrange a variety of fresh fruit and cheese on a tray. Serve with dessert plates and small knives.

Select fresh fruits in season: apples, bananas, cherries, grapes, oranges, pears, pineapple, raspberries, strawberries, tangerines. Fill in with dates, figs, prunes and shell nuts.

As a guide to cheese selection, choose at least one soft, one semisoft and one firm-to-hard cheese, some mild and some sharp. Try one of the following combinations:

Gourmandise (soft; cherry brandy-flavored)
Port du Salut (semisoft; mild to robust)
Swiss (firm to hard; mild, nutty, sweet) or **Fontina** (firm to hard; mellow, scattered "eyes")

Liederkranz (soft; edible crust, pungent)
Bel Paese (semisoft; mild)
Cheddar (firm to hard; mild to very sharp) or
Gruyère (firm to hard; nutty, sharper than Swiss)

Camembert (soft; edible crust, pungent) or **Brie** (soft; edible crust, pungent)
Roquefort (semisoft; sharp, salty)
Edam or Gouda (firm to hard; inedible casing, mild)

Or make substitutions or additions as desired from the following:

Club (soft; often flavored)
Cream (soft; very mild, chill slightly)
Blue (firm to hard; tangy, sharp)
Gorgonzola (firm to hard; piquant flavor, crumbly)
Kashkaval (firm to hard; salty)

STRAWBERRIES TO DIP

Wash 1 pint fresh strawberries; do not hull. Chill. To serve, divide berries among individual serving dishes. Pass bowls of sour cream and brown sugar to be spooned onto dishes. Berries are first dipped into sour cream, then into sugar. *4 servings.*

STRAWBERRIES ROMANOFF

1 quart strawberries, hulled
½ cup confectioners' sugar
1 cup chilled whipping cream
¼ cup orange-flavored liqueur

Sprinkle strawberries with sugar; stir gently. Cover; refrigerate at least 2 hours.

Just before serving, beat cream in chilled bowl until stiff. Gradually stir in liqueur. Fold in the strawberries. *6 servings.*

Substitution

For liqueur: ¼ cup orange juice.

MINTED GRAPEFRUIT

1 can (16 ounces) grapefruit sections
12 peppermint candy circles, crushed

Mix grapefruit (with syrup) and candy. Cover; refrigerate at least 1 hour. *4 servings.*

Substitution

For canned grapefruit sections: 2 medium grapefruit, pared and sectioned (about 2 cups sections and juice).

PEARS AU CHOCOLAT

Chill can of pear halves. For each serving, put 2 well-drained pear halves together with 1 tablespoon canned chocolate frosting in cavity. Stand pear upright in individual serving dish; chill.

Just before serving, melt 1 tablespoon chocolate frosting per serving (in custard cup placed in boiling water); pour on pears.

FRUITED SHERBET

Sprinkle cubes of pineapple or other fresh fruit with confectioners' sugar; cover and refrigerate. Just before serving, scoop lime sherbet into individual serving dishes; surround with the fruit.

FRUIT IN SOUR CREAM

 2 cups seedless green grapes
 1 can (13½ ounces) pineapple tidbits, drained
 ¼ cup brown sugar (packed)
 ⅓ cup dairy sour cream

Mix grapes and pineapple. Reserving 1 tablespoon of the brown sugar, stir remaining sugar into sour cream. Toss with fruit; chill. Just before serving, sprinkle with reserved brown sugar.   *4 servings.*

Substitutions

For fresh grapes: 1 can (16 ounces) seedless grapes, drained.

For sour cream: ⅓ cup unflavored yogurt.

VARIATION

■ *Strawberries in Sour Cream:* Substitute 3 cups fresh strawberry halves (about 1 pint) for the grapes and pineapple.

PINEAPPLE ZIP

> 2 cans (about 8½ ounces each)
>   pineapple tidbits
> 2 tablespoons maraschino cherry syrup
> ½ cup orange juice
> ¼ cup confectioners' sugar
> ⅛ teaspoon cinnamon

Mix pineapple tidbits (with syrup) and remaining ingredients. Cover; refrigerate at least 1 hour.

4 to 6 servings.

PINEAPPLE DATE DESSERT

Prepare 1 package (14 ounces) date bar mix as directed except—decrease hot water to ¼ cup and stir 1 can (8½ ounces) crushed pineapple, drained, into date filling. Serve with sweetened whipped cream or frozen whipped topping (thawed).   *9 servings.*

RUBY-JEWELED PEARS

> 1 can (16 ounces) whole cranberry sauce
> ¼ cup sugar
> 2 tablespoons lemon juice
> ¼ teaspoon cinnamon
> 4 pears, pared and cored

Heat oven to 350°. Mix cranberry sauce, sugar, lemon juice and cinnamon in saucepan. Cook over low heat, stirring occasionally, until the sugar is dissolved.

Stand pears upright in ungreased baking pan, 8x8x2 inches; pour sauce on pears. Bake 30 minutes or until tender, basting occasionally.   *4 servings.*

BROILED FRUIT KABOBS

Set oven control at broil and/or 550°. Cut a variety of fresh or canned fruits into uniform pieces, about ¾-inch cubes. (Try pineapple, pitted cooked prunes, peaches, pears, maraschino cherries, bananas or apples.) Alternate fruits on long skewers; place on well-greased rack in broiler pan.

Blend ¼ cup honey and 1½ teaspoons lemon juice; brush on fruit. Broil kabobs about 5 inches from heat 1½ minutes or until light brown. Turn carefully; brush with honey mixture. Broil 1½ minutes longer or until heated through.

APPLE CRISP

Butter Crunch (below)
1 can (21 ounces) apple pie filling
1 teaspoon lemon juice
½ teaspoon cinnamon
1 or 2 drops aromatic bitters, if desired

Prepare Butter Crunch. Heat oven to 450°. Mix remaining ingredients. Place apple mixture in ungreased 9-inch pie pan or in baking dish, 8x8x2 inches. Sprinkle 1 cup of the Butter Crunch evenly on top. Bake 10 minutes or until golden brown and bubbly. Serve warm. Delicious topped with ice cream.   *4 servings.*

BUTTER CRUNCH

½ cup butter or margarine
¼ cup brown sugar (packed)
1 cup all-purpose flour*
½ cup chopped pecans, walnuts or coconut

Heat oven to 400°. Mix all ingredients with hands. Spread in ungreased baking pan, 13x9x2 inches. Bake 15 minutes. Stir with spoon; cool. (Store in covered container in refrigerator.)

---

* Do not use self-rising flour in this recipe.

HOT FRUIT COMPOTE

 1 banana
  Corn syrup
 1 jar (30 ounces) fruits for salad, drained
 2 tablespoons brown sugar
 1 tablespoon butter or margarine

Heat oven to 350°. Slice banana; dip into corn syrup. Arrange all fruit in ungreased baking pan, 13x9x2 inches. Sprinkle with sugar; dot with butter. Bake 20 minutes. For a topping, mix 1 cup canned vanilla pudding and 2 tablespoons water. *4 to 6 servings.*

Substitution

 For fruits for salad: 2 cans (17 ounces each) fruits for salad.

CARAMEL PEACH CRISPS

 1 can (16 ounces) cling peach halves, drained
 2 tablespoons brown sugar
 ⅔ cup whole wheat flakes cereal
 ¼ cup brown sugar (packed)
 3 tablespoons butter or margarine, melted
 2 tablespoons raisins
 2 tablespoons broken pecans
  Vanilla ice cream

Set oven control at broil and/or 550°. Place peach halves cut side up in ungreased baking pan, 8x8x2 inches; sprinkle with 2 tablespoons brown sugar. Broil peaches 5 inches from heat 2 to 3 minutes or until light brown.

Mix remaining ingredients except ice cream; spoon onto peaches. Broil about 1 minute longer or until mixture is bubbly and brown. Serve with ice cream.
 4 to 6 servings.

CHERRY COBBLER

> 1 can (21 ounces) cherry pie filling
> ½ teaspoon almond extract
> 1 cup buttermilk baking mix
> 1 tablespoon sugar
> ¼ cup milk
> 1 tablespoon soft butter
> 2 tablespoons toasted slivered blanched almonds

Heat oven to 400°. In 1½-quart casserole, mix pie filling and almond extract. Place in oven 15 minutes or until hot and bubbly.

Mix baking mix, sugar, milk and butter with fork until a soft dough forms; beat vigorously 20 strokes. Stir in almonds. Drop 6 spoonfuls of dough onto hot cherry mixture. Bake 20 to 25 minutes or until topping is light brown. For a touch of tradition, serve with light cream. *6 servings.*

VARIATIONS

■ *Blueberry Cobbler:* Omit cherry pie filling and almond extract; substitute 1 can (21 ounces) blueberry pie filling and ½ teaspoon grated orange peel.

■ *Peach Cobbler:* Omit cherry pie filling and almond extract; substitute 1 can (21 ounces) peach pie filling and ½ teaspoon cinnamon.

CHOCOLATE FONDUE

Heat 1 can (16.5 ounces) chocolate frosting over low heat, stirring frequently. Pour into fondue pot or chafing dish to keep warm. Offer pineapple chunks, banana slices, fresh strawberries and cubes of angel food cake to dip into the fondue.

VARIATIONS

■ *Almond Chocolate Fondue:* Stir ½ teaspoon vanilla and ¼ teaspoon almond extract into frosting.

■ *Mint Chocolate Fondue:* Stir ½ teaspoon mint extract into frosting.

Puddings

CHOCOLATE-CHERRY PARFAIT

For each serving, alternate layers of canned chocolate pudding and cherry pie filling in parfait glass or individual serving dish. Garnish with whipped cream and a maraschino cherry.

ROCKY ROAD PUDDING

    1 can (18 ounces) chocolate pudding
    1½ cups miniature marshmallows
    Whipped cream

Mix pudding and marshmallows; pour into individual serving dishes. Garnish with whipped cream.

4 or 5 servings.

FRUIT DELIGHT

    1 can (11 ounces) mandarin orange segments,
      well drained
    1 can (13¼ ounces) pineapple tidbits,
      well drained
    1 can (18 ounces) vanilla pudding

Mix all ingredients. Spoon into individual serving dishes. Toasted coconut makes a nice garnish.

8 servings.

FRUIT 'N RICE DESSERT

  1 can (17 ounces) rice pudding
  1 can (17 ounces) fruit cocktail, well drained
  1 jar (12 ounces) apricot jam

Mix rice pudding and fruit cocktail; chill. Just before serving, heat apricot jam until melted, stirring occasionally. Spoon pudding into individual serving dishes and top with apricot sauce.   *6 servings.*

COCONUT PUDDING

Mix ½ cup flaked coconut and 1 can (18 ounces) vanilla pudding. Spoon into individual serving dishes. Garnish with sliced strawberries.   *4 servings.*

PUDDING-PIE DESSERT

For each serving, spoon ¼ cup apricot, blueberry, cherry, peach or strawberry pie filling into individual serving dish or glass. Top with ½ cup rice pudding. Garnish with a spoonful of pie filling.   *4 servings.*

RICH VANILLA PUDDING

  1 cup dairy sour cream
  1 can (18 ounces) vanilla pudding
  Canned sliced peaches, drained

Fold sour cream into pudding; pour into individual serving dishes. Top with peaches.   *5 or 6 servings.*

LEMON PUDDING SHELLS

  3 egg whites
¼ teaspoon cream of tartar
¾ cup sugar
  1 package (3¼ ounces) lemon pudding
   and pie filling
  1 cup sweetened whipped cream
  8 fresh strawberries

Heat oven to 275°. Cover baking sheet with heavy brown paper. In small mixer bowl, beat egg whites and cream of tartar until foamy. Beat in sugar, 1 tablespoon at a time; continue beating until stiff and glossy. Do not underbeat.

Drop meringue by ⅓ cupfuls onto brown paper. Shape mounds into circles with back of spoon, building up sides. Bake 1 hour. Turn off oven; leave meringues in oven with door closed 1½ hours. Remove from oven; finish cooling meringues away from draft. Cook pudding as directed on package; cool. Fill shells with pudding. Top with whipped cream and a strawberry.

8 servings.

Chilled and Frozen Desserts

RASPBERRY-RASPBERRY

>   1 cup boiling water
>   1 package (3 ounces) raspberry-flavored gelatin
>   4 to 6 ice cubes
>   1 carton (8 ounces) raspberry-flavored yogurt

Pour boiling water on gelatin in large bowl, stirring until gelatin is dissolved. Add ice cubes; stir until gelatin begins to thicken. Remove any remaining ice cubes.

Add yogurt; beat until smooth with rotary beater. Pour into individual serving dishes, glasses or molds. Chill until firm, about 45 minutes. Serve with a dollop of whipped topping.   *5 or 6 servings.*

Note: Try other gelatin and yogurt combinations.

STRAWBERRY ICE

>   1 package (3 ounces) strawberry-flavored gelatin
>   ½ cup sugar
>   1½ cups boiling water
>   1 package (16 ounces) frozen sliced strawberries, partially thawed
>   ¼ cup orange juice
>   ¼ cup lemon juice

Blend gelatin and sugar; pour boiling water on gelatin mixture in large bowl, stirring until gelatin is dissolved. Stir in remaining ingredients.

Pour into 2 refrigerator trays; freeze until mushy, about 1 hour. Remove from trays; beat until smooth. Return to trays; freeze until firm, about 1 hour.

8 to 10 servings.

FRUIT DESSERT FREEZE

>   1 package (15.4 ounces) creamy white frosting mix
>   2 cups whipping cream
>   1 large banana
>   1 can (8¾ ounces) crushed pineapple, drained
>   1 can (11 ounces) mandarin orange segments,
>   drained
>   ⅓ cup halved maraschino cherries, drained
>   ⅓ cup cut-up dates
>   ⅓ cup chopped pecans, if desired
>   2 tablespoons lemon juice

In small mixer bowl, chill frosting mix (dry) and whipping cream at least 1 hour. Beat until soft peaks form. Slice banana into frosting mixture; fold in remaining ingredients. Pour into 2 refrigerator trays or a baking pan, 9x9x2 inches. Freeze until firm. Cut into squares.   *12 servings.*

VARIATION

■ *Fruit Salad Freeze:* Fold ⅓ cup mayonnaise into beaten frosting mix and whipping cream.

COOKIE REFRIGERATOR DESSERT

>   About twenty 2-inch vanilla wafers
>   1 envelope (about 2 ounces) dessert topping mix
>   ½ cup flaked coconut, if desired
>   1 can (18 ounces) vanilla pudding
>   ¼ cup finely chopped nuts

Arrange vanilla wafers in bottom of ungreased baking pan, 9x9x2 inches. Prepare dessert topping as directed on package. Fold topping and coconut into pudding; spread on wafers. Sprinkle with nuts. Chill at least 1 hour or until firm.   *9 servings.*

Substitution

For vanilla pudding: chocolate pudding.

CHERRIES SUPREME

  ½ cup butter or margarine, softened
  ¼ cup brown sugar (packed)
  1 cup all-purpose flour°
  ½ cup chopped pecans
  ½ gallon vanilla ice cream, softened
  1 can (21 ounces) cherry pie filling
  2 tablespoons rum flavoring, if desired

Heat oven to 400°. Mix butter, brown sugar, flour and pecans with hands. Press mixture evenly in bottom of baking pan, 9x9x2 inches. Bake about 12 minutes or until light brown. Crumble with spoon; cool.

Reserving 1 cup of the crumbs, press remaining crumbs evenly in pan. Pack ice cream evenly on crumbs. Sprinkle reserved crumbs on top. Freeze until firm. Just before serving, heat pie filling and rum flavoring; spoon onto each serving.   *9 servings.*

° *Do not use self-rising flour in this recipe.*

ICE-CREAM WAFFLES

  1 package (5 ounces) frozen waffles
  1 pint vanilla ice cream
  1 pint strawberries, sliced and sweetened

Toast waffles as directed on package. Top each with scoop of ice cream. Spoon berries on ice cream.

                               6 servings.

Substitution

For fresh strawberries: 1 package (16 ounces) frozen sliced strawberries, partially thawed.

VARIATION

■ *Sundae Waffles:* Omit strawberries. Pour warm chocolate sauce on ice cream; top with nuts.

CREAMY LEMON SHERBET

> 1 can (13 ounces) evaporated milk, chilled
> 1 can (6 ounces) frozen lemonade concentrate,
>   partially thawed
> 5 drops yellow food color

Beat chilled milk until stiff. Stir in lemonade concentrate and food color. Pour into 2 refrigerator trays; freeze until firm. If desired, serve with a sprinkling of chopped crystallized ginger.   *6 to 8 servings.*

PARTY PEACH MELBA

> 1 can (16 ounces) peach halves, drained
>   Toasted almonds
> 1 package (10 ounces) frozen raspberries,
>   partially thawed
> 1 pint vanilla ice cream

Place a peach half in each individual serving dish; sprinkle with almonds. Spoon raspberries on peach halves. Cover; refrigerate at least 1 hour. Just before serving, top each serving with a scoop of ice cream.
5 or 6 servings.

CHOCOLATE-MINT PARFAITS

> ¼ cup mint jelly
> 2 tablespoons water
> ½ cup chilled whipping cream
> 3 pints chocolate ice cream

Heat mint jelly and water until smooth, stirring constantly; cool. In chilled bowl, beat whipping cream until stiff; stir in jelly mixture. Alternate layers of ice cream and whipped cream mixture in parfait glasses or other individual serving dishes. Freeze until firm.
8 servings.

INDIVIDUAL BAKED ALASKAS

1 package sponge shortcakes (4)
1 pint ice cream
1 package (7.2 ounces) fluffy white frosting mix

Cover baking sheet with aluminum foil. Arrange short-cakes on foil. Place scoop of ice cream in each short-cake; freeze at least 1 hour.*

Heat oven to 500°. Prepare frosting as directed on package. Completely cover shortcake and ice cream with frosting, sealing it to foil on baking sheet. Bake on lowest rack in oven 3 to 5 minutes or until frosting is light brown. Serve immediately.   *4 servings.*

---

* *Shortcakes can be frozen up to 24 hours at this point.*

Cookies

GINGERBREAD DROPS

Heat oven to 375°. Blend 1 package (14.5 ounces) gingerbread mix (dry) and ½ cup water. Drop by teaspoonfuls about 2 inches apart onto lightly greased baking sheet. Bake 10 to 12 minutes.

About 3 dozen cookies.

VARIATIONS

■ *Chocolate Chip Ginger Drops:* Stir in 1 package (6 ounces) semisweet chocolate pieces and ½ cup chopped nuts.

■ *Coconut Ginger Drops:* Stir in 1 cup shredded coconut.

■ *Date-Nut Ginger Drops:* Stir in ½ cup cut-up dates and ½ cup chopped nuts.

■ *Fruit Ginger Drops:* Stir in 1 cup cut-up candied fruit and ½ cup sugared chopped nuts.

■ *Jeweled Ginger Drops:* Stir in ⅔ cup cut-up gumdrops and ½ cup chopped nuts.

■ *Mincemeat Ginger Drops:* Stir in 1 cup prepared mincemeat and ½ cup chopped nuts.

■ *Orange-Coconut Ginger Drops:* Omit water; stir in 1 cup shredded coconut, 1 tablespoon grated orange peel and the juice from 1 orange plus enough water to measure ½ cup.

■ *Peanut Butter Ginger Drops:* Add ½ cup peanut butter.

■ *Peanut Ginger Drops:* Stir in 1 cup chopped peanuts.

■ *Raisin-Nut Ginger Drops:* Stir in 1 cup raisins and ½ cup chopped nuts.

Starting with a mix . . .
BROWNIE VARIATIONS

Prepare 1 package (15.5 ounces) fudge brownie mix as directed except—try one of the following variations:

■ *Almond:* Stir in ½ teaspoon almond extract.

■ *Cherry:* Stir in ¼ cup drained chopped maraschino cherries (about 16).

■ *Coconut:* Omit nuts; stir in 1 cup flaked coconut.

■ *Date:* Omit nuts; stir in 1 cup chopped dates. Coat baked squares with confectioners' sugar.

■ *Fruit:* Stir in ⅓ cup chopped candied fruit.

■ *Mint:* Immediately after removing brownies from oven, place 16 chocolate-covered mint patties (about 1½ inches in diameter) on top. Allow mints to soften; spread evenly.

■ *Mocha:* Add 1½ tablespoons powdered instant coffee.

■ *Peanut:* Stir in ½ cup chopped peanuts. Frost with a peanut butter icing.

■ *Peanut Butter:* Omit nuts; add 3 tablespoons chunky peanut butter.

■ *Peppermint:* Add ¼ teaspoon peppermint extract.

SOUR CREAM BROWNIES

    1 package (22.5 ounces) fudge brownie mix
    2 eggs
    ¾ cup dairy sour cream

Heat oven to 350°. Grease baking pan, 13x9x2 inches. Mix brownie mix (dry), eggs and sour cream. Spread in pan. Bake 23 to 27 minutes. Cool; cut into 1½-inch squares.   *4 dozen cookies.*

Starting with a mix . . .
DATE BAR VARIATIONS

Prepare 1 package (14 ounces) date bar mix as directed except—try one of the following easy variations:

■ *Almond:* Stir ¾ teaspoon almond extract into date filling.

■ *Apple:* Stir ½ cup finely chopped pared tart apples into date filling.

■ *Apricot:* Stir ½ cup finely cut dried apricots into date filling.

■ *Cherry:* Stir ¼ cup drained chopped maraschino cherries (about 16) into date filling.

■ *Coffee:* Stir 1 tablespoon powdered instant coffee into date filling.

■ *Raisin:* Stir ½ cup raisins into date filling.

■ *Spice:* Stir 1 teaspoon cinnamon, ¼ teaspoon cloves or ½ teaspoon nutmeg into date filling.

■ *Walnut:* Stir ½ cup chopped walnuts into date filling.

PEANUT BUTTER COOKIES

> 1 cup peanut butter
> ¼ cup water
> ¼ cup butter or margarine, softened
> 2 eggs
> 1 package (18.5 ounces) yellow cake mix

Heat oven to 375°. Beat peanut butter, water, butter, eggs and half the cake mix (dry) until smooth. Stir in remaining cake mix.

Drop dough by teaspoonfuls 3 inches apart onto ungreased baking sheet. With fork dipped in flour, flatten in crisscross pattern. Bake 8 to 10 minutes or until golden brown. Cool slightly before removing from baking sheet. *4 dozen cookies.*

FUDGE CRINKLES

    2 eggs
    ½ cup shortening
    1 package (18.5 ounces) devils food cake mix
    1 package (15.4 ounces) chocolate fudge
        frosting mix

Heat oven to 375°. Beat eggs, shortening and half the cake mix (dry) until light and fluffy. Stir in remaining cake mix.

Shape into 1-inch balls. Place about 2 inches apart on ungreased baking sheet. Bake 10 to 12 minutes. Cool slightly before removing from baking sheet.

Prepare frosting as directed on package; frost cooled cookies. You can decorate with raisins, red cinnamon candies, colored nonpareils or candy corn. Or, put cookies together in pairs with frosting.

4 dozen cookies (2 dozen cookie sandwiches).

The Case for Keeping Cookies

Soft cookies: Store in any container with a tight-fitting cover. To keep them soft, tuck in a fresh slice of bread or apple every couple of days.

Crisp cookies: Store in any container, but cover loosely. If they soften, recrisp by placing them in a 300° oven for 3 to 5 minutes. Crunch!

Freezing? Arrange baked cookies in a foil- or plastic wrap-lined box, separating the layers with foil or wrap. Or, store small batches in freezer bags, plastic wrap or foil. They'll keep for 9 to 12 months!

REFRIGERATOR COOKIES

   1 package (15.4 ounces) creamy white frosting mix
   2 cups all-purpose flour*
   1 cup butter or margarine, softened
   ½ cup chopped pecans
   1½ tablespoons butter or margarine, softened
   2 tablespoons hot water

Measure 1½ cups of the frosting mix (dry) into large bowl. With hands, mix in flour, 1 cup butter and the pecans. Divide dough in half; shape each half into roll, about 1½ inches in diameter and about 7½ inches long. Wrap; chill at least 4 hours.

Heat oven to 400°. Cut rolls into ⅛-inch slices. Place 1 inch apart on ungreased baking sheet. Bake 4 to 6 minutes. Cool slightly before removing from baking sheet.

Mix remaining frosting mix, 1½ tablespoons soft butter and the water until smooth. (Add 1 to 2 teaspoons water if necessary.) Frost cookies. (Enough frosting for about 4 dozen cookies.)

About 8 dozen cookies.

---

* Do not use self-rising flour in this recipe.

VARIATION

■ *Chocolate Refrigerator Cookies:* Substitute chocolate fudge frosting mix for the creamy white.

GOLDEN GOOD BARS

   2 cups buttermilk baking mix
   1½ cups brown sugar (packed)
   3 eggs
   1 teaspoon vanilla
   1 cup chopped nuts
   ½ cup flaked coconut

Heat oven to 350°. Grease and flour baking pan, 13x9x2 inches. In large bowl, mix all ingredients. Spread in pan. Bake about 35 minutes. Cool; cut into bars, 2x1 inch.   *4½ dozen cookies.*

ALMOND SHORTBREADS

>   1 packet free-flowing pie crust mix
>   1 cup confectioners' sugar
>   ½ cup chopped blanched almonds
>   1 teaspoon almond extract

Heat oven to 350°. Prepare pastry for Two-crust Pie as directed on package except—before adding water to pie crust mix, mix in sugar, nuts and almond extract.

Roll dough ½ inch thick on lightly floured board. Cut into 1¼-inch diamonds. Place ½ inch apart on ungreased baking sheet. Bake about 15 minutes or until set. Immediately remove from baking sheet.

About 3 dozen cookies.

Substitution

For free-flowing mix: 2 sticks pie crust mix.

CHOCOLATE CHIP BARS

>   ⅓ cup shortening
>   ⅓ cup butter or margarine, softened
>   ½ cup granulated sugar
>   ½ cup brown sugar (packed)
>   1 egg
>   1 teaspoon vanilla
>   1½ cups all-purpose flour*
>   ½ teaspoon soda
>   ½ teaspoon salt
>   ½ cup chopped pecans
>   1 package (6 ounces) semisweet
>   chocolate pieces

Heat oven to 375°. Mix shortening, butter, sugars, egg and vanilla. Stir in remaining ingredients.

Spread in ungreased baking pan, 13x9x2 inches. Bake 20 to 25 minutes or until light brown. Cool; cut into bars, about 3x1 inch.   *About 3 dozen cookies.*

---

* *If using self-rising flour, omit soda and salt.*

BUTTER PECAN COOKIES

1 package (12.5 ounces) butter pecan muffin mix
⅓ cup salad oil
1 egg
2 tablespoons milk

Heat oven to 375°. Mix muffin mix (dry), oil, egg and milk. Drop by teaspoonfuls 2 inches apart onto ungreased baking sheet. Flatten slightly with bottom of glass that has been greased and dipped in sugar. Bake 8 to 10 minutes or until light brown on edges. Immediately remove from baking sheet.

About 3 dozen cookies.

APPLESAUCE BARS

1 cup all-purpose flour*
⅔ cup brown sugar (packed)
1 teaspoon soda
1 teaspoon pumpkin pie spice
½ teaspoon salt
¼ cup shortening
1 cup applesauce
1 egg
½ cup raisins
Browned Butter Icing (below)

Heat oven to 350°. Grease baking pan, 13x9x2 inches. Mix all ingredients except icing. Spread in pan. Bake about 25 minutes. Cool; frost with icing. Cut into bars, about 3x1 inch.   *32 cookies.*

If using self-rising flour, decrease soda to ½ teaspoon and omit salt.

BROWNED BUTTER ICING

Heat 3 tablespoons butter over medium heat until golden. Remove from heat; blend in 1½ cups confectioners' sugar, 1 teaspoon vanilla and about 1 tablespoon milk. Beat until smooth.

COCONUT-TOFFEE BARS

¼ cup butter or margarine, softened
¼ cup shortening
½ cup brown sugar (packed)
1 cup all-purpose flour°
Almond-Coconut Topping (below)

Heat oven to 350°. Cream butter, shortening and sugar. Blend in flour. Press evenly in bottom of ungreased baking pan, 13x9x2 inches. Bake 10 minutes.

Spread Almond-Coconut Topping on baked layer. Bake 25 minutes longer or until topping is golden brown. Cool cookies slightly; cut into bars, about 3x1 inch.   *32 cookies.*

° *If using self-rising flour, omit baking powder and salt from Almond-Coconut Topping.*

ALMOND-COCONUT TOPPING

2 eggs
1 cup brown sugar (packed)
1 teaspoon vanilla
2 tablespoons flour
1 teaspoon baking powder
½ teaspoon salt
1 cup shredded coconut
1 cup chopped almonds

Beat eggs in large mixing bowl; stir in remaining ingredients.

CHOCOLATE CHIP COOKIES

⅔ cup shortening
⅔ cup butter or margarine, softened
1 cup granulated sugar
1 cup brown sugar (packed)
2 eggs
2 teaspoons vanilla
3 cups all-purpose flour*
1 teaspoon soda
1 teaspoon salt
1 cup chopped nuts
2 packages (6 ounces each) semisweet
  chocolate pieces

Heat oven to 375°. Mix shortening, butter, sugars, eggs and vanilla. Stir in remaining ingredients. (For a softer, rounder cookie, add ½ cup flour.)

Drop dough by rounded teaspoonfuls 2 inches apart onto ungreased baking sheet. Bake 8 to 10 minutes or until light brown. Cool slightly before removing from baking sheet.   *About 7 dozen cookies.*

---

* *If using self-rising flour, omit soda and salt.*

VARIATION

■ *Salted Peanut Cookies:* Substitute 2 cups salted peanuts for the chopped nuts and chocolate pieces. Before baking, flatten each cookie with bottom of glass that has been greased and dipped in sugar.

BROWN SUGAR PECAN ROUNDS

½ cup butter or margarine, softened
1¼ cups brown sugar (packed)
1 egg
1¼ cups all-purpose flour°
¼ teaspoon soda
⅛ teaspoon salt
½ cup coarsely chopped pecans

Heat oven to 350°. Mix butter, brown sugar and egg. Stir in remaining ingredients.

Drop dough by teaspoonfuls about 2 inches apart onto ungreased baking sheet. (Dough will flatten and spread.) Bake 12 to 15 minutes or until set.

About 3 dozen cookies.

° *If using self-rising flour, omit soda and salt.*

POLYNESIAN COOKIES

1 cup shortening
1½ cups sugar
1 egg
1 can (8½ ounces) crushed pineapple
3½ cups all-purpose flour°
1 teaspoon soda
½ teaspoon salt
¼ teaspoon nutmeg
½ cup chopped macadamia nuts

Heat oven to 400°. Mix shortening, sugar and egg. Stir in pineapple (with syrup) and remaining ingredients.

Drop dough by teaspoonfuls about 2 inches apart onto ungreased baking sheet. Bake 8 to 10 minutes or until golden brown and no imprint remains when touched lightly with finger.   *About 5 dozen cookies.*

° *If using self-rising flour, omit soda and salt.*

Substitution

For macadamia nuts: ½ cup chopped walnuts or pecans.

VARIATIONS

■ *Pineapple Coconut Cookies:* Omit nutmeg; stir in 1 cup flaked coconut.

■ *Pineapple Raisin Cookies:* Stir in 1 cup raisins.

Take Care with Your Cookie-baking

☐ Make sure your baking sheets are in good condition—nice and smooth. They should be at least 2 inches narrower and shorter than your oven.

☐ Don't grease unless the recipe tells you so.

☐ Always place cookie dough on a cool sheet.

☐ It's best to bake cookies one sheet at a time, in the center of the oven.

☐ With drop cookies, you can take a trial run: bake a test cookie. If it spreads more than you like, add 1 or 2 tablespoons flour to the dough. If it's too dry or crumbly, add 1 or 2 tablespoons cream or milk.

☐ Don't overbake. Check cookies at the end of the minimum baking time. One minute can make a big difference.

☐ When cookies are done, remove from the baking sheet immediately—unless the recipe directs otherwise. Cool on a wire rack.

PEANUT BREAK

    1 cup butter or margarine, melted
1½ cups brown sugar (packed)
    2 cups all-purpose flour°
    ¼ cup dark corn syrup
    1 egg
    2 cups salted peanuts

Heat oven to 375°. Line jelly roll pan, 15½ x 10½ x 1 inch, with waxed paper. Cream butter and sugar. Mix in flour, syrup and egg. Stir in peanuts.

Spread in pan. Bake about 25 minutes or until light brown. Loosen layer from sides of pan; invert onto wire rack. Carefully remove paper. Cool; break into pieces.

° *Self-rising flour can be used in this recipe.*

Candies

CHOCOLATE FUDGE

>   2 tablespoons butter or margarine
> ¼ cup plus 2 teaspoons milk
>   1 package (15.4 ounces) chocolate fudge
>   frosting mix

Butter loaf pan, 9x5x3 inches. In medium saucepan, melt butter in milk. Blend in frosting mix (dry). Heat over low heat, stirring constantly, 1 to 2 minutes or until smooth and glossy. Spread mixture evenly in buttered pan. Cool until firm. Cut into 1-inch squares.
32 candies.

VARIATION

■ *Chocolate-Nut Fudge:* Stir in ½ cup chopped nuts.

OPERA FUDGE

>   2 tablespoons butter or margarine
> ¼ cup milk
>   1 package (15.4 ounces) creamy white frosting mix
> ½ cup chopped nuts

Butter loaf pan, 9x5x3 inches. In medium saucepan, melt butter in milk. Blend in frosting mix (dry). Heat over low heat, stirring constantly, 1 to 2 minutes or until smooth and glossy. Remove from heat; stir in nuts.

Spread mixture evenly in buttered pan. Cool until firm. Cut into 1-inch squares.   *32 candies.*

VARIATION

■ *Cherry Opera Fudge:* Stir in ½ cup candied cherry halves with the nuts.

FUDGE CLUSTERS

    2 tablespoons butter or margarine
    ¼ cup plus 2 teaspoons milk
    1 package (15.4 ounces) chocolate fudge
      frosting mix
    1 cup pecans or salted peanuts

In medium saucepan, melt butter in milk. Blend in frosting mix (dry). Heat over low heat, stirring constantly, 1 to 2 minutes or until smooth and glossy. Remove from heat; stir in nuts.

   Drop by teaspoonfuls onto waxed paper. (Keep mixture warm, stirring occasionally, while making candies.) Cool until firm.   *3 to 4 dozen candies.*

CRUNCHY COFFEE DROPS

    2 tablespoons butter or margarine
    ¼ cup milk
    1 package (15.4 ounces) creamy white frosting mix
    1 to 2 tablespoons powdered instant coffee
    1½ cups toasted flaked coconut

In medium saucepan, melt butter in milk. Blend in frosting mix (dry) and instant coffee. Heat over low heat, stirring constantly, 1 to 2 minutes or until smooth and glossy. Remove from heat; stir in coconut.

   Drop by teaspoonfuls onto waxed paper. (Keep mixture warm, stirring occasionally, while making candies.) Cool until firm.   *4 to 5 dozen candies.*

MARGUERITES

    1 package (7.2 ounces) fluffy white frosting mix
    1 cup chopped nuts
    About 4 dozen soda crackers

Heat oven to 350°. Prepare frosting as directed on package. Fold in nuts. Drop by tablespoonfuls onto soda crackers. Bake 4 to 6 minutes or until light brown.
      About 4 dozen confections.

PEANUT BUTTER FUDGE BALLS

 1 package (15.4 ounces) chocolate fudge frosting mix
 ½ cup creamy peanut butter
 ¼ cup butter or margarine, softened
 2 tablespoons hot water
 ½ teaspoon vanilla
 2 cups O-shaped puffed oat cereal

In large bowl, mix frosting mix (dry), peanut butter, butter, water and vanilla until blended. Mix in cereal. Shape into 1-inch balls.   *About 4 dozen candies.*

CHOCOLATE BONBONS

 1 package (15.4 ounces) chocolate fudge
    frosting mix
 ½ cup butter or margarine, softened
 1 teaspoon vanilla

Mix frosting mix (dry), butter and vanilla with fork. Work into a ball with hands. Knead 20 to 30 times on board lightly dusted with confectioners' sugar. Wrap fondant around candied fruit such as cherries, ginger, pineapple or walnut halves.

Garnish candies with finely chopped coconut pressed on top or roll in finely chopped nuts, chocolate shot and the like. Store in tightly covered container in cool place.   *4 to 5 dozen candies.*

VARIATION

■ *Vanilla Bonbons:* Substitute 1 package (15.4 ounces) creamy white frosting mix for the chocolate fudge frosting mix. Tint fondant with food color if desired.

ALMOND DROPS

    1 can (16.5 ounces) vanilla frosting
    ¾ teaspoon almond extract
    ½ teaspoon vanilla
    ½ cup slivered almonds, toasted

Mix all ingredients. Drop by level teaspoonfuls onto waxed paper-covered baking sheet. Chill until set, about 4 hours. Store in refrigerator.   *7 dozen candies.*

CREAMY VANILLA FONDANT

Mix 1 package (15.4 ounces) creamy white frosting mix (dry), ½ cup butter or margarine, softened, and 1 teaspoon vanilla with fork. Work into a ball with hands. Knead 20 to 30 times on board lightly dusted with confectioners' sugar. (Fondant can be divided and tinted with various food colors; knead again to distribute color evenly in each portion.)

Shape mixture into 1-inch balls. Press tops into, or roll completely in, finely crushed peppermint-stick candy, chopped nuts, multicolored candies or flaked coconut.   *About 4 dozen candies.*

VARIATIONS

■ *Peppermint Creams:* Substitute ½ teaspoon peppermint extract for the vanilla.

■ *Toasted Almond Bonbons:* Omit vanilla and stir in ½ cup finely chopped toasted almonds. Roll balls in finely chopped toasted almonds if desired.

CHOCOLATE NUT CREAMS

    1 package (15.4 ounces) chocolate fudge
      frosting mix
    ½ cup butter or margarine, softened
    1 teaspoon vanilla
    ½ cup finely chopped nuts

Mix frosting mix (dry), butter and vanilla with fork. Stir in nuts. Work into a ball with hands. Knead 20 to 30 times on board lightly dusted with confectioners' sugar.

Shape mixture into 1-inch balls. (If desired, roll in mixture of 1 teaspoon cinnamon and 1 tablespoon granulated sugar.) Store in tightly covered container in cool place.   *About 5 dozen candies.*

VARIATION

■ *Vanilla Nut Creams:* Substitute 1 package (15.4 ounces) creamy white frosting mix for the chocolate fudge frosting mix.

Cakes

Starting with a mix ...
WHITE CAKE VARIATIONS

Prepare 1 package (18.5 ounces) white cake mix as directed except—try one of these variations:

■ *Cherry:* Stir in ½ cup drained finely chopped maraschino cherries.

■ *Cherry-Nut:* Stir in ½ cup finely chopped nuts and ½ cup drained finely chopped maraschino cherries.

■ *Coconut:* Stir in 1 to 1½ cups flaked coconut.

■ *Mint:* Add ¼ teaspoon peppermint extract and stir in red or green food color.

■ *Orange:* Add 2 tablespoons grated orange peel.

STRAWBERRY CHANTILLY TORTE

> 1 package (18.5 ounces) white cake mix
> 1 package (15.4 ounces) creamy white frosting mix
> 1 package (8 ounces) cream cheese, softened
> 1 tablespoon milk
> 1 teaspoon almond extract
> 1 pint strawberries

Bake cake in 2 layer pans, 8 or 9x1½ inches, as directed on package. Cool; split to make 4 layers.

In small mixer bowl, beat frosting mix (dry), cream cheese, milk and almond extract until smooth. Slice strawberries lengthwise, reserving ½ cup of the outer slices for top layer.

Stack layers, spreading each with about ½ cup frosting and about ½ cup strawberries. Place reserved strawberry slices cut side down on top layer. Chill at least 1 hour before serving. Because of the cream cheese, refrigerate leftover cake.

Starting with a mix...
YELLOW CAKE VARIATIONS

Prepare 1 package (18.5 ounces) yellow cake mix as directed except—try one of the following variations:

■ *Banana:* Use ¼ cup less water and add 1 cup mashed banana (2 to 3 medium) and ⅛ teaspoon soda. Stir in ½ cup finely chopped nuts.

■ *Maple-Nut:* Add 2 teaspoons maple flavoring and stir in ⅓ cup finely chopped nuts.

■ *Nutmeg-Mace:* Add ½ teaspoon each nutmeg and mace.

■ *Orange:* Add 2 tablespoons grated orange peel.

■ *Toasted Coconut:* Stir in 1 to 1½ cups toasted flaked coconut.

BUTTERSCOTCH CRUNCH CAKE

> 1 package (18.5 ounces) yellow cake mix
> 2 cans (5 ounces each) butterscotch pudding
> 1 cup crushed peanut brittle

Bake cake in baking pan, 13x9x2 inches, as directed on package. Cool; spread pudding on cake. Sprinkle with peanut brittle.

PEANUT BUTTER CAKE

Prepare 1 package (18.5 ounces) yellow cake mix as directed except—before blending, add 1 cup peanut butter. Cool.

Prepare 1 package (15.4 ounces) creamy white frosting mix as directed except—substitute peanut butter for the butter. If frosting is too thick, add a few drops of hot water. Frost cake.

BUSY DAY CUPCAKES

Bake cupcakes in greased muffin cups as directed on 1 package (18.5 ounces) white, yellow or devils food cake mix. Place chocolate-covered thin mint candy on each cupcake.

Set oven control at broil and/or 550°. Broil cupcakes 3 inches from heat 1 to 2 minutes or until candy is soft. Spread candy to frost cupcakes.

Starting with a mix . . .
DEVILS FOOD CAKE VARIATIONS

Prepare 1 package (18.5 ounces) devils food cake mix as directed except—try one of the following variations:

■ *Banana:* Use ¼ cup less water and add ¾ cup mashed banana (1½ to 2 medium) and ⅛ teaspoon soda. Stir in ½ cup chopped nuts.

■ *Cherry Chocolate:* Stir in ½ cup well-drained chopped maraschino cherries.

■ *Fudge Nut:* Stir in ½ cup chopped nuts.

■ *Mocha:* Use 1 cup cold strong coffee for part of the water and add 3 tablespoons instant coffee.

■ *Peppermint:* Stir in ¼ teaspoon peppermint extract.

PARTY DEVILS FOOD CAKE

    1 package (18.5 ounces) devils food cake mix
    1 package (7.2 ounces) fluffy white frosting mix
    8 maraschino cherries, chopped
    1 can (4 ounces) shredded coconut
    ½ teaspoon almond extract

Bake cake in 2 layer pans, 8 or 9x1½ inches, as directed on package. Cool.

Prepare frosting as directed on package except—fold in almond extract; frost cake. Mix cherries and coconut until coconut is a delicate pink. Sprinkle on frosted cake.

TRIPLE FUDGE CAKE

> 1 package (3¾ ounces) chocolate pudding
> and pie filling
> 1 package (18.5 ounces) devils food cake mix
> ½ cup semisweet chocolate pieces
> ½ cup coarsely chopped nuts

Heat oven to 350°. Grease and flour baking pan, 13x9x2 inches. In large saucepan, cook pudding as directed on package. Stir cake mix (dry) into hot pudding. Beat 2 minutes on medium speed.

Pour into pan. Sprinkle batter with chocolate pieces and nuts. Bake 35 to 40 minutes. If you like, serve with whipped cream.

BROWNIE FUDGE CAKE

> 1 package (15.5 ounces) fudge brownie mix
> 2 eggs
> ½ cup water
> ½ cup finely chopped nuts
> Creamy Cocoa Frosting (below)

Heat oven to 350°. Grease baking pan, 9x9x2 inches. In small mixer bowl, blend brownie mix (dry), eggs and ¼ cup of the water on low speed, scraping bowl constantly. Beat 1 minute medium speed, scraping bowl occasionally. Add remaining ¼ cup water; beat 1 minute longer. Stir in nuts.

Pour into pan. Bake about 30 minutes or until top springs back when touched lightly with finger. Cool and frost.

CREAMY COCOA FROSTING

> 1 cup confectioners' sugar
> 2 tablespoons cocoa
> 1 tablespoon soft butter or margarine
> 1½ tablespoons milk

Beat all ingredients until smooth.

COUNTRY LOAF CAKE

Heat oven to 350° (325° for glass pans). Grease and flour 2 loaf pans, 9x5x3 inches. Prepare 1 package (18.5 ounces) layer cake mix (chocolate, yellow or white) as directed except—use 2 tablespoons less water.

Pour into pans. Bake 30 to 35 minutes or until wooden pick inserted in center comes out clean. Cool. If desired, dust cake with confectioners' sugar or frost with your favorite frosting and trim with candied fruits or chopped nuts.

VARIATION

■ *Cake Sandwiches:* Cut loaf cake into ½-inch slices; put slices together in pairs with favorite pudding, marshmallow crème or slice of ice cream.

HAWAIIAN CREAM PIE

     1 package (21.5 ounces) pineapple upside-down
        cake mix
  ½ can (18-ounce size) vanilla pudding
     Brown Sugar Glaze (below)

Heat oven to 350°. Drain pineapple from 1 package pineapple upside-down cake mix; fold into 1 cup vanilla pudding. Chill.

Generously grease and flour layer pan, 8x1½ inches. Prepare cake as directed on package. Pour into pan. Bake 35 to 40 minutes or until wooden pick inserted in center comes out clean. Cool slightly; remove from pan. Cool thoroughly. Split layer; fill with pudding mixture and refrigerate.

Just before serving, spread with hot Brown Sugar Glaze. (If glaze hardens, stir over low heat.) Because of the pudding, refrigerate leftover pie.

BROWN SUGAR GLAZE

Mix Topping Mix, 2 tablespoons butter and 1 tablespoon light cream in small saucepan. Heat to boiling, stirring constantly.

TRIPLE LEMON CAKE

Bake 1 package (18.5 ounces) lemon chiffon cake mix
as directed. Cool; split to make 3 layers. Stack layers,
filling each with 1 can (5 ounces) vanilla pudding
(1 cup).

Prepare 1 package (6.5 ounces) lemon fluff frosting
mix as directed. Frost side and top of cake. Because
of the pudding, refrigerate leftover cake.

FUDGY PECAN PUDDING CAKE

   1 package (12.5 ounces) butter pecan
     muffin mix
   ½ cup milk
   1 cup brown sugar (packed)
   ¼ cup cocoa
   1¼ cups hot water

Heat oven to 350°. Grease baking pan, 9x9x2 inches.
Stir together muffin mix (dry) and milk just until mix
is moistened. Spread in pan.

Mix sugar and cocoa; sprinkle evenly on batter. Pour
hot water carefully on batter. (Do not stir.) Bake 35
minutes. Cool slightly; cut into squares. Invert onto
dessert plates and top with sauce.   *9 servings.*

QUICK DATE CAKE

   1 package (14 ounces) date bar mix
   ½ cup hot water
   2 eggs
   1 teaspoon baking powder
   ½ cup chopped walnuts

Heat oven to 375°. Grease baking pan, 8x8x2 inches.
Mix date filling and hot water. Stir in crumbly mix,
eggs, baking powder and nuts.

Spread in pan. Bake about 30 minutes or until top
springs back when touched lightly with finger. Cool.

Starting with a mix . . .
POUND CAKE VARIATIONS

Prepare 1 package (16 ounces) golden pound cake mix as directed except—try one of the following variations:

■ *Chocolate-Nut:* Stir in 2 squares (1 ounce each) unsweetened chocolate, grated, and ½ cup nuts.

■ *Fruit-Nut:* Stir in ½ cup finely chopped mixed candied fruit and ½ cup finely chopped nuts.

■ *Lemon:* Stir in 1 tablespoon grated lemon peel.

■ *Pecan:* Stir in 1 cup finely chopped pecans.

■ *Raisin-Nut:* Stir in ½ cup finely chopped raisins and ½ cup chopped nuts.

ROOT BEER ANGEL CAKE

Prepare 1 package (15 or 16 ounces) angel food cake mix as directed except—substitute root beer-flavored carbonated beverage for the water. Cool. Pour or spoon small amount of Root Beer Glaze (below) at a time on cake and spread, allowing some to drizzle unevenly down side.

ROOT BEER GLAZE

Melt ⅓ cup butter or margarine in saucepan. Remove from heat. Blend in 2 cups confectioners' sugar and ¼ cup finely crushed root beer-flavored hard candies. Stir in 2 to 4 tablespoons root beer-flavored carbonated beverage, 1 tablespoon at a time, until glaze is of proper consistency.

VARIATION

■ *Cotton Candy Angel Cake:* Substitute strawberry-flavored soda for the root beer-flavored carbonated beverage. In the glaze, omit crushed hard candies and use water or strawberry-flavored soda.

MOCK PISTACHIO CAKE

> ½ cup diced almonds
> 4 or 5 drops green food color
> 1 package (15 or 16 ounces) angel food cake mix
>   Glaze (below)

Heat oven to 375°. In plastic bag or tightly covered jar, shake almonds and food color until almonds are evenly colored. Spread in ungreased baking pan. Bake 8 to 10 minutes. Cool.

Prepare cake as directed on package except—fold almonds into batter. Cool.

Pour or spoon small amount of Glaze at a time on top of cake and spread, allowing some to drizzle unevenly down side. (Glaze will set within ½ hour.)

GLAZE

Mix 1½ cups confectioners' sugar and 1 to 2 tablespoons water until smooth.

VARIATION

■ *Chocolate Chip Angle Cake:* Omit almonds and green food color. Fold in ½ cup chocolate shot.

GRAHAM CRACKER TORTE

> ⅔ cup walnuts
> 1¼ cups graham cracker crumbs
>   1 tablespoon plus 1 teaspoon flour
> 1½ teaspoons baking powder
>   2 eggs
> ⅓ cup butter or margarine, softened
> ⅔ cup sugar
> ½ cup milk
>   1 can (18 ounces) chocolate pudding
>   Dessert topping or whipped cream
>   Chopped crystallized ginger

Heat oven to 350°. Grease and flour layer pan, 9x1½ inches. Chop nuts 10 seconds in blender. Mix nuts, crumbs, flour and baking powder in bowl.

In blender, whip eggs, butter and sugar ½ minute while adding milk. Whip 1 minute longer, adding crumb mixture and stopping blender occasionally to scrape sides and guide mixture toward blades.

Pour batter into pan. Bake 40 minutes. Cool 10 minutes in pan; remove and cool. Split to make 2 layers. Fill layers and frost top with pudding. Garnish with dessert topping and ginger. Because of the pudding, refrigerate leftover torte. *8 to 10 servings.*

Substitution

For chocolate pudding: 1 can (18 ounces) vanilla or butterscotch pudding or 2 cups sweetened whipped cream.

BLENDER ORANGE-RAISIN CAKE

    1 orange
    1 egg
    ⅓ cup shortening
    ¾ cup milk
    1 teaspoon vanilla
    1¼ cups all-purpose flour°
    1 cup sugar
    1½ teaspoons baking powder
    ½ teaspoon salt
    ½ cup walnuts
    ½ cup raisins
    Creamy Orange Frosting (page 186)

Heat oven to 350°. Grease and flour baking pan, 9x9x2 or 8x8x2 inches. With vegetable parer, remove thin outer layer of peel from orange. (Set orange aside and use for juice in frosting.) Place peel in blender; chop on low speed and set chopped peel aside.

In order listed, measure egg, shortening, milk, vanilla, flour, sugar, baking powder, salt, walnuts and raisins into blender; add 1 tablespoon of the chopped peel (reserve ½ teaspoon chopped peel for frosting). Mix ½ minute on high speed, stopping blender occa-

---

° *If using self-rising flour, omit baking powder and salt.*

sionally to scrape sides with rubber spatula. (Batter may be slightly lumpy.)

Pour batter into pan. Bake 9-inch square about 35 minutes, 8-inch square about 40 minutes or until wooden pick inserted in center comes out clean. Cool; frost with Creamy Orange Frosting.

Note: To prepare cake with electric mixer, measure all ingredients except orange and frosting into large mixer bowl, using 1 teaspoon grated orange peel, ½ cup chopped walnuts and ½ cup chopped raisins. Blend ½ minute on low speed, scraping bowl constantly. Beat 3 minutes high speed, scraping bowl occasionally.

CREAMY ORANGE FROSTING

⅓ cup butter or margarine, softened
1½ teaspoons vanilla
2 tablespoons orange juice
½ teaspoon reserved chopped orange peel
2 cups confectioners' sugar

Mix all ingredients until smooth.

The Cake Pan Counts—a Lot

Obvious but important, use the right size pan. Shiny metal ones give you tender, light brown crusts. (With heat-resistant glass pans, just lower the oven temperature 25°.) Non-stick finishes are great, too. Simply do as the manufacturer says.

For layer or loaf cakes (mix or scratch), grease pans generously with shortening—not butter, margarine or oil. Dust with abandon, shaking out the excess flour. Place pans on the middle rack of the oven and don't let them touch—the sides or each other.

SPICE CAKE

  1¼ cups all-purpose flour°
   1 cup sugar
  1½ teaspoons baking powder
   1 teaspoon cinnamon
  ½ teaspoon salt
  ½ teaspoon nutmeg
  ¼ teaspoon cloves
  ¾ cup milk
  ⅓ cup shortening
   1 egg
     Browned Butter Icing (below)

Heat oven to 350°. Grease and flour baking pan,
8x8x2 or 9x9x2 inches. Measure all ingredients except
Browned Butter Icing into large mixer bowl. Blend
½ minute on low speed, scraping bowl constantly.
Beat 3 minutes high speed, scraping bowl occasionally.

Pour into pan. Bake 35 to 40 minutes or until wooden
pick inserted in center comes out clean. Cool; frost
with Browned Butter Icing.

° If using self-rising flour, omit baking powder and salt.

BROWNED BUTTER ICING

   3 tablespoons butter or margarine
  1½ cups confectioners' sugar
   1 teaspoon vanilla
     About 1 tablespoon milk

Heat butter in saucepan over medium heat until a
delicate brown. Blend in sugar. Stir in vanilla and milk;
beat until frosting is smooth and of spreading consistency.

Substitution

For all-purpose flour: 1½ cups cake flour.

Starting with a mix . . .
CHOCOLATE FROSTING VARIATIONS

Prepare 1 package (15.4 ounces) chocolate fudge frosting mix as directed except—try one of the following variations:

- *Mocha:* Add 1 tablespoon powdered instant coffee.
- *Peppermint:* Sprinkle top of frosted cake with ½ cup crushed peppermint candy.
- *Peppermint Fudge:* Stir in ¼ to ½ teaspoon peppermint extract.
- *Rocky Road:* Stir in ½ cup miniature marshmallows and ½ cup chopped nuts.

Starting with a mix . . .
CREAMY WHITE FROSTING VARIATIONS

Prepare 1 package (15.4 ounces) creamy white frosting mix as directed except—try one of the following variations:

- *Browned Butter:* Lightly brown butter over low heat.
- *Chocolate:* Add ½ cup cocoa.
- *Cocoa Mocha:* Substitute strong coffee for the water and add ½ cup cocoa.
- *Lemon, Orange or Lime:* Substitute lemon, orange or lime juice for the water.
- *Peppermint:* Add ½ teaspoon peppermint extract and 3 to 4 drops food color.
- *Raisin-Nut:* Stir in ½ cup cut-up raisins and ½ cup finely chopped nuts.
- *Raspberry or Strawberry:* Substitute crushed fresh or thawed frozen raspberries or strawberries for the water.

Starting with a mix . . .
FLUFFY WHITE FROSTING VARIATIONS

Prepare 1 package (7.2 ounces) fluffy white frosting mix as directed except—try one of the following variations:

- *Almond:* Fold in ½ teaspoon almond extract.

- *Cherry-Nut:* Fold in ⅓ cup drained chopped maraschino cherries and ½ cup chopped nuts.

- *Chocolate Chip:* Fold in ½ cup semisweet chocolate pieces.

- *Cinnamon:* Add 1 teaspoon cinnamon.

- *Clove:* Add ¼ teaspoon cloves.

- *Lemon:* Fold in ½ teaspoon lemon extract.

- *Maple-Nut:* Fold in ½ teaspoon maple flavoring and ½ cup chopped pecans.

- *Mocha:* Add 2 teaspoons powdered instant coffee.

- *Nutmeg:* Add ½ teaspoon nutmeg.

- *Orange-Coconut:* Fold in 1 tablespoon grated orange peel and ½ cup finely cut-up coconut.

- *Orange-Raisin:* Fold in ½ cup chopped nuts, 1½ cups raisins and 2 tablespoons coarsely grated orange peel.

- *Peppermint:* Fold in ¼ teaspoon peppermint extract. Red or green food color can be added.

- *Spice:* Add ½ teaspoon cinnamon, ¼ teaspoon nutmeg and ¼ teaspoon cloves.

Frosting a Layer Cake?

Is the cake nice and cool? Okay, begin. Lift one layer in your hand. With your free hand, brush the sides and edges gently to remove excess crumbs. Do the same with the other layer.

Place one layer upside down on the cake plate. Use about ½ cup frosting to fill—but don't spread to the edge; leave about ¼ inch free of filling. Then place the second layer right side up on the filling.

Now to the business of frosting. Do the sides first. Start with a thin coat to seal in the crumbs, then once again lavishly. Bring the frosting up high on the side, forming a ridge above the top. Spread the remaining frosting on top, meeting the ridge. It's picture pretty this way—agree?

VANILLA BUTTER FROSTING

⅓ cup soft butter or margarine
3 cups confectioners' sugar
1½ teaspoons vanilla
About 2 tablespoons milk

Blend butter and sugar. Stir in vanilla and milk; beat until frosting is smooth and of spreading consistency. *Fills and frosts two 8- or 9-inch layers or frosts a 13x9-inch cake.*

VARIATIONS

■ *Browned Butter Frosting:* Heat butter in saucepan over medium heat until a delicate brown.

■ *Cherry Butter Frosting:* Stir in 2 tablespoons drained chopped maraschino cherries and 2 drops red food color.

■ *Orange Butter Frosting:* Omit vanilla and substitute orange juice for the milk; stir in 2 teaspoons grated orange peel.

■ *Peanut Butter Frosting:* Substitute peanut butter for the butter; increase milk to ¼ to ⅓ cup.

CHOCOLATE BUTTER FROSTING

⅓ cup soft butter or margarine
2 ounces melted unsweetened chocolate (cool)
2 cups confectioners' sugar
1½ teaspoons vanilla
About 2 tablespoons milk

Mix thoroughly butter and cooled chocolate. Blend in sugar. Stir in vanilla and milk; beat until frosting is smooth and of spreading consistency.
Fills and frosts two 8- or 9-inch layers or frosts a 13x9-inch cake.

VARIATIONS

■ *Chocolate-Nut Butter Frosting:* Stir in ¼ cup finely chopped nuts.

■ *Cocoa Butter Frosting:* Substitute ⅓ cup cocoa for the chocolate.

■ *Mocha Butter Frosting:* Blend in 1½ teaspoons powdered instant coffee with the sugar.

CHOCOLATE GLAZE

In small bowl, blend ¼ cup canned chocolate frosting and 2 teaspoons hot water. If necessary, add a few drops of water until of desired consistency.

Glazes an 8- or 9-inch layer cake.

Hideaways for Frosted Cakes

With a creamy-type frosting: Keep under a cake safe or an inverted large bowl. Or cover *loosely* with foil, plastic wrap or waxed paper.

With a fluffy-type frosting: Eat right away! If you must store, or have some left over, use a cake safe. But keep a knife under the edge to let a bit of air in.

With a whipped cream-type frosting: Store in the refrigerator —no need to cover. Do the same for any cake with a cream filling or topping.

BUTTERSCOTCH BROILED TOPPING

  ¼ cup soft butter or margarine
  ⅔ cup brown sugar (packed)
  1 cup finely chopped nuts
  2 tablespoons milk

Mix thoroughly butter, brown sugar and nuts. Stir in milk. Spread mixture evenly on warm 13x9-inch cake.

Set oven control at broil and/or 550°. Place cake 5 inches from heat; broil about 3 minutes or until topping bubbles and browns slightly. (Watch carefully—mixture burns easily.)   *Frosts a 13x9-inch cake.*

VARIATIONS

■ *Coconut Broiled Topping:* Decrease nuts to ½ cup; add 1 cup flaked coconut with the nuts and increase milk to 3 tablespoons.

■ *Crunchy Broiled Topping:* Decrease nuts to ½ cup; add ½ cup whole wheat flakes cereal with the nuts and increase milk to 3 tablespoons.

BROWN SUGAR MERINGUE

  2 egg whites (¼ cup)
  1 cup brown sugar (packed)
  1 tablespoon lemon juice
  ½ cup finely chopped nuts

Just before cake is removed from oven, beat egg whites until foamy. Gradually beat sugar and lemon juice into egg whites, beating until stiff. Carefully spread on hot 13x9-inch cake. Sprinkle with nuts. Bake in 400° oven 8 to 10 minutes or until brown.

Frosts a 13x9-inch cake.

Pies

APPLE-CHEESE PIE

Pastry for 9-inch Two-crust Pie (page 202)
1 cup shredded Cheddar cheese (4 ounces)
2 cans (21 ounces each) apple pie filling

Heat oven to 425°. Prepare pastry except—add cheese before mixing. Fill pastry-lined pie pan with apple pie filling.

Cover with top crust which has slits cut in it; seal and flute. Cover edge with 2- to 3-inch strip of aluminum foil to prevent excessive browning; remove foil for the last 15 minutes of baking. Bake 35 to 40 minutes.

Starting with a frozen pie . . .
APPLE PIE FIX-UPS

Bake 8-inch frozen ready-to-bake apple pie as directed on package except—try one of the following variations:

■ *Cheesey Apple Pie:* Five minutes before end of baking time, spread ½ cup pasteurized process cheese spread on pie.

■ *Raspberry-glazed Apple Pie:* Five minutes before end of baking time, spread 2 tablespoons raspberry jam on pie.

■ *Vanilla Apple Pie:* After baking, pour 2 teaspoons vanilla into slits in crust. Best served warm.

■ *Orange-glazed Apple Pie:* Mix ½ cup confectioners' sugar, 2 teaspoons grated orange peel and 1 tablespoon orange juice. Spoon on warm baked pie; garnish with orange slices.

APPLE PANDOWDY

Pastry for 8- or 9-inch Two-crust Pie (page 202)
1 can (20 ounces) apple slices, drained
½ cup brown sugar (packed)
3 tablespoons butter or margarine, melted
6 tablespoons maple-flavored syrup

Heat oven to 425°. Prepare pastry. Mix apple slices and brown sugar. Fill pastry-lined pie pan with apple mixture; top with butter and 3 tablespoons of the syrup.

Cover with top crust which has slits cut in it; seal and flute. Bake 15 minutes. Remove from oven; make crisscross cuts about 1 inch apart through top crust and apples. Pour remaining syrup on crust.

Cover edge with a 2- to 3-inch strip of aluminum foil to prevent excessive browning. Bake 25 minutes. Serve warm and, if you like, with maple-flavored syrup.

VARIATION

■ *Molasses Pandowdy:* Substitute 3 tablespoons corn syrup for first 3 tablespoons maple-flavored syrup and 3 tablespoons molasses for the second.

RASPBERRY PIE

Pastry for 9-inch Two-crust Pie (page 202)
¼ cup sugar
3 tablespoons flour
3 packages (10 ounces each) frozen raspberries,
   thawed and drained (reserve ½ cup syrup)
2 tablespoons butter or margarine

Heat oven to 425°. Prepare pastry. Combine sugar and flour; mix with raspberries and reserved syrup. Pour into pastry-lined pie pan; dot with butter.

Cover with top crust which has slits cut in it; seal and flute. Cover edge with 2- to 3-inch strip of aluminum foil to prevent excessive browning; remove foil for the last 15 minutes of baking. Bake 35 to 40 minutes.

Starting with a frozen pie ...
CHERRY PIE FIX-UPS

Bake 8-inch frozen ready-to-bake cherry pie as directed on package except—try one of the following variations:

■ *Candy-topped Cherry Pie:* Five minutes before end of baking time, sprinkle 1 bar (1⅛ ounces) chocolate toffee candy, chopped, on pie. After baking, pour 1 tablespoon crème de cacao or chocolate syrup into slits in crust.

■ *Lemon-glazed Cherry Pie:* Ten minutes before end of baking time, spread pie with Lemon Glaze: Mix ½ cup confectioners' sugar, 1 teaspoon grated lemon peel and 1 tablespoon lemon juice until smooth. (Be sure to drizzle some of the glaze into slits in crust.)

ORANGE-CHERRY PIE

Pastry for 8-inch Two-crust Pie (page 202)
1 tablespoon finely shredded orange peel
1 can (21 ounces) cherry pie filling
½ cup confectioners' sugar
1 teaspoon shredded orange peel
1 tablespoon orange juice

Heat oven to 425°. Prepare pastry except—add 1 tablespoon orange peel. Mix remaining ingredients. Fill pastry-lined pie pan with cherry mixture.

Cut second half of pastry into eight ½-inch strips. Arrange 4 pastry strips 1 inch apart across filling. Weave first cross-strip, folding back every other strip going the other way. Continue weaving cross-strips in this manner until lattice is complete.

Fold lower crust over ends of pastry strips, building up edge; seal and flute. Cover edge with 2- to 3-inch strip of aluminum foil to prevent excessive browning; remove foil for the last 15 minutes of baking. Bake 35 to 40 minutes.

BERRY BASKET PIE

> 9-inch Cookie Pat Crust (page 204)
> 4 cups fresh strawberries (about 2 pints)
> 1 envelope (about 2 ounces) dessert topping mix
> 1 can (18 ounces) vanilla pudding

Bake crust; cool. Reserve about 8 strawberries for garnish. Arrange remaining whole berries in baked crust. Prepare dessert topping as directed on package. Fold topping into pudding; pour on berries in crust. Chill at least 4 hours. Garnish with reserved berries. For easier cutting, let stand at room temperature 10 minutes before serving.

Substitution

For Cookie Pat Crust: Vanilla Wafer Cookie Crumb Crust (page 203).

PERFECT PINEAPPLE PIE

> Pastry for 9-inch Two-crust Pie
> (page 202)
> 3 eggs
> ⅓ cup butter or margarine, melted
> 2 tablespoons lemon juice
> ½ cup water
> 1 cup sugar
> ¼ cup all-purpose flour*
> ¼ teaspoon salt
> 1 can (20½ ounces) crushed pineapple,
> drained

Heat oven to 400°. Prepare pastry. In small mixer bowl, beat eggs until blended. Add butter, lemon juice and water; blend on low speed. Add sugar, flour and salt; beat until smooth. Stir in pineapple. Fill pastry-lined pie pan with pineapple mixture.

---

* If using self-rising flour, omit salt.

Cut second half of pastry into ten ½-inch strips. Arrange 5 pastry strips 1 inch apart across filling. Weave first cross-strip through center. Add another cross-strip, first folding back every other strip going the other way. Continue weaving until lattice is complete.

Fold lower crust over ends of pastry strips, building up edge; seal and flute. Cover edge with 2- to 3-inch strip of aluminum foil to prevent excessive browning; remove foil for the last 15 minutes of baking. Bake 35 to 40 minutes.

PECAN PIE

> 3 eggs
> ⅔ cup sugar
> ½ teaspoon salt
> ⅓ cup butter or margarine, melted
> 1 cup light or dark corn syrup
> 1 cup pecan halves or broken pieces
> 9-inch frozen ready-to-bake pie crust shell

Heat oven to 375°. Beat eggs, sugar, salt, butter and syrup with rotary beater. Stir in nuts. Pour into frozen pie crust shell. Bake 40 to 50 minutes or until filling is set.

Substitution

For ready-to-bake pie crust shell: Pastry for 9-inch One-crust Pie (page 202).

Starting with a frozen pie ...
MINCEMEAT PIE FIX-UPS

Bake 8-inch frozen ready-to-bake mincemeat pie as directed on package. Then try one of the following variations:

■ *Mincemeat Pie with Hard Sauce:* Cool pie about 1 hour. In small mixer bowl, beat ¼ cup soft butter at high speed until very creamy and light in color, about 5 minutes. Gradually beat in ½ cup confectioners' sugar; stir in 1 teaspoon rum or ½ teaspoon rum flavoring. Just before serving, spread on warm pie.

■ *Pudding-topped Mincemeat Pie:* Cool pie about 1 hour. Mix ½ cup canned vanilla pudding and 3 or 4 drops almond extract; just before serving, spread on warm pie.

Starting with a frozen pie ...
PUMPKIN PIE FIX-UPS

Bake 8-inch frozen ready-to-bake pumpkin pie as directed on package. Then try one of the following variations:

■ *Maple Pumpkin Pie:* Cool pie about 30 minutes. Drizzle 2 tablespoons maple-flavored syrup on warm pie; sprinkle with 2 tablespoons chopped pecans. Serve warm.

■ *Pumpkin Pie with Rum Whipped Topping:* Cool pie about 1 hour. Mix ½ carton (8-ounce size) whipped cream cheese, 2 tablespoons confectioners' sugar and 1 tablespoon rum or ½ teaspoon rum flavoring; spread topping on warm pie. Serve immediately.

Pastry a Problem?

It needn't be—if you follow directions carefully and add these tips to your repertoire:

Rolling out: Keep the pastry circle round by pushing in gently around the edge with slightly cupped hands.

Patching up: Moisten the edge or tear; press the pastry patch into place. Who can tell?

Transferring: Fold the pastry round in quarters, then place in the pie pan with the point at center; unfold. It's an easy job this way.

LEMON PUDDING CAKE PIE

Pastry for 9-inch One-crust Pie (page 202)
1 package (11 ounces) lemon pudding cake mix
1 egg
2 tablespoons water
1 cup boiling water

Heat oven to 425°. Prepare pastry. In small mixer bowl, blend Cake Mix, egg and 2 tablespoons water; beat 1 minute on medium speed. Spread batter evenly in pastry-lined pie pan.

Sprinkle Pudding Mix evenly over batter. Do not mix. Pour 1 cup boiling water slowly over mix to moisten top. Do not stir. Cover edge of crust with 2- to 3-inch strip of aluminum foil to prevent excessive browning.

Bake about 25 minutes. Cool pie at least 15 minutes before serving. If desired, top with sweetened whipped cream or ice cream.

BANANA CREAM PIE

> 9-inch Cookie Pat Crust (page 204)
> 1 banana, sliced
> 1 cup miniature marshmallows
> 1 can (18 ounces) vanilla pudding

Bake crust; cool. Fold banana slices and marshmallows into pudding; pour into baked crust. Chill at least 4 hours. For easier cutting, let stand at room temperature 10 minutes before serving.

Substitution

For Cookie Pat Crust: 9-inch Graham Cracker Crust (page 204).

STRAWBERRY CREAM PIE

> 9-inch Graham Cracker Crust (page 204)
> 1 package (10 ounces) frozen strawberries
> 1 package (3 ounces) strawberry-flavored gelatin
> 1 pint vanilla ice cream

Bake crust; cool. Heat strawberries to boiling, breaking apart with fork. Stir in gelatin until dissolved. Mix in ice cream until melted. Chill until thickened but not set.

Pour into baked crust. Chill until firm, about 2 hours. If desired, serve with frozen dessert topping (thawed) or sweetened whipped cream.

Substitution

For Graham Cracker Crust: 9-inch purchased graham cracker crust, baked.

RICH CHOCOLATE PIE

> 9-inch Cookie Pat Crust (page 204)
> ½ cup dairy sour cream
> 1 can (18 ounces) chocolate or chocolate
> fudge pudding
> Sweetened whipped cream
> Chocolate curls

Bake crust; cool. Fold sour cream into 1 cup of the pudding; pour into baked crust. Spread remaining pudding on top. Chill at least 8 hours.

Garnish with whipped cream and chocolate curls. For easier cutting, let stand at room temperature 10 minutes before serving.

GRASSHOPPER PIE

> Chocolate Wafer Cookie Crumb Crust
> (page 203)
> 3 cups miniature marshmallows
> ½ cup milk
> 1½ cups chilled whipping cream
> ¼ cup green crème de menthe
> 3 tablespoons white crème de cacao
> Few drops green food color

Bake crust; cool. Melt marshmallows in milk over low heat, stirring constantly. Chill until thickened.

In chilled bowl, beat cream until stiff. Stir marshmallow mixture to blend; stir in liqueurs and fold into cream. Fold in food color. Pour into baked crust. If desired, sprinkle grated semisweet chocolate on top. Chill at least 4 hours.

Substitution

For miniature marshmallows: 32 large marshmallows, cut up.

ELECTRIC MIXER PASTRY

8- OR 9-INCH ONE-CRUST PIE

> 1 cup all-purpose flour*
> ½ teaspoon salt
> ⅓ cup plus 1 tablespoon shortening
> 2 to 3 tablespoons cold water

8- OR 9-INCH TWO-CRUST PIE

> 2 cups all-purpose flour*
> 1 teaspoon salt
> ⅔ cup plus 2 tablespoons shortening
> 4 to 5 tablespoons cold water

Measure flour, salt and shortening into large mixer bowl; blend 1 minute on low speed, scraping bowl

---

If using self-rising flour, omit salt. Pie crusts made with self-rising flour differ in flavor and texture from those made with plain flour.

Getting the Edge on Pastry

You don't have to be a pro to put a fancy fluting on your pie. All you need is a fork, a spoon or your fingers. Here's how:

Fork Edge: Press tines all around edge—press firmly.

Spoon Scallop: Leaving a ½-inch overhang at rim, cut scallops with tip of inverted teaspoon.

Pinch Edge: With one index finger inside upright pastry fold and other index finger and thumb outside, pinch into V-shape.

---

constantly. Add water; mix until all flour is moistened and dough begins to gather into beaters, about 10 seconds. (If using quick-mixing flour, dough will begin to gather into beater in about 1 minute.) Scrape bowl constantly.

Press dough firmly into a ball. Shape into flattened round on lightly floured cloth-covered board. (For Two-crust Pie, divide dough in half and shape into 2 flattened rounds.) With floured stockinet-covered rolling pin, roll dough 2 inches larger than inverted pie pan.

Fold pastry into quarters; unfold and ease into pan.

For One-crust Pie: Trim overhanging edge of pastry 1 inch from rim of pan. Fold and roll pastry under, even with pan; flute. Fill and bake as directed in recipe.

For Baked Pie Shell: Prick bottom and side thoroughly with fork. Bake in 475° oven 8 to 10 minutes.

For Two-crust Pie: Pour desired filling into pastry-lined pie pan. Trim overhanging edge of pastry ½ inch from rim of pan. Roll second round of dough. Fold into quarters; cut slits so steam can escape. Place over filling and unfold. Trim overhanging edge of pastry 1 inch from rim of pan. Fold and roll top edge under lower edge, pressing pastry on rim of pan to seal; flute. Bake as directed in recipe.

COOKIE CRUMB CRUST

1½ cups cookie crumbs (vanilla or chocolate
    wafers or gingersnaps)
2 tablespoons sugar
¼ cup butter or margarine, melted

Heat oven to 350°. Mix crumbs, sugar and butter. (If desired, reserve 2 to 3 tablespoons crumb mixture for a garnish.) Press mixture firmly and evenly against bottom and side of 9-inch pie pan. Bake 10 minutes. Cool.

GRAHAM CRACKER CRUST

> 1½ cups graham cracker crumbs
>   (about 20 crackers)
> 3 tablespoons sugar
> ⅓ cup butter or margarine, melted

Heat oven to 350°. Mix crumbs, sugar and butter. (If desired, reserve 2 to 3 tablespoons crumb mixture for a garnish.) Press mixture firmly and evenly against bottom and side of 9-inch pie pan. Bake 10 minutes. Cool.

COOKIE PAT CRUST

> 1 cup all-purpose flour°
> ½ cup butter or margarine, softened
> ¼ cup finely chopped pecans
> ¼ cup confectioners' sugar

Heat oven to 400°. With hands mix all ingredients to form a soft dough. Press firmly and evenly against bottom and side of 9-inch pie pan. (Do not press on rim.) Bake 12 to 15 minutes or until light brown. Cool.

° *Self-rising flour can be used in this recipe. If using quick-mixing flour, add 1 tablespoon milk.*

Pastry from a Package

Skip the preliminaries. Get right down to the pastry rolling with a never-fail pie crust mix—either pie crust sticks or free-flowing mix. And since a mix puts you a jump ahead, think about this: do two shells at one time—one for today's pie and one to freeze, baked or unbaked.

Beverages

DEMITASSE

Prepare coffee, using ¼ cup ground coffee for each
¾ cup water. Serve with a twist of lemon peel. Sugar
may be used but cream is usually shunned.

2 servings (about ⅓ cup each).

INSTANT DEMITASSE

Measure ½ cup instant coffee into heatproof container.
Stir in 1 quart boiling water. Cover; let stand 5 minutes.

12 servings (about ⅓ cup each).

MOCHA DESSERT COFFEE

For each serving, place 1 to 2 tablespoons canned
chocolate frosting in cup. Fill with hot coffee; stir
until blended. If desired, garnish with whipped topping.

RED-HOT CINNAMON COFFEE

For each serving, place 1 tablespoon red cinnamon
candies in mug. Fill with hot coffee; stir. Serve with
a cinnamon stick.

CAFÉ MEXICAN

⅛ teaspoon cinnamon
⅛ teaspoon nutmeg
1 cup frozen whipped topping (thawed)
2 cups hot strong coffee

Fold spices into whipped topping. Serve coffee in demitasse cups and top with the spiced whipped topping.   *6 servings (about ⅓ cup each).*

CALIFORNIA COFFEE

For each serving, pour 1 ounce (2 tablespoons) brandy into mug. Fill ⅔ full with hot strong coffee. Top with a small scoop of chocolate ice cream.

IRISH COFFEE

1 cup chilled whipping cream
¼ cup confectioners' sugar
1 teaspoon vanilla
¾ cup ground coffee
3 cups water
4 ounces (½ cup) Irish whiskey or brandy
4 to 8 teaspoons granulated sugar

In chilled bowl, beat cream, confectioners' sugar and vanilla until stiff; refrigerate.

Prepare coffee, using the ¾ cup ground coffee and 3 cups water.

Heat 4 mugs by rinsing with boiling water; drain. Mix 1 ounce (2 tablespoons) whiskey and 1 to 2 teaspoons granulated sugar in each mug; add hot coffee. Top with the whipped cream.

4 servings (¾ cup each).

COFFEE À LA MODE

For each serving, fill mugs about ¾ full with steaming hot strong coffee. Top with a small scoop of vanilla or coffee ice cream. Serve at once.

SPICED TEA

4 cups boiling water
4 teaspoons loose tea
6 whole cloves, broken into pieces
½ teaspoon dried orange peel
⅛ teaspoon cinnamon

Pour boiling water over tea, cloves, orange peel and cinnamon in heatproof container. Cover tightly; let steep 3 to 5 minutes. Stir and strain.

6 servings (⅔ cup each).

ICE-CREAM SODA

For each serving, place 2 to 3 tablespoons any flavor syrup (or ice-cream topping) or ¼ cup crushed fruit with 1 teaspoon sugar in tall glass. Fill ½ full with chilled sparkling water. Top with a scoop of ice cream; stir vigorously. Fill with sparkling water.

FRUIT FIZZ

For each serving, place ¼ cup chilled pineapple juice and 1 scoop vanilla ice cream in tall glass. Fill with chilled sparkling water; stir lightly.

Substitution

For pineapple juice: ¼ cup grape, cherry or raspberry juice or cranberry cocktail.

STRAWBERRY CREAM

For each serving, blend ½ pint vanilla ice cream (1 cup) and ½ cup chilled strawberry soda in blender or with rotary beater.

ORANGE FREEZE

For each serving, place 2 tablespoons frozen orange juice concentrate (thawed) and 1 scoop vanilla ice cream in tall glass. Fill with chilled ginger ale; stir lightly. Serve with a halved orange slice.

ORANGE FROST SODA

> 1 quart orange sherbet
> 2 bottles (14 ounces each)
>   carbonated orange beverage, chilled

Place 2 scoops orange sherbet in each of 5 tall glasses. Fill with orange beverage.   *5 servings.*

CRANBERRY FROST

For each serving, place 1 scoop lime sherbet in tall glass. Fill with cranberry cocktail.

Substitution
  For lime sherbet: Lemon or orange sherbet.

CREAMY PEACH CUP

> 1 package (12 ounces) frozen sliced peaches
> ¼ cup canned vanilla pudding
> ¾ cup milk
> ¼ teaspoon almond extract

Thaw peaches just until they can be removed from package; cut into chunks. Pour into blender; blend until thoroughly chopped. Add remaining ingredients; mix until smooth. Serve immediately in chilled cups or individual serving dishes.   *3 or 4 servings.*

BREAKFASTS AND BRUNCHES

∎

Hot soup for breakfast? A strawberry sundae on your cereal? How about fish sticks on a bun? Why not! There are no hard and fast rules about breakfast— except that you have a nutritious one, every day.

TRY SOME SURPRISES

Face it, the merrier the menu, the more likely your family is to sit down and eat it. Milk shakes, for instance, are deliciously nutritious. Likewise peanut butter sandwiches. And if you're a finicky eater, age 4, that's really good news. Bring on Breakfast Burgers (page 228) to snag a reluctant teenager. You speak his language; he gets his morning protein. And if Dad has a passion for apple pie, go ahead—slip him a piece, à la mode, before he gets out the door. Counting calories? Think about open-face grilled cheese sandwiches with a bunch of grapes alongside, or cottage cheese with orange slices.

Or be conventional, almost. Don't just serve a glass of fruit juice—stage it as a breakfast cocktail, on the rocks. Dress up the cereal bowl, too, with fruit or a scoop of ice cream. How about some eggstravaganzas: a fancy Rolled Egg (page 227); or Shirred Eggs (page 220), baked and brought to the table in individual ramekins. When you spare an extra 15 minutes, add a new twist to your breakfast repertoire with Chicken Livers with Mushrooms (page 229) or Jam Grill (page 233). Above all, don't be a slave to custom. You have nothing to lose but breakfast boredom.

MAKE IT A BIG DEAL MEAL

Nutritionally speaking, breakfast should provide ¼ to ⅓ of your daily food requirements. So, no matter what you decide to serve your family, make sure it's something wholesome and nutritious. And be careful not to confuse eating lots with eating well. (To brush up on nutritional needs, see page 285.)

Plan ahead. Each member of your family deserves a well-balanced meal to start off his day. After all, what with late nights at the office and those can't-be-missed football practices, chances are that breakfast is one of the few meals that a family's sure to eat at home. And it's one of the easiest for you to prepare. So go ahead—seize the opportunity to wake up those sleepy morning appetites. How you do it and the foods you choose are up to you and the willingness of your family to try something new.

BUY EXTRA TIME IN THE A.M.

It happens in the most organized household—you grab a few extra winks and the breakfast scene falls apart at the seams. So stay a jump ahead. Set the table the night before; have cereals out, fruits chilled. Rely on convenience foods. Think about pre-preparation: mix up the batter for Potato Pancakes (page 239) or put together a Dried Fruit Compote (page 213) or bake muffins on the weekend, tuck them in the freezer and reheat them during the week. And if the family simply must eat on the run, plan ahead for Breakfast Bars (page 218). Or, at that eat-and-run moment, pour out a breakfast in a glass. You'll find a different one for every day of the week on pages 244–245.

MORNING TIME . . . PARTY TIME?

Turn a late-morning breakfast into two meals in one —otherwise known as brunch. Stick strictly to traditional breakfast menus, ending with coffee cake or doughnuts for dessert; or try something continental like Quiche Lorraine (page 225). It's elegant, but simple to do. Serve with a salad; finish with fruit. Think about it. It's one of the easiest ways to entertain.

Now who says breakfast is a bore? Not you. You believe in giving that early-morning meal lots of encouragement. And it shows on those happy faces going out your door.

Breakfast Fruits

HONEY BEE AMBROSIA

   4 medium oranges, chilled
   1 medium banana
   ½ cup orange juice
   ¼ cup honey
   2 tablespoons lemon juice
   ¼ cup flaked coconut

Pare oranges and cut into thin slices. Peel banana and cut into slices. Mix fruits carefully. Blend orange juice, honey and lemon juice; pour on fruit. Sprinkle with coconut.   *4 to 6 servings.*

FRUIT WITH YOGURT

   1 can (30 ounces) fruit cocktail, drained
   ½ cup unflavored yogurt
   2 tablespoons honey
   2 teaspoons lemon juice
   Dash aromatic bitters, if desired

Spoon fruit into individual serving dishes. Blend yogurt, honey, lemon juice and bitters; pour over fruit. Nice served with Almond Flatbread (page 144).
                                   4 or 5 servings.

Substitutions

   For fruit cocktail: 1 can (30 ounces) apricot halves or peach halves or about 4 cups cut-up fresh fruit.
   For yogurt: ½ cup dairy sour cream.

PAPAYA

Cut 2 large ripe papayas in half lengthwise; remove seeds. Pare and cut into slices. Serve with lime wedges.

4 servings.

FROZEN FRUIT SLICES

Remove wrapping from 1 package (16 ounces) frozen melon balls. Cut frozen fruit into ⅜- to ½-inch slices with serrated knife. Place slices on salad plates with curly endive or sprigs of watercress or parsley.

4 or 5 servings.

Substitution

For melon balls: 1 package (10 ounces) frozen peach slices, 1 package (10 ounces) frozen strawberry halves or 1 can (13½ ounces) frozen pineapple chunks.

STRAWBERRY-RHUBARB COMPOTE

    ½ cup water
    1 package (16 ounces) frozen rhubarb
    2 tablespoons sugar
    2 cups fresh strawberries
    ⅛ teaspoon ginger

Heat water to boiling; stir in rhubarb and sugar. Reduce heat; simmer 5 minutes, breaking fruit apart with fork. Remove from heat; stir in strawberries and ginger. Serve warm or cold.

Remember this fruit refresher as a first course for dinner, too.   *6 servings.*

MELON AND PROSCIUTTO

Cut a ripe cantaloupe, casaba, honeydew or Spanish melon (about 3 pounds) in half; scoop out seeds and fibers. Cut each half into 6 lengthwise wedges. Remove rind. Cut crosswise slits 1½ inches apart in each melon wedge.

Cut ¼ pound sliced prosciutto (Italian ham) into 1-inch strips. Place several strips of ham on each wedge; push ham into slits. *12 servings.*

VARIATION

■ *Bite-size Melon and Prosciutto:* Cut pared melon into bite-size pieces. Wrap each piece in strips of prosciutto; secure with picks.

DRIED FRUIT COMPOTE

    1 package (10 ounces) mixed dried fruit
    One 3-inch stick cinnamon
 ¼ cup brown sugar (packed)
    3 slices lemon
    2 cups water
    1 can (21 ounces) cherry pie filling

Mix dried fruit, cinnamon stick, sugar, lemon slices and water in saucepan. Heat to boiling, stirring occasionally. Reduce heat; simmer uncovered 30 minutes. Stir in cherry pie filling. Serve warm or cold. This fruit combo also makes a particularly nice accompaniment for ham or roast beef. *4 to 6 servings.*

VARIATION

■ *Currant-Raspberry Compote:* Omit cherry pie filling. Drain cooked fruit, reserving liquid. Measure reserved liquid and, if necessary, add enough water to measure 2½ cups. Prepare 1 package (4¾ ounces) currant-raspberry-flavored dessert mix as directed on package for fruit sauce except—substitute the reserved 2½ cups liquid for the water.

CINNAMON FRUITS

Drain 1 can (16 ounces) peaches or pears, reserving
½ cup syrup. In small saucepan, heat reserved syrup
and ¼ cup red cinnamon candies to boiling; boil 1
minute. Remove from heat. Cover tightly; let stand
10 minutes or until candies are dissolved. Stir in fruit.
Serve warm or chilled.   *4 servings.*

HOT BREAKFAST FRUITS

    ¼ cup butter or margarine
    ¼ cup brown sugar (packed)
    1 tablespoon lemon juice
    1 can (30 ounces) fruits for salad, drained

Melt butter in medium skillet over low heat; blend
in sugar and lemon juice. Cook until smooth and
bubbly. Stir in fruit; heat through.
    Nice to serve on oatmeal or farina. Good for dessert,
too—on rice pudding, custard or ice cream.
                        4 or 5 servings.

CRUNCHY BROILED GRAPEFRUIT

    2 grapefruit, halved
    1 cup whole wheat flakes cereal, crushed
    ⅓ cup brown sugar (packed)
    ¼ cup butter or margarine, melted

Remove seeds from grapefruit halves. Cut around
edges and sections to loosen; remove centers. Mix
cereal, sugar and butter; spread on grapefruit.
    Set oven control at broil and/or 550°. Broil grape-
fruit 5 inches from heat 3 to 4 minutes or until golden
brown.   *4 servings.*

BROILED HONEY GRAPEFRUIT

> 2 grapefruit, halved
> ¼ cup honey
> 10 drops aromatic bitters

Remove seeds from grapefruit halves. Cut around edges and sections to loosen; remove centers. Mix honey and bitters; spoon about 1 tablespoon honey mixture on each grapefruit half.

Set oven control at broil and/or 550°. Broil grapefruit 5 inches from heat about 5 minutes.   *4 servings.*

MARSHMALLOW APRICOTS

Heat oven to 400°. Divide 1 can (17 ounces) apricot halves among 4 or 5 individual ovenproof dishes (about 3 apricot halves and 1 tablespoon syrup per dish). Top each with 6 to 8 miniature marshmallows. Bake 5 minutes or until puffed.   *4 or 5 servings.*

BAKED BANANAS

Heat oven to 375°. For each serving, peel a large firm banana and cut lengthwise in half. Place halves cut side down in buttered baking dish. Brush with lemon juice. Sprinkle each half with ½ teaspoon grated lemon peel and ½ tablespoon brown sugar. Drizzle each banana with ½ tablespoon butter, melted. Bake 20 minutes. Serve warm. Top with ice cream, for dessert or breakfast.

Cereals

MOCK APPLE DUMPLINGS

2 cups whole wheat flakes cereal, crushed
2 tablespoons sugar
⅛ teaspoon salt
⅛ teaspoon nutmeg
⅛ teaspoon cinnamon
3 cups applesauce
Milk

Mix cereal, sugar, salt, nutmeg and cinnamon. Spoon applesauce into individual serving dishes. Sprinkle cereal mixture on applesauce. Serve with milk.

4 servings.

SOUP 'N CEREAL

½ soup can milk
½ soup can water
1 can (10¾ ounces) condensed tomato soup
¼ teaspoon salt
Favorite unsweetened dry cereal

In saucepan, gradually stir milk and water into soup and salt. Heat through over low heat, stirring frequently. Serve on cereal immediately.   *3 servings.*

FRUITED HOT CEREAL

Prepare cereal as directed on package except—when heating water to boiling, add one of the following for each serving:

2 tablespoons raisins
4 to 5 dried apricot halves, cut up
4 to 5 prunes, cut up
3 to 4 dates, cut up

PEANUT MALLOW CHEWS

⅓ cup butter or margarine
3 cups miniature marshmallows
½ cup peanut butter
5 cups fruit-flavored corn puffs cereal

In large saucepan, melt butter and marshmallows over low heat, stirring constantly. Stir in peanut butter until melted. Remove from heat; fold in cereal, stirring until evenly coated.

With buttered hands, pat evenly into buttered baking pan, 9x9x2 inches. Cool; cut into bars, about 3x2 inches.

12 bars.

Substitution

For miniature marshmallows: 32 large marshmallows, cut up.

HOT CEREAL STIR-INS

Prepare your favorite hot cereal as directed on package except—for each serving, stir in one of the following:

1 teaspoon fruit-flavored gelatin (swirled in)
¼ cup miniature marshmallows
1 to 2 tablespoons maple syrup, light molasses or honey
1 tablespoon instant cocoa mix
1 to 2 tablespoons jam, jelly or marmalade
2 tablespoons brown sugar
2 tablespoons applesauce and 1 tablespoon brown sugar
2 tablespoons mandarin orange segments and 1 tablespoon brown sugar

BREAKFAST BARS

½ cup butter or margarine
3 cups miniature marshmallows
½ cup peanut butter
½ cup nonfat dry milk
¼ cup orange-flavored instant breakfast drink
1 cup raisins
4 cups O-shaped puffed oat cereal

In large saucepan, melt butter and marshmallows over low heat, stirring constantly. Stir in peanut butter until melted. Mix in milk and breakfast drink.

Remove from heat; fold in raisins and cereal, stirring until evenly coated. With buttered hands, pat evenly into buttered baking pan, 9x9x2 inches. Cool; cut into bars, about 3x1 inch.

Two bars and a glass of skimmed milk make a nutritious breakfast-on-the-run, furnishing ¼ of the Minimum Daily Requirements.   *24 bars (12 servings).*

Substitution

For miniature marshmallows: 32 large marshmallows, cut up.

CEREAL TOPPINGS

Try one of these flavored milks on your favorite unsweetened cereal. To ¾ cup milk in blender, add one of the following:

½ banana, cut up
2 teaspoons sugar and 1 teaspoon powdered
   instant coffee
½ teaspoon sugar-sweetened soft drink mix
1 or 2 canned peach halves
1 tablespoon peanut butter and
   1 teaspoon sugar

CEREAL SWEETENERS

Substitute one of the following for sugar on your favorite unsweetened cereal:

Mixture of 2 teaspoons sugar and
   1 teaspoon cinnamon

Brown sugar

Maple syrup

Ice-cream sundae topping

Instant cocoa mix

Fruit-flavored gelatin

Jam or jelly

Colored sugars

Eggs

SOFT-COOKED EGGS

Place eggs in saucepan; add enough cold water to come at least 1 inch above eggs. Heat rapidly to boiling. Remove from heat. Cover tightly; let stand 1 to 3 minutes, depending on desired doneness.

Immediately cool eggs in cold water several seconds to prevent further cooking. Cut eggs in half; scoop from shell.

HARD-COOKED EGGS

Place eggs in saucepan; add enough cold water to come at least 1 inch above eggs. Heat rapidly to boiling. Remove from heat. Cover tightly; let stand 25 minutes.

Immediately cool eggs in cold water to prevent further cooking. Tap egg to crackle shell. Roll between hands to loosen shell, then peel. Hold egg under running cold water to help ease off shell.

BAKED (SHIRRED) EGGS

Heat oven to 325°. For each serving, break an egg carefully into buttered 5- or 6-ounce baking dish. Season with salt and pepper. If desired, top each egg with 1 tablespoon milk or light cream, dot with soft butter or sprinkle with 1 tablespoon shredded Cheddar cheese.

Bake eggs uncovered 15 to 18 minutes, depending on desired doneness and depth of baking dish. Whites should be set, but yolks soft. Serve in baking dish.

FRIED EGGS

In heavy skillet, heat butter or bacon fat (⅛ inch deep) until just hot enough to sizzle a drop of water. Break each egg into a measuring cup or saucer; carefully slip eggs one at a time into skillet. Immediately reduce heat to low.

Cook slowly, spooning butter on eggs until whites are set and a film forms over yolks (sunny-side up). Or when whites are set, turn eggs over gently and cook until desired doneness.

VARIATION

■   *Poached-fried Eggs:* Heat just enough butter or bacon fat to grease skillet. Cook eggs over low heat until edges turn white. Add ½ teaspoon water for 1 egg, decreasing the proportion slightly for each additional egg. Cover tightly.

POACHED EGGS

In saucepan or skillet, heat water, bouillon or milk (1½ to 2 inches) to boiling; reduce to simmer. Break each egg into a measuring cup or saucer; carefully slip eggs one at a time into water. (Eggs shouldn't touch each other while cooking.)

Cook 3 to 5 minutes or until desired doneness. Lift eggs from water with slotted spatula. Season with salt and pepper.

Note: To poach eggs in an egg poacher, pour water into poacher to just below bottom of egg cups; heat water to boiling. Butter metal egg cups; break eggs into cups. Set egg cups in frame over boiling water. Cover tightly; steam 3 to 5 minutes or until desired doneness.

EGGS ON CORNED BEEF HASH

>   1 can (15 ounces) corned beef hash
>   6 eggs
>   Salt and pepper
>   ⅓ cup shredded Cheddar cheese

Heat oven to 350°. In each of six 5- or 6-ounce baking dishes, press about ¼ cup hash against bottom and side. Break an egg on hash in each dish. Season with salt and pepper. Sprinkle each with about 1 tablespoon cheese. Bake uncovered 20 to 25 minutes, depending on desired doneness.   *6 servings.*

GOLDEN EGGS ON TOAST

>   1 can (10¾ ounces) condensed Cheddar
>   cheese soup
>   ⅓ cup milk
>   6 hard-cooked eggs, sliced
>   6 slices toast

Heat soup and milk, stirring constantly. Gently stir in egg slices; heat through. Spoon on toast. For extra color and flavor, garnish with snipped chives and crisply fried bacon.   *4 to 6 servings.*

SCRAMBLED EGGS

For each serving, break 2 eggs into bowl; add 2 tablespoons milk or cream, ¼ teaspoon salt and dash pepper. Mix with fork, stirring thoroughly for a uniform color, or mixing just slightly if streaks of white and yellow are preferred.

Heat ½ tablespoon butter or margarine in skillet over medium heat until just hot enough to sizzle a drop of water. Pour egg mixture into skillet.

As mixture begins to set at bottom and side, gently lift cooked portions with spatula so that thin, uncooked

portion can flow to bottom. Avoid constant stirring.
Cook until eggs are thickened throughout but still
moist, about 3 to 5 minutes.

VARIATIONS

■ *Creamy Scrambled Eggs:* Cook egg mixture in top of
double boiler over simmering, not boiling, water. Stir occasionally until thick and creamy.

■ *Flavored Scrambled Eggs:* For each serving, stir one
of the following into egg mixture in bowl:

  2 tablespoons shredded Cheddar, Monterey (Jack)
    or Swiss cheese
  2 tablespoons chopped mushrooms
  2 tablespoons snipped chives
  2 tablespoons snipped parsley
  2 tablespoons crispy fried and crumbled bacon*
  2 tablespoons finely shredded dried beef*
  2 tablespoons chopped cooked ham*

Omit salt in egg mixture.

POTATO SCRAMBLE

      6 slices bacon, diced
      2 cups diced cooked potatoes
      1 medium onion, diced
      1 teaspoon salt
    ¼ teaspoon pepper
      4 eggs, beaten

Fry bacon until crisp; drain off all but 3 tablespoons
fat. Cook and stir potatoes, onion, salt and pepper in
fat until light brown. Pour eggs into skillet. Cook uncovered until eggs are thickened.   *4 servings.*

Substitution

  For cooked potatoes: 1 package (9 ounces) frozen
French fried potatoes, diced.

HOME-STYLE SCRAMBLED EGGS

    4 eggs
    1 tablespoon instant minced onion
    ¾ teaspoon salt
    3 tablespoons water
    ¼ cup butter or margarine
    1 cup diced tomatoes
    1 cup diced cooked potatoes
    1 cup diced zucchini

Beat eggs, onion, salt and water. Melt butter in large
skillet over medium heat; cook and stir vegetables in
butter 2 minutes. Pour on egg mixture.

As mixture begins to set at bottom and side, gently
lift cooked portions with spatula so that thin, uncooked
portion can flow to bottom. Avoid constant stirring.
Cook until eggs are thickened throughout but still
moist, 3 to 5 minutes.   *3 servings.*

Substitutions

   For instant onion: 3 tablespoons minced onion.
   For zucchini: ½ cup chopped green pepper.

VARIATION

■ *Eggs Mexicali:* Decrease salt to ½ teaspoon. Omit instant onion and vegetables; stir ⅔ cup crushed corn chips
into butter. Serve with hot green chili relish.

QUICHE LORRAINE

    12 slices bacon (about ½ pound), crisply
       fried and crumbled
     1 cup shredded natural Swiss cheese (4 ounces)
   ⅓ cup minced onion
      9-inch frozen ready-to-bake pie crust shell
     4 eggs
     2 cups whipping cream or light cream (20%)
    ¾ teaspoon salt
    ¼ teaspoon sugar
    ⅛ teaspoon cayenne red pepper

Heat oven to 425°. Sprinkle bacon, cheese and onion
in frozen pie crust shell. Beat eggs slightly; beat in
remaining ingredients. Pour cream mixture into pie
shell. Bake 15 minutes.

   Reduce oven temperature to 300° and bake 30 minutes longer or until knife inserted 1 inch from edge
comes out clean. Let stand 10 minutes before cutting.
Serve in wedges.

           6 main-dish servings (8 appetizer servings).

Substitution

   For ready-to-bake pie crust shell: Pastry for 9-inch
One-crust Pie (page 202).

HAM AND CHEESE OVEN OMELET

    8 eggs
    1 cup milk
    ½ teaspoon seasoned salt
    1 package (3 ounces) thin-sliced ham
    1 cup shredded Cheddar cheese (4 ounces)
    1 tablespoon instant minced onion

Heat oven to 325°. Beat eggs, milk and seasoned salt.
Tear ham in small pieces into egg mixture. Stir in
cheese and onion.

Pour into greased baking dish, 11½x7½x1½ or
8x8x2 inches. Bake uncovered 40 to 45 minutes or
until omelet is set and top is golden brown.

4 to 6 servings.

Note: Remember this for a late-evening supper. Prepare mixture ahead of time and refrigerate until
needed.

Substitutions

For ham: 1 package (3 ounces) thin-sliced corned
beef or dried beef.

For Cheddar cheese: 1 cup shredded mozzarella, Swiss
or other cheese.

For instant onion: 3 tablespoons minced onion.

ROLLED EGG

For each Rolled Egg, beat 1 egg and ⅛ teaspoon salt until foamy. Melt 2 teaspoons butter, margarine or bacon fat in hot 10-inch skillet; rotate pan to coat bottom with butter.

Pour egg into skillet; slowly rotate pan to spread mixture into thin circle. Cook over medium heat about 2 minutes. Loosen edge; roll up, using small spatula and fork.

When preparing more than one, keep Rolled Eggs warm on ungreased baking sheet in 275° oven. Nice served with our cheese or mushroom sauce.

VARIATION

■ *Cheese Egg Roll:* Before rolling circle, sprinkle with 1 tablespoon Parmesan cheese.

PUFFY CHEESE BAKE

        4 slices bread, buttered
        2 eggs
        1 cup light cream (20%)
        2 tablespoons butter or margarine, melted
        ½ teaspoon salt
        ½ teaspoon dry mustard
        ¼ teaspoon paprika
            Dash cayenne red pepper
     1½ cups shredded process American
            cheese (6 ounces)

Heat oven to 350°. Butter baking dish, 8x8x2 inches. Cut each slice of bread diagonally into 4 triangles. Line bottom and sides of baking dish with bread triangles. (For a crown effect, place 8 triangles upright against sides of dish. Arrange remaining triangles on bottom of dish.)

Beat eggs slightly; add remaining ingredients and mix well. Pour mixture into baking dish. Bake uncovered 30 to 40 minutes.   *4 servings.*

Breakfast Meats

MEAT 'N POTATO ROLL-UPS

    Instant mashed potato puffs
    (enough for 4 servings)
  1 tablespoon finely chopped green pepper
  ¼ teaspoon instant chopped onion
  ½ teaspoon prepared mustard
  8 slices large bologna

Heat oven to 350°. Prepare potato puffs as directed on package. Stir in green pepper, onion and mustard.

    Place about ¼ cup potato mixture on each bologna slice; roll up and secure with wooden pick. Place on ungreased baking sheet. Bake 10 to 15 minutes.

    An unusual lunch, brunch or hearty breakfast served with Frozen Fruit Slices (page 212).   *4 servings.*

BREAKFAST BURGERS

  1 pound ground beef
  ¼ cup applesauce
  1 teaspoon salt
  1 teaspoon Worcestershire sauce
  ½ teaspoon allspice

Mix all ingredients. Shape mixture by tablespoonfuls into 2-inch patties. Cook in skillet over medium-high heat, about 2 to 3 minutes on each side. *6 to 8 servings.*

VARIATION

■ *Baked Breakfast Burgers:* Shape mixture into 5 patties, about 3 inches in diameter and ½ inch thick. Bake in 350° oven 20 minutes. Serve on a bun or toasted French bread.

FINNAN HADDIE

1 package (16 ounces) frozen finnan haddie, thawed
¼ cup butter or margarine

Cut fish into serving pieces. Melt butter in skillet. Add fish; reduce heat. Cover tightly; simmer 30 minutes or until fish flakes easily with a fork. To serve, spoon butter over fish.

Traditionally served on buttered toast—but why not try an English muffin and cinnamon apple rings.

4 servings.

Substitution

For finnan haddie: 1 package (16 ounces) frozen walleye pike, Northern pike or pollack. Rinse under cold water to remove wrapping. Let fish stand 5 minutes, then saw into serving pieces. Brush with 2 tablespoons liquid smoke; add to butter in skillet. Cover tightly; simmer 30 minutes.

CHICKEN LIVERS WITH MUSHROOMS

¼ cup butter or margarine
½ pound chicken livers, halved
¼ pound fresh mushrooms, sliced
¼ teaspoon salt
2 teaspoons Worcestershire sauce

Melt butter in large skillet; brown livers. Push livers to one side. Add mushrooms; cook and stir until mushrooms are light brown. Mix livers and mushrooms.

Sprinkle with salt and Worcestershire sauce. Reduce heat. Cover tightly; simmer 5 minutes or until liver is done.

Serve with an omelet or scrambled eggs for a special brunch.

2 or 3 servings.

Substitution

For fresh mushrooms: 1 can (4 ounces) mushroom stems and pieces, drained.

FISH STICK BREAKFAST

1 package (16 ounces) frozen fish sticks
1 can (8½ ounces) sliced pineapple, drained
2 tablespoons cranberry-orange relish
4 English muffins, split and toasted

Arrange fish sticks and pineapple slices on lightly buttered baking sheet. Fill each pineapple slice with a rounded teaspoonful of cranberry-orange relish.

Set oven control at broil and/or 550°. Broil fish sticks and pineapple slices 5 inches from heat about 5 minutes or until fish sticks are golden. Serve with English muffins. And don't forget to serve this treat for lunch or dinner sometime. *4 servings.*

BACON

To Panfry: Place bacon slices in cold skillet. Cook over low heat 8 to 10 minutes, turning to brown evenly.

To Bake: Place separated slices of bacon on rack in broiler pan. Bake in 400° oven 10 minutes or until brown. Do not turn.

To Broil: Place separated slices of bacon on rack in broiler pan. Set oven control at broil and/or 550°. Broil bacon 3 inches from heat until brown, about 2 minutes. Turn slices; broil 1 minute longer.

Merry Up the Menu—Maybe Then They'll Eat

Soup for breakfast? Why not! It's filling . . . and fast. Try any of the soups on pages 248–252, or even those in our lunch chapter. And how about breakfast sandwiches? Plain old peanut butter goes over big with You Know Who, and Breakfast Burgers (page 228) are sure to draw the teenagers to the scene. And Denvers (page 262). They ought to give you a full table. Another day, surprise them with Baked Meatballs (page 19) or Oven-fried Fillets (page 82). Morning monotony? Not for your family!

CANADIAN-STYLE BACON

To Panfry: Place ⅛-inch slices of Canadian-style bacon in cold skillet. Cook over low heat 8 to 10 minutes, turning to brown evenly.

To Bake: If necessary, remove casing from 2-pound piece of Canadian-style bacon. Place bacon fat side up on rack in open shallow baking pan. Insert meat thermometer so tip is in center of bacon. Bake uncovered in 325° oven 1 to 1¼ hours or until thermometer registers 160°.

To Broil: Place ¼-inch slices Canadian-style bacon on rack in broiler pan. Set oven control at broil and/or 550°. Broil bacon 2 to 3 inches from heat until brown, about 3 minutes. Turn slices; broil 3 minutes longer.

SAUSAGE (Uncooked Smoked or Fresh)

To Panfry: Place sausage links or patties in cold skillet. Add 2 to 4 tablespoons water. Cover tightly; cook slowly 5 to 8 minutes, depending on size or thickness of sausages. Uncover; cook until well done, turning to brown evenly.

To Bake: Arrange sausages in single layer in ungreased shallow baking pan. Bake uncovered in 400° oven 20 to 30 minutes or until well done, turning sausages to brown evenly. Drain off fat as it accumulates.

YORKSHIRE SAUSAGE

> 1 cup all-purpose flour*
> ½ teaspoon salt
> 1 cup milk
> 2 eggs
> 1 package (10 ounces) brown and serve
>   smoked sausages (10)

Heat oven to 425°. Butter baking pan, 9x9x2 inches. Mix flour, salt, milk and eggs with rotary beater just until smooth. (Do not overbeat.) Pour into pan.

Arrange sausages on batter. Bake 25 minutes or until puffed and brown. Delicious with warm applesauce. For a complete breakfast add a glass of orange juice and a glass of milk.   *4 or 5 servings.*

---

* *Do not use self-rising flour in this recipe.*

Substitution

For salt: ½ teaspoon favorite seasoned salt.

Breakfast Breads

FLAVORED OVEN TOAST

Heat oven to 400°. Cut unsliced loaf of bread into desired number of 1-inch slices. Spread both sides of slices with butter. Arrange on ungreased baking sheet. Bake 10 to 12 minutes or until golden brown. Sprinkle with one of the following:

> Chocolate-flavored malted milk (dry)
>
> Instant cocoa
>
> Orange-flavored instant breakfast drink (dry)
>
> Fruit-flavored gelatin

Substitution

For 1-inch slices bread: Commercially sliced bread; bake 3 or 4 minutes, then turn and bake 4 or 5 minutes or until golden brown.

BREAKFAST HOT SWEETS

Heat oven to 400°. Cut unsliced nut bread into desired number of ½-inch slices. Spread with soft butter or margarine. Arrange buttered side up on ungreased baking sheet. Bake 6 to 8 minutes or until light brown.

JAM GRILL

For each serving, spread 1 slice bread with 2 tablespoons strawberry or raspberry jam; top with second slice bread. Spread outside of sandwich with about 1 tablespoon soft butter or margarine. Cook on both sides in skillet or on grill. Sprinkle with confectioners' sugar.

JAM CRUMPETS

   6 English muffins, split
¼ cup soft butter or margarine
¼ cup jam or preserves
¼ cup brown sugar (packed)
¼ cup flaked coconut or sliced almonds

Heat oven to 450°. Spread cut surface of each muffin half with 1 teaspoon each butter and jam. Sprinkle with brown sugar and coconut. Bake on ungreased baking sheet 5 minutes or until bubbly and brown.

12 crumpets.

PEANUTTY POP-UPS

Heat oven to 350°. For each serving, spread peanut butter on flat side of your favorite toaster pop-up; top with second pop-up, flat side down. Arrange on ungreased baking sheet. Bake about 10 minutes or until heated through.

Note: Remember pop-ups for a quick dessert, too. Toast in oven. Top each with ice cream and ice-cream topping.

VARIATION
■ *Cheese Pop-ups:* Substitute pasteurized process cheese spread for the peanut butter.

MARMALADE PINWHEELS

2 cups buttermilk baking mix
½ cup cold water
½ cup orange marmalade
1 tablespoon butter or margarine, melted
1 tablespoon sugar

Heat oven to 425°. Grease 9-inch pie pan or 10 medium muffin cups. Stir baking mix and water with fork until a soft dough forms. Gently smooth dough into a ball on floured cloth-covered board. Knead 5 times. Roll dough into rectangle, 12x9 inches. Spread with marmalade; roll up, beginning at wide side. Pinch edge of dough into roll to seal well.

Cut roll into 10 slices. Place cut side up with sides touching in pan. Brush with butter; sprinkle with sugar. Bake about 15 minutes or until golden brown.

10 pinwheels.

PEANUT BUTTER AND JELLY COFFEE CAKE

2 cups buttermilk baking mix
2 tablespoons sugar
¼ cup creamy peanut butter
⅔ cup milk
1 egg
½ cup favorite jam or jelly

Heat oven to 400°. Grease layer pan, 9x1½ inches. Mix baking mix and sugar; cut in peanut butter. Mix in milk and egg; beat vigorously ½ minute.

Spread in pan; spread with jam. Bake 20 to 25 minutes or until light brown.   *9 servings.*

Substitution

For jam or jelly: ½ cup orange marmalade.

ORANGE ROLLS

>1 loaf (1 pound) frozen bread dough
>   Salad oil
>3 tablespoons soft butter or margarine
>1 tablespoon grated orange peel
>2 tablespoons orange juice
>1½ cups confectioners' sugar

Brush frozen loaf with oil. Place on lightly greased baking sheet; cover and thaw up to 12 hours in refrigerator or about 3 hours at room temperature.

Beat butter, orange peel, juice and confectioners' sugar until creamy and smooth. On lightly floured board, roll dough into rectangle, 15x8 inches. Spread with half the orange mixture; roll up, beginning at wide side. Pinch edge of dough into roll to seal well. Stretch to make even.

Cut roll into 15 slices. Place slightly apart in greased baking pan, 13x9x2 inches, or in greased muffin cups. Let rise until double, about 1 hour.

Heat oven to 350°. Bake 35 to 40 minutes or until golden brown. While warm, remove from pan and frost with remaining orange filling.   *15 rolls.*

VARIATIONS

■ *Caramel Rolls:* Before rolling dough, melt ¼ cup butter or margarine; stir in ½ cup brown sugar (packed), 2 tablespoons corn syrup and ½ cup pecan halves and spread over bottom of baking pan. Omit orange peel, juice and confectioners' sugar. Spread rectangle with 3 tablespoons butter; sprinkle with mixture of ¼ cup granulated sugar and 2 teaspoons cinnamon. After baking, immediately turn pan upside down on large tray. Let pan remain on a minute so caramel drizzles over rolls.

■ *Cinnamon Rolls:* Omit orange peel, orange juice and confectioners' sugar. Spread rectangle with 3 tablespoons butter and sprinkle with mixture of ¼ cup sugar, 2 teaspoons cinnamon and ½ cup chopped nuts. While rolls are warm, frost with mixture of 1½ cups confectioners' sugar and 1 tablespoon milk.

CARROT-ORANGE MUFFINS

    1 package (14 ounces) orange muffin mix
    1 cup shredded carrot
½ cup raisins
¼ teaspoon cinnamon
¼ teaspoon nutmeg
¼ teaspoon allspice

Prepare muffin mix as directed on package except—stir in carrot, raisins and spices. Bake about 20 minutes.

About 15 muffins.

STREUSEL COFFEE CAKE

Heat oven to 400°. Grease baking pan, 9x9x2 inches. Prepare any flavor muffin mix except corn as directed on package. Spread in pan. Sprinkle with Streusel Topping (below). Bake 20 to 25 minutes or until wooden pick inserted in center comes out clean. Serve warm. *9 servings.*

STREUSEL TOPPING

Mix ½ cup brown sugar (packed), ⅓ cup all-purpose flour, ¼ cup firm butter and ½ teaspoon cinnamon until crumbly.

ORANGE PECAN BREAD

Heat oven to 350°. Grease and flour 2 loaf pans, 9x5x3 inches. Prepare 1 package (19 ounces) orange cake mix as directed except—use 2 tablespoons less water and add ½ cup chopped pecans. Pour into pans. Bake 35 to 40 minutes or until wooden pick inserted in center comes out clean. Cool thoroughly before slicing. Nice served with hard sauce.

BLUEBERRY-ORANGE BREAD

    2 eggs
    1 cup milk
    1 package (14 ounces) orange muffin mix
    1 package (13.5 ounces) wild blueberry muffin mix

Heat oven to 350°. Grease loaf pan, 9x5x3 inches.
Blend eggs and milk; add muffin mixes (dry). Stir
with fork. (Batter will be slightly lumpy.) Pour into
pan. Bake 50 to 60 minutes or until wooden pick inserted in center comes out clean. Cool thoroughly before slicing.

HAM WAFFLES

    2 cups buttermilk baking mix
    2 tablespoons shortening, melted, or salad oil
    1⅓ cups milk
    1 egg
    1 package (3 ounces) smoked pressed ham

Heat waffle iron. Beat baking mix, shortening, milk
and egg with rotary beater until smooth. Stir in ham.
Pour batter from cup or pitcher onto center of hot
waffle iron. Bake about 5 minutes or until steaming
stops. Lift waffle carefully with fork.

Three 9-inch waffles.

Note: To freeze waffles, bake, cool, and wrap individually in foil. To reheat, unwrap and arrange on baking
sheet. Bake in 400° oven 8 to 10 minutes or until hot.

VARIATION

■ *Orange-Nut Waffles:* Omit ham. Substitute orange juice
for the milk and stir ¾ cup finely chopped nuts into batter.

Starting with a mix ...
PANCAKE VARIATIONS

Prepare Pancakes as directed on buttermilk baking
mix package except—try one of the following variations:

■ *Cheese:* Fold in ½ to 1½ cups shredded sharp
cheese.

■ *Corn:* Fold in 1 cup drained whole kernel corn.

■ *Ham:* Fold in 1 to 1½ cups ground or chopped
cooked ham.

POTATO PANCAKES

> 1¾ cups boiling water
> 1 package (5.5 ounces) hash browns with onions
> ¼ cup salad oil
> 2 eggs
> 2 tablespoons flour
> 1 teaspoon salt

Pour boiling water over potatoes; set aside about 30
minutes, tossing occasionally, until liquid is absorbed.
(At this point, potatoes can be covered and refrigerated up to 12 hours.)

Pour oil over potatoes; toss. Beat eggs, flour and salt;
pour over potatoes and mix. For each pancake, spread
¼ cup batter into 4-inch round on medium-hot griddle.
Cook 3 to 4 minutes; turn and cook 3 to 4 minutes
longer or until golden.   *12 pancakes.*

VARIATION

■ *Corned Beef-Potato Pancakes:* Flake 1 can (12 ounces)
corned beef; mix into batter.

OVEN FRENCH TOAST

        4 slices white bread, 1 inch thick
        3 eggs, slightly beaten
    ¾ cup milk
        1 tablespoon sugar
    ¼ teaspoon salt

Heat oven to 500°. Arrange bread in ungreased baking dish, 13½ x9x2 inches. Beat eggs, milk, sugar and salt. Pour egg mixture on bread; turn each slice to coat well.

With pancake turner, arrange bread on greased baking sheet. Bake about 8 minutes. Turn and bake about 8 minutes longer or until golden brown. Serve with warm cranberry sauce.   *4 servings.*

Note: The toast can also be cooked in buttered skillet or on a griddle.

Substitution

For 1-inch slices bread: 4 to 6 ½-inch slices white bread or 8 1¼-inch slices French bread; cover baking dish and refrigerate at least 8 hours.

VARIATION

■ *Waffled French Toast:* Heat waffle iron. Use 1-inch or ½-inch slices white bread; arrange on hot ungreased waffle iron and bake 3 to 5 minutes or until golden brown.

Note: To freeze Waffled French Toast, bake, cool and wrap individually in foil. To reheat, unwrap and arrange on baking sheet. Heat in 400° oven 8 to 10 minutes.

CONTINENTAL BRUNCH TOAST

> ½ loaf (1-pound size) French bread
> 3 eggs
> ⅓ cup sugar
> ½ teaspoon cinnamon
> Dash salt
> 1½ cups milk
> 2 tablespoon raisins
> 2 tablespoons brown sugar

Butter baking pan, 9x9x2 inches. Into pan, tear bread into 1- to 1½-inch pieces, each with a little crust (about 8 cups). Beat eggs, sugar, cinnamon and salt; stir in milk and raisins. Pour egg mixture on bread pieces; sprinkle with brown sugar. Cover; refrigerate at least 8 hours for best results. (Can be baked immediately if you like.)

Heat oven to 325°. Bake uncovered 1 hour or until crust is golden brown. Serve warm.   *6 or 7 servings.*

Note: For 8 to 10 servings, double amounts of all ingredients except French bread; bake 1 hour in buttered baking pan, 13x9x2 inches.

Breakfast Beverages

BREAKFAST PUNCH

>   1 cup orange juice, chilled
>   ½ cup lemon juice, chilled
>   2 cups apple cider, chilled
>   ¼ cup sugar

Stir juices and sugar until sugar is dissolved. Pour over ice cubes. Garnish with mint leaves.

4 or 5 servings.

MULLED APRICOT NECTAR

>   1 can (46 ounces) apricot nectar
>   ½ lemon, sliced
>   2 cinnamon sticks
>   15 whole cloves
>   8 whole allspice

Mix all ingredients in heavy saucepan; heat to boiling. Reduce heat; simmer gently 5 minutes. Remove from heat. Cover tightly; allow to stand 30 minutes. Strain. Reheat before serving.   *12 servings (½ cup each).*

SPARKLING ORANGE JUICE

For each serving, fill glass with 2 parts orange juice and 1 part chilled carbonated lemon beverage. Float a half-slice of orange or a fresh mint sprig in each glass.

OYSTER STEW

¼ cup butter or margarine
1 pint fresh oysters
2 cups milk
½ cup light cream (20%)
1 teaspoon salt
Dash pepper

Melt butter in small saucepan. Add oysters (with liquor); cook and stir over low heat just until edges curl. Heat milk and cream in another saucepan. Stir in salt, pepper and oysters.   *4 servings (1 cup each).*

HERBED CREAM OF CHICKEN SOUP

1 can (10½ ounces) condensed
cream of chicken soup
1 can (10½ ounces) condensed
chicken with rice soup
½ cup milk
1 teaspoon tarragon leaves

Heat all ingredients over low heat, stirring occasionally. For an unusual garnish, top each serving with a spoonful of whipped cream and sprinkle with paprika.
3 servings (1 cup each).

MUSHROOM-CORN SOUP

2 slices bacon
1 medium onion, chopped (about ½ cup)
1 can (8 ounces) cream-style corn
1 can (10½ ounces) condensed cream of
mushroom soup
1 soup can milk

In saucepan, fry bacon until crisp; remove bacon and drain. Add onion to bacon fat in saucepan; cook and stir until onion is tender. Stir in corn, soup and milk; heat through, stirring occasionally. Crumble bacon; sprinkle over each serving.   *3 servings (1 cup each).*

TOMATO BOUILLON

¾ cup tomato juice
¼ cup water
1 teaspoon instant beef bouillon

Heat all ingredients to boiling over medium-high heat, stirring occasionally. Serve hot or cold.   *2 servings.*

COCOA-CEREAL MILK SHAKE

1 cup milk
1 pint chocolate ice cream, slightly softened
2 cups chocolate-flavored corn puffs cereal
1 tablespoon malted milk powder, if desired

Measure all ingredients into blender. Cover; blend at high speed about 30 seconds. Complete this breakfast with Honey Bee Ambrosia (page 211).   *2 servings.*

BLENDER BREAKFAST COMBOS

Blend any of the following combinations 5 to 10 seconds at high speed:

1 cup milk
1 envelope (1.22 ounces) strawberry-flavored
   instant breakfast drink
¼ cup crushed pineapple

1 cup milk
1 envelope (1.22 ounces) vanilla-flavored instant
   breakfast drink
1 jar (4¾ ounces) pureed fruits (baby food)
   or 6 canned apricot halves

1 cup milk
1 envelope (1.22 ounces) chocolate-flavored
   instant breakfast drink
1 small banana, cut up

1 serving.

ORANGE EGGNOG

1 can (6 ounces) frozen orange juice
concentrate (thawed)
2 cups milk
2 cups eggnog

Beat orange juice and milk with rotary beater or in blender. Stir in eggnog. A sprinkling of colored sugar or nutmeg makes a pretty topping.   *4 servings.*

BANANA ORANGE FROST

1 ripe banana
½ cup orange juice
½ cup cold milk
½ pint (1 cup) orange sherbet

Mash banana with fork; stir in orange juice. Beat with rotary beater or in blender. Add milk and orange sherbet; beat until smooth. Serve on scoops of orange sherbet. An orange slice makes a pretty decoration.
2 or 3 servings.

FLAVORED MILKS

For each serving, add one of the following to a tall glass:

2 tablespoons caramel syrup

1 maraschino cherry and 2 tablespoons
maraschino cherry juice

1 tablespoon chocolate syrup and
1 tablespoon chunky peanut butter

1 to 2 tablespoons chocolate syrup,
cocoa mix or ice-cream topping

1 tablespoon honey, 1 tablespoon grape juice,
orange juice or lemonade or limeade concentrate

Fill glass with milk and stir thoroughly. Serve immediately.

SUNNY SIPPER

    ¼ cup honey
    ½ cup orange juice
       Juice of 1 lemon
     1 can (6 ounces) evaporated milk (undiluted)
     1 can (12 ounces) apricot nectar

Blend honey, orange juice and lemon juice. Add
evaporated milk and apricot nectar; beat until foamy.
Chill. Just before serving, beat again. Serve in small
cups.   *4 servings.*

CHOCOLATE MILK SHAKE

Measure ¼ cup Chocolate Fudge Sauce (below) and
¾ cup milk into blender. Cover; blend 2 seconds.
Add 3 scoops vanilla ice cream; blend at low speed
5 seconds. (Or, beat all ingredients with rotary beater.)
                                                 1 serving.

CHOCOLATE FUDGE SAUCE

     1 package (15.4 ounces) chocolate fudge
       frosting mix
     2 tablespoons light corn syrup
     3 tablespoons butter or margarine
    ⅔ cup milk

Mix frosting mix (dry), corn syrup, butter and milk
in saucepan. Cook, stirring frequently, until mixture
boils. Boil 1 minute.

Substitution

    For Chocolate Fudge Sauce: ¼ cup chocolate ice-
cream topping.

VARIATIONS

■ *Chocolate Mint Shake:* Add ⅛ teaspoon peppermint
extract.

■ *Chocolate Mocha Shake:* Add ½ teaspoon powdered
instant coffee.

COCOA-FLAVORED COFFEE

For each serving, stir ½ teaspoon cocoa into 1 cup hot coffee.

PINEAPPLE MILK SHAKE

Measure ¼ cup pineapple ice-cream topping and ¾ cup milk into blender. Cover; blend 2 seconds. Add 3 scoops vanilla ice cream; blend at low speed 5 seconds. (Or, use rotary beater.)   *1 serving.*

VARIATIONS

■ *Cherry Milk Shake:* Substitute cherry ice-cream topping for the pineapple ice-cream topping.

■ *Strawberry Milk Shake:* Substitute strawberry ice-cream topping for the pineapple ice-cream topping.

CONTINENTAL COCOA

> 2 cups milk
> ⅓ cup Chocolate Fudge Sauce (page 246)
> ¼ teaspoon cinnamon
> 3 or 4 large marshmallows

Mix milk, Chocolate Fudge Sauce and cinnamon in saucepan. Heat through, stirring occasionally, but do not boil. Drop a marshmallow into each cup and pour hot cocoa over it.   *3 or 4 servings (½ to ⅔ cup each).*

HOT CHOCOLATE MILK

Heat 1 quart chocolate-flavored milk over medium-low heat until small bubbles form around edge of pan. Beat with rotary beater until foamy.

6 servings (⅔ cup each).

■

Soups

VEGETABLE CHEESE CHOWDER

1 package (10 ounces) frozen mixed vegetables
1 can (10½ ounces) condensed cream of chicken soup
1 soup can milk
1 cup shredded Cheddar cheese (4 ounces)

Cook vegetables as directed on package; drain. Return to saucepan. Stir in soup and milk. Heat through, stirring occasionally. Sprinkle cheese on each serving.

4 servings (about 1 cup each).

CREAM OF CORN SOUP

1 can (10½ ounces) condensed cream of
chicken soup
1½ cups milk
½ cup mayonnaise
1 can (16 ounces) whole kernel corn
Chopped pimiento
Snipped parsley

Heat soup, milk, mayonnaise and corn, stirring occasionally. Garnish with pimiento and parsley.

5 servings (1 cup each).

antclothreasonughly

SHRIMP BISQUE

  1 can (10¾ ounces) condensed tomato soup
  1 can (10¾ ounces) condensed cream of shrimp soup
  2 cups milk
  1 can (4½ ounces) broken shrimp, rinsed and drained

Heat tomato soup, shrimp soup and milk, stirring occasionally. Stir in shrimp; heat through.

4 servings (1 cup each).

HERBED SOUPS

For a new flavor in soup, heat one of the following combinations:

  1 can (10½ ounces) condensed chicken noodle soup
  1 can (10½ ounces) condensed chicken with
    rice soup
  1 soup can water
  ½ teaspoon marjoram

  1 can (10¾ ounces) condensed tomato soup
  1 soup can milk
  ¼ teaspoon cloves

  1 can (10½ ounces) condensed cream of
    chicken soup
  1 soup can water
  ¼ teaspoon curry powder

  1 can (11½ ounces) condensed green pea soup
  1 soup can water or milk
  ¼ teaspoon chili powder

3 servings (about ¾ cup each).

QUICK SOUP COMBOS

Create a new soup treat by combining and heating old favorites, for example:

> 1 can (10½ ounces) condensed beef noodle soup
> 1 can (10¾ ounces) condensed tomato soup
> 1 soup can water
> 1 soup can milk

> 1 can (10¾ ounces) condensed Cheddar cheese soup
> 1 can (10¾ ounces) condensed tomato soup
> 1 soup can water
> 1 soup can milk

> 1 envelope (1¾ ounces) chicken noodle soup mix, prepared
> 1 envelope (about 1½ ounces) onion soup mix, prepared

> 1 can (10¾ ounces) condensed vegetable soup
> 1 can (11½ ounces) bean with bacon soup
> 2 soup cans water

5 servings (1 cup each).

CLAM AND TOMATO BISQUE

> 1 can (7 to 8 ounces) minced clams
> 1 can (10¾ ounces) condensed tomato soup
> 1 soup can water
> 1 teaspoon salt
> ⅛ teaspoon pepper
> 1 teaspoon lemon juice

Heat clams (with liquor) and remaining ingredients to boiling. Reduce heat; simmer 5 minutes.

4 servings (about ¾ cup each).

CLAM-POTATO CHOWDER

>   1 package (5.5 ounces) scalloped potatoes
>   1 can (7 to 8 ounces) minced clams, drained
>   (reserve liquor)
> 2½ cups milk
>   1 tablespoon butter or margarine

In large saucepan, heat potato slices, sauce mix, amounts of water and milk called for on package and clam liquor to boiling, stirring occasionally. Reduce heat.

Cover tightly; simmer about 25 minutes or until potatoes are tender, stirring occasionally. Stir in clams, 2½ cups milk and the butter; heat through.

6 servings (about 1 cup each).

VARIATIONS

■ *Clam-Corn Chowder:* Stir in 1 can (8 ounces) whole kernel corn, drained, with the clams.

■ *Lobster Chowder:* Omit clams and liquor; stir in 1 can (5 ounces) lobster, drained and broken into small pieces, with the milk and butter.

SHERRIED MADRILENE

>   2 cans (13 ounces each) clear madrilene
>   2 cans (13 ounces each) red madrilene
>   ½ cup sherry

Heat madrilenes to boiling. Remove from heat; stir in wine. Serve immediately.

5 servings (about ¾ cup each).

CREAMY POTATO SOUP

     2 tablespoons butter or margarine
     2 tablespoons finely chopped onion
  1½ teaspoons salt
   ¼ teaspoon celery salt
   ⅛ teaspoon pepper
  3½ cups milk
  1⅓ cups instant mashed potato puffs
     Paprika
     Snipped parsley

In medium saucepan, heat butter, onion, salt, celery salt, pepper and milk *just* to boiling. Stir in potato puffs (dry); continue cooking until smooth, stirring constantly. Garnish with paprika and parsley.

4 servings (1 cup each).

Substitution

For fresh onion: 1 tablespoon instant minced onion.

SOUTH-OF-THE-BORDER BEAN SOUP

     1 can (11½ ounces) condensed bean and bacon soup
     1 can (10¾ ounces) condensed tomato soup
     1 can (10½ ounces) chili without beans
     1 soup can water
   ⅛ to ¼ teaspoon garlic powder
     Corn chips

Heat all ingredients except corn chips to boiling. Garnish soup with corn chips.

5 servings (1 cup each).

Sandwiches

MEAT ROLL SANDWICHES

4 frankfurter buns
  Soft butter or margarine
2 hard-cooked eggs, chopped
2 tablespoons chopped ripe olives
2 teaspoons pickle relish, drained
2 teaspoons prepared mustard
8 slices large bologna

Spread buns with butter. Mix eggs, olives, pickle relish and mustard. Arrange bologna in stacks of two slices each. Spoon ¼ of the egg mixture down center of each stack; roll up. Place meat rolls in buns. Secure with wooden picks. *4 sandwiches.*

INDIVIDUAL SUBMARINE SANDWICHES

4 loaves French bread, each 6 inches long
  Soft butter or margarine
4 lettuce leaves
2 to 3 tablespoons Italian salad dressing
4 slices salami
4 slices American cheese
4 slices boiled ham
4 slices Provolone cheese
4 to 8 slices tomato
  Thin slices onion
4 endive leaves

Cut loaves in half horizontally. Spread cut sides with butter. Dip lettuce leaves into salad dressing. On bottom halves of loaves, layer lettuce, salami, American cheese, ham, Provolone cheese, tomato and onion slices.

Dip endive into remaining salad dressing; place on onion slices and top with remaining halves of loaves. Secure with wooden picks. *4 sandwiches.*

SANDWICH FILLING CHART (for 5 or 6 sandwiches)

Make your own combinations of ingredients from the chart below, being careful not to choose too many. Stir together and chill if necessary. Remember to serve fillings on a variety of breads. Try any one of the many available sliced breads, but don't forget biscuits, corn muffins, hard rolls and buns.

Basic Ingredient (Choose one to total 2 cups)	Add Interest with ... (Choose one or combine to total ½ to ¾ cup)	Spread with ... (Use one or combine to total ½ cup)	If Desired, Season with	Garnish with
Chopped, ground or minced cooked meat (veal, ham, pork, lamb, beef, corned beef, chicken or frankfurter)	Chopped or minced vegetables (celery, onion, radishes, cucumber, carrot or green pepper)	Mayonnaise or salad dressing	Salt	Lettuce
		Thousand Island dressing	Pepper	Spinach
			Garlic salt	Watercress
Shrimp, rinsed and drained	Chopped fruits (apples, avocado, oranges or pineapple)	Dairy sour cream	Onion salt	Endive
		French dressing (for only partial amount)	Onion juice	Bermuda onion slices
Crabmeat, drained and cartilage removed			Lemon juice	Orange slices
	Pickle relish, drained, or chopped dill or sweet pickles		Worcestershire sauce	Radish slices
Tuna, drained			Red pepper sauce	Tomato slices
Salmon, drained and boned	Chopped olives (green, ripe or pimiento-stuffed)		Prepared mustard	Pear slices
6 hard-cooked eggs, chopped	Crumbled crisply fried bacon		Horseradish	Pineapple slices or spears
American or Cheddar cheese, shredded	Chopped nuts		Dill weed	Green pepper slices
Creamed cottage cheese, drained			Chili powder	Paprika
Baked beans, drained			Ground cloves	

CONEY ISLAND HOT DOGS

    1 can (15 ounces) chili with beans
    1 can (6 ounces) tomato paste
    ¼ cup chopped green pepper
    ¼ cup chopped onion
    1 teaspoon prepared mustard
    ½ teaspoon salt
    ½ teaspoon chili powder
    8 to 10 frankfurters
    8 to 10 frankfurter buns, buttered

In saucepan, mix all ingredients except frankfurters
and buns. Heat to boiling. Reduce heat; simmer uncovered 10 minutes.

Drop frankfurters into boiling water; reduce heat.
Cover tightly; simmer 5 to 8 minutes.

Toast buns. Serve frankfurters in buns; top frankfurters with chili mixture.   *8 to 10 sandwiches.*

GRILLED REUBEN SANDWICHES

    ⅓ cup mayonnaise or salad dressing
    1 tablespoon chili sauce
    12 slices rye bread, buttered
    ½ pound sliced Swiss cheese
    ½ pound sliced cooked corned beef brisket
    1 can (16 ounces) sauerkraut, drained
      Soft butter or margarine

Mix mayonnaise and chili sauce; spread on 6 bread
slices. Top with cheese slices, corned brisket, sauerkraut and remaining bread slices.

Butter outside of sandwiches. Grill in skillet over
low to moderate heat 5 to 7 minutes on each side or
brown in sandwich grill 5 to 7 minutes.   *6 sandwiches.*

VARIATION

■ *Rachel Sandwiches:* Substitute 1½ cups coleslaw for
the sauerkraut.

GRILLED HAM AND SWISS SANDWICHES

>　1 package (3 ounces) sliced ready-to-serve
>　　smoked ham
>　4 slices Swiss cheese
>　8 slices bread
>　½ cup soft butter or margarine

Place ham and cheese slices on 4 slices of bread; top
with remaining bread slices. Butter outsides of sandwiches. Grill in skillet over low to moderate heat
5 to 7 minutes on each side or brown in sandwich grill
5 to 7 minutes.　　　　　　　　　　　*4 sandwiches.*

Substitution

　For smoked ham: 4 to 8 thin slices fully cooked ham.

HASH AND CHEESE GRILL

>　1 can (16 ounces) roast beef hash
>　⅓ cup catsup
>　¾ teaspoon oregano
>　1 teaspoon parsley flakes
>　2 teaspoons instant minced onion
>　4 English muffins, split and buttered
>　8 slices American cheese, cut into strips

Mix hash, catsup, oregano, parsley flakes and onion;
spread evenly on muffin halves. Top with cheese strips.
Set oven control at broil and/or 550°. Broil 8 to 10
inches from heat until cheese melts and hash mixture
is bubbly and hot.　　　　　　　　　　*8 sandwiches.*

Substitutions

　For parsley flakes: 1 tablespoon snipped parsley.
　For instant onion: 2 tablespoons minced onion.

HAMBURGERS

   1 pound ground beef
   1 tablespoon instant minced onion
   ½ teaspoon salt
   ¼ teaspoon pepper
   4 hamburger buns, split

Mix ground beef, onion, salt and pepper. Shape mixture into four 4½-inch patties. Set oven control at broil and/or 550°. Broil hamburgers 3 inches from heat 2 minutes on each side for rare, 3 to 4 minutes on each side for medium. Serve in buns.   *4 sandwiches.*

To Charcoal-grill: Add ¼ cup water to ground beef mixture; shape into 5 patties. Place on grill 4 to 6 inches from hot coals; cook 12 minutes or until done, turning once.

Substitution

For instant onion: 3 tablespoons minced onion.

VARIATIONS

■ *California Hamburgers:* Top each with lettuce, onion slice, tomato slice and a dab of mayonnaise.

■ *Cheeseburgers:* About 1 minute before hamburgers are done, top each with cheese slice. Continue cooking until cheese melts.

■ *Panfried Hamburgers:* Turning frequently, fry patties in medium skillet in ½ teaspoon hot shortening over medium heat, about 7 minutes.

FREEZER BURGERS

    1 pound ground beef
    1 envelope (about 1½ ounces) onion soup mix
    ½ cup finely crushed cracker crumbs
    8 hamburger buns, split

Mix ground beef, onion soup mix and cracker crumbs.
Shape mixture into eight 4½-inch patties. Wrap each
patty in single thickness aluminum foil; freeze. (Keep
no longer than 3 months.) Wrap each bun in aluminum
foil; freeze.

Heat frozen hamburgers and buns (in foil wrap-
pings) in 425° oven 10 minutes.   *8 sandwiches.*

BARBECUED HAMBURGER
MAKE-AHEAD MIX

    4 pounds ground beef
    2 medium onions, chopped (about 1 cup)
    1 bottle (14 ounces) catsup
    1 cup water
    ½ cup chopped celery
    ¼ cup lemon juice
    2 tablespoons brown sugar
    1 tablespoon Worcestershire sauce
    1 tablespoon salt
    2 teaspoons vinegar
    ½ teaspoon dry mustard

In Dutch oven, cook and stir ground beef and onion
until meat is brown and onion is tender. Drain off
fat. Stir in remaining ingredients; heat to boiling,
stirring frequently.

Reduce heat. Cover tightly; simmer 30 minutes.
Cool; divide among pint-freezer containers and freeze
for future use. Or, use portion of hot mixture for variations on page 259, freeze remainder.   *5 pints.*

Note: To thaw frozen Make-ahead Mix, heat slowly in
saucepan or thaw in refrigerator.

VARIATIONS

■ *Baked Frank Rolls:* If desired, stir 1 cup shredded American cheese (about 4 ounces) into 1 pint Make-ahead Mix. Split 8 to 10 frankfurter buns; scoop part of bread from center of each. Spoon mixture into buns; wrap individually in aluminum foil. Heat in 350° oven 30 to 35 minutes.

■ *Barbecued Burger Buns:* Fill each buttered hamburger bun with about ¼ cup hot Make-ahead Mix. The entire recipe will fill 30 to 40 hamburger buns.

■ *Easy Chili:* Stir 1 can (15½ ounces) kidney beans (with liquid), ½ to 1 cup tomato juice and 2 to 3 teaspoons chili powder into 1 pint Make-ahead Mix; heat through. *4 servings.*

■ *Mock Pizza:* Split 6 to 8 hamburger buns; toast. Place on rack in broiler pan. Spoon 1 pint Make-ahead Mix on halves; sprinkle with shredded American cheese and dash oregano. Set oven control at broil and/or 550°. Broil 3 to 4 inches from heat just until cheese is bubbly.

SLOPPY JOES

    1 pound ground beef
   ¾ cup chopped onion
    1 can (10½ ounces) condensed chicken gumbo soup
    3 tablespoons catsup
    3 tablespoons prepared mustard
    6 hamburger buns, split and toasted

Cook and stir ground beef and onion until meat is brown. Drain off fat. Stir in soup, catsup and mustard. Simmer uncovered 15 minutes, stirring occasionally. Serve in buns.   *6 sandwiches*

Substitution

For chicken gumbo soup and catsup: 1 can (10¾ ounces) condensed tomato soup; decrease prepared mustard to 1 tablespoon.

SPREAD-A-BURGER

  1 can (10¾ ounces) condensed tomato soup
  ½ cup shredded Cheddar or American cheese
  ¼ cup chopped onion
  2 teaspoons salt
  1 teaspoon dry mustard
  ¼ teaspoon pepper
  1 pound ground beef
  8 hamburger buns, split and toasted
  16 thin green pepper rings
     Pimiento-stuffed olives, sliced

Heat oven to 350°. Mix soup, cheese, onion, salt, mustard and pepper. Stir in ground beef; spread evenly on bun halves, being careful to bring mixture to the edges.

Place eight of the bun halves on ungreased baking sheet. Bake 15 to 20 minutes or until meat is done. Set oven control at broil and/or 550°. Broil 6 to 8 inches from heat about 3 minutes or until brown. Repeat with remaining bun halves. Garnish with pepper rings and olive slices.   *16 sandwiches.*

CHEESE CLUB SANDWICH

Set oven control at broil and/or 550°. Toast bread slice 5 inches from heat until golden brown on one side; toast lightly on second side. Butter second side; top with tomato slice. Place 2 or 3 slices crisply fried bacon on tomato and top with cheese slice. Broil until cheese melts.   *1 sandwich.*

TOMATO SHORTCAKES

2⅓ cups buttermilk baking mix
3 tablespoons butter, melted and cooled slightly
½ cup milk
6 slices bacon
1 can (10¾ ounces) condensed Cheddar cheese soup
⅓ cup milk
Soft butter
3 medium tomatoes, sliced

Heat oven to 450°. Mix baking mix, 3 tablespoons butter and ½ cup milk wth fork until a soft dough forms. Knead 8 to 10 times on lightly floured cloth-covered board. Roll dough ½ inch thick. Cut with floured 3-inch cutter. Bake on ungreased baking sheet about 10 minutes.

Fry bacon until crisp; remove and drain. Heat soup and ⅓ cup milk over low heat, stirring frequently. Split warm shortcakes crosswise; spread with butter. Place tomato slices between layers and on top of each shortcake. Spoon hot cheese sauce onto shortcakes; garnish with bacon.   *6 sandwiches.*

HAM-BROCCOLI SANDWICHES

1 package (10 ounces) frozen broccoli spears
1 can (10¾ ounces) condensed Cheddar cheese soup
⅓ cup milk
4 slices toast, buttered
4 slices cooked ham

Cook broccoli as directed on package; drain. Heat cheese soup and milk just to boiling, stirring frequently. Top each toast slice with ham slice, broccoli spears and about ⅓ cup cheese sauce.

4 open-face sandwiches.

DENVER SANDWICHES

    ¼ cup minced onion
    ¼ cup minced green pepper
     2 tablespoons shortening (half butter)
     4 eggs
    ½ cup minced cooked ham
    ¼ teaspoon salt
    ⅛ teaspoon pepper
     8 slices bread or toast, buttered

In 10-inch skillet, cook and stir onion and green pepper
in hot shortening until onion is tender. Beat eggs
slightly; stir in ham, salt and pepper. Pour egg mixture
into skillet. Cook over low heat *just* until set. Cut into
4 wedges; turn. Brown slightly. Serve between bread
slices.   *4 sandwiches.*

Substitution

    For ham: 1 can (2¼ ounces) deviled ham and ¼
teaspoon Worcestershire sauce.

SHRIMP TOWERS

     2 hamburger buns, split and toasted
       Soft butter or margarine
     1 tomato, sliced
    16 cleaned, cooked shrimp
       Bacon-flavored vegetable protein chips
     4 slices process Cheddar cheese

Spread cut sides of buns with butter. Top each bun
half with tomato slice, shrimp, chips and cheese slice.
    Set oven control at broil and/or 550°. Broil 5 or 6
inches from heat 2 to 3 minutes or until cheese melts
and bubbles.   *4 open-face sandwiches.*

TUNA BURGERS

1 can (6½ ounces) tuna, drained
1 cup chopped celery
½ cup diced American cheese
1 tablespoon instant minced onion
¼ teaspoon salt
⅛ teaspoon pepper
¼ cup mayonnaise or salad dressing
6 hamburger buns, split and buttered

Heat oven to 350°. Mix all ingredients except buns. Fill buns with tuna mixture. Place each sandwich on square of aluminum foil; fold foil over sandwich and seal securely. Place on baking sheet. Bake 20 minutes or until heated through.   *6 sandwiches.*

Lunch Main Dishes

BEEF AND MUSHROOM SALAD

    1½-pound sirloin steak, 1½ inches thick
      1 jar (4½ ounces) sliced mushrooms, drained
      1 medium green pepper, sliced into thin rings
     ⅓ cup red wine vinegar
     ¼ cup salad oil
      1 teaspoon salt
     ½ teaspoon onion salt
     ½ teaspoon Worcestershire sauce
     ¼ teaspoon pepper
     ¼ teaspoon tarragon leaves
      2 cloves garlic, crushed
        Lettuce cups
        Cherry tomatoes

Set oven control at broil and/or 550°. Place top of steak 3 to 4 inches from heat. Broil until medium, about 15 minutes on each side; cool.

Cut steak into ⅜-inch strips; arrange in baking dish, 13½x9x2 inches. Top meat with mushrooms and pepper rings. Mix vinegar, oil and seasonings; pour on meat and vegetables. Cover; refrigerate at least 3 hours, spooning marinade over vegetables occasionally.

With a slotted spoon, remove vegetables to lettuce cups. Arrange strips of meat beside vegetables; garnish with tomatoes.

Chocolate cake for dessert makes this a man-designed lunch.   *4 servings.*

SIRLOIN STROGANOFF

    1-pound sirloin steak, 1 inch thick
    1 tablespoon butter or margarine
    ⅛ teaspoon garlic salt
    ⅛ teaspoon pepper
    1 package (5.5 ounces) noodles Stroganoff dinner
1⅔ cups milk
    ⅓ cup red Burgundy, if desired
    1 tablespoon soft butter or margarine
    1 teaspoon poppy seed

Cut meat across the grain into ½-inch strips, about
1½ inches long. Melt 1 tablespoon butter in large
skillet; cook meat until light brown. Season with
garlic salt and pepper.

Mix in sauce mix (from noodles Stroganoff) and
milk; heat to boiling, stirring constantly. Reduce heat;
stir in wine. Cover tightly; simmer 20 minutes, stirring
occasionally.

Cook noodles as directed on package; drain. Return to saucepan. Stir in 1 tablespoon butter and the
poppy seed. Serve sauce on noodles.   *4 servings.*

BEEF STEW LUNCH

    1 can (16 ounces) sliced carrots
    1 can (8 ounces) whole potatoes
    1 can (8 ounces) cut green beans
    ¼ cup all-purpose flour
    1 envelope (about 1½ ounces) onion soup mix
    3 cups cut-up cooked beef

Drain vegetables, reserving liquid. Combine flour and
soup mix in large skillet. Add enough water to reserved
vegetable liquid to measure 3 cups; stir into mixture in
skillet. Heat to boiling, stirring constantly. Boil and
stir 1 minute.

Stir in vegetables and beef. Cover tightly; cook
over low heat about 10 minutes or until heated through.
                        4 servings (about 1½ cups each).

CHILI CASSEROLE

1 can (15½ ounces) chili without beans
1 tablespoon instant minced onion
1 can (12 ounces) vacuum-pack whole kernel
   corn with sweet peppers, drained
½ cup shredded Cheddar cheese

Heat oven to 350°. Pour chili into greased baking dish,
8x8x2 or 9x9x2 inches. Top with onion and corn;
sprinkle with cheese. Bake uncovered 20 to 25 minutes
or until cheese is bubbly.

Plan a Mexicali menu with shredded lettuce, fried
tortillas (they come frozen, you know) and Pears au
Chocolat (page 148).   *4 to 6 servings.*

Substitutions

For instant onion: 3 tablespoons minced onion.
For Cheddar cheese: ½ cup shredded Swiss cheese.

CHOW MEIN CASSEROLE

1¼ cups boiling water
½ cup uncooked converted rice
½ teaspoon salt
1 pound ground beef
¾ cup chopped celery
3 tablespoons instant minced onion
1 can (10½ ounces) condensed chicken with
   rice soup
1 can (4 ounces) mushroom stems and pieces,
   drained
2 tablespoons soy sauce
1 tablespoon brown sugar
1 teaspoon butter or margarine

Heat oven to 350°. Mix water, rice and salt; cover.
Cook and stir ground beef, celery and onion until meat
is brown. Drain off fat.

Mix all ingredients. Pour into greased 2-quart casserole. Cover tightly; bake 30 minutes. Uncover and
stir; bake 30 minutes longer.   *4 or 5 servings.*

HAM AND NOODLE COOLER

> 1 package (5.5 ounces) noodles Romanoff
> ½ teaspoon grated onion
> 2 teaspoons lemon juice
> 1½ cups seedless green grapes
> 1½ cups cubed cooked ham

Prepare noodles Romanoff as directed on package; cool slightly. Stir in remaining ingredients; chill. *6 servings.*

Substitution

For ham: 1 can (12 ounces) pork luncheon meat, cubed.

HAM 'N HASH

> 1 package (5.5 ounces) hash browns with onions
> 1 cup cubed cooked ham
> 2 tablespoons chopped green pepper

Prepare hash browns as directed on package except—decrease salt to ½ teaspoon and stir in ham and green pepper before cooking.

Start the lunch with Tomato Bouillon (page 244) and finish with Dried Fruit Compote (page 213).
4 servings.

FRANKFURTER CHOWDER

> 1 tablespoon butter or margarine
> 6 frankfurters, cut into ½-inch pieces
> ¼ cup chopped green pepper
> 2 tablespoons chopped onion
> 1 can (16 ounces) cream-style corn
> 3 dashes red pepper sauce

Melt butter in large skillet; cook and stir frankfurters, green pepper and onion over medium heat until brown. Stir in corn and pepper sauce; heat through.
4 to 6 servings.

SPANISH RICE

       6 slices bacon
    ¼ cup chopped onion
    ¼ cup chopped green pepper
       3 cups cooked rice
       1 can (16 ounces) tomatoes
    1½ teaspoons salt
    ⅛ teaspoon pepper

Fry bacon in large skillet until crisp; remove bacon
and drain. Drain off all but 2 tablespoons fat. Stir in
onion and green pepper; cook and stir until onion is
tender.

Crumble bacon; stir in with remaining ingredients.
Cook uncovered over low heat about 15 minutes.

4 to 6 servings.

Note: To bake casserole in oven, heat oven to 400°;
pour mixture into greased 1½-quart casserole and
bake uncovered 25 to 30 minutes.

VARIATION

■ *Spanish Rice with Sausage:* Omit bacon and substitute 7 to 8 pork sausage links, cut into ¾-inch pieces (2
cups); cook sausages until brown.

Nobody Lunches at Home?

Your husband works in the city; the kids eat at school. And
maybe you're tied to a desk all day too. Then keep these hearty
recipes in mind for other things . . . for sending off something
hot in the lunchbox thermos or for the day when it's your turn
to entertain the girls. And nothing says you can't take any one
of them to the table later and call it dinner.

CHEF'S SALAD

1 head lettuce, washed and chilled
1 small bunch romaine or endive, washed and chilled
1 cup julienne strips cooked meat (beef,
    ham, tongue)
1 cup julienne strips cooked chicken or turkey
1 cup julienne strips Swiss cheese
½ cup chopped green onions
½ cup sliced celery
1 can (2 ounces) anchovy fillets, if desired
2 tomatoes, cut into wedges
½ cup mayonnaise or salad dressing
¼ cup French dressing
    Ripe olives
1 hard-cooked egg, sliced

Into large salad bowl, tear lettuce and romaine into bite-size pieces (about 12 cups). Reserve few strips of meat and cheese. Toss remaining meat and cheese strips, the onion, celery, anchovies and tomatoes with the salad greens.

Blend mayonnaise and French dressing; pour on salad and toss. (If you prefer a clear dressing, use the traditional oil and vinegar.) Garnish with reserved meat and cheese strips, the olives and egg slices.

4 servings.

HOT CHICKEN SALAD

2 cups cubed cooked chicken
2 cups thinly sliced celery
1 cup toasted bread cubes
1 cup mayonnaise
½ cup chopped or slivered almonds, toasted
2 tablespoons lemon juice
2 teaspoons instant minced onion
½ teaspoon salt
½ cup shredded cheese
1 cup toasted bread cubes or crushed potato chips

Heat oven to 450°. Mix all ingredients except cheese and 1 cup toasted bread cubes. Pile lightly into ungreased 1-cup baking dishes. Sprinkle with cheese and remaining bread cubes. Bake 10 to 15 minutes or until bubbly.   *6 servings.*

Substitution

For instant onion: 2 tablespoons minced onion.

VARIATIONS

■ *Hot Tuna, Turkey or Veal Salad:* Substitute 2 cans (6½ ounces each) tuna, drained, or 2 cups cubed cooked turkey or veal for the chicken.

CHICKEN À LA KING

1 can (10½ ounces) condensed cream of celery soup
1 cup cut-up cooked chicken
1 tablespoon chopped pimiento
1 teaspoon parsley flakes
1 can (4 ounces) mushroom stems and pieces, drained
Chow mein noodles or hot rice

Heat soup. Stir in chicken, pimiento, parsley flakes and mushrooms; heat through. Serve on chow mein noodles.   *3 or 4 servings.*

Substitution

For parsley flakes: 1 tablespoon snipped parsley.

VARIATION

■ *Turkey à la King:* Substitute cut-up cooked turkey for the chicken.

CHICKEN AND MACARONI SALAD

>   1 cup uncooked elbow macaroni
>   1 cup diced cucumber
>   1½ cups cut-up cooked chicken
>   1 tablespoon grated onion
>   1 tablespoon snipped parsley
>   ½ cup mayonnaise or salad dressing
>   ½ teaspoon salt
>   ¼ teaspoon pepper
>   4 cups bite-size pieces lettuce

Cook macaroni as directed on package; drain and rinse in cold water. Mix all ingredients except lettuce. Cover and refrigerate.

Just before serving, toss with lettuce. Garnish with parsleyed tomato wedges.   *4 to 6 servings.*

Substitutions

For fresh onion: 1 teaspoon instant minced onion.
For fresh parsley: 1 teaspoon parsley flakes.

VARIATIONS

■ *Tuna or Turkey and Macaroni Salad:* Substitute 1 can (9¾ ounces) tuna, drained, or 1½ cups cut-up cooked turkey for the chicken.

SPEEDY CHICKEN AND SHRIMP

>   1 medium onion, chopped
>   1 can (8½ ounces) pineapple tidbits, drained
>   3 to 4 tablespoons butter or margarine
>   2 cans (10½ ounces each) chicken à la king
>   1 can (4½ ounces) shrimp, rinsed and drained
>   2 tablespoons lemon juice
>   3 to 4 cups hot cooked rice
>   Bacon-flavored vegetable protein chips

In large skillet, cook and stir onion and pineapple tidbits in butter until onion is tender. Stir in chicken à la

king, shrimp and lemon juice; heat through. Serve on
rice; sprinkle with chips.   *4 to 6 servings.*

Substitution

For pineapple tidbits: 1 medium apple, pared and
diced; omit chips and add 2 to 3 teaspoons curry powder
with the lemon juice.

TUNA ON A SHOESTRING

> 1 can (6½ ounces) tuna, drained
> 1 cup shredded carrots
> 1 cup diced celery
> ¼ cup minced onion
> ¾ to 1 cup salad dressing or mayonnaise
> 1 can (4 ounces) shoestring potatoes

In large bowl, separate tuna into chunks. Add carrots,
celery, onion and salad dressing; toss until tuna is well
coated with dressing. Cover and chill.

Just before serving, fold in potatoes. Add a bright
touch with parsley and carrot curls. *4 to 6 servings.*

TUNA-POTATO SCALLOP

> 1 package (5.5 ounces) scalloped potatoes
> 1 can (9¼ ounces) tuna, drained
> 1 can (10½ ounces) condensed cream of celery soup
> 2 tablespoons chopped pimiento

Heat oven to 400°. Empty potato slices into ungreased
2-quart casserole; sprinkle with packet of sauce mix.
Stir in amount of boiling water as directed on package,
the tuna, soup and pimiento. Bake uncovered 35 to
40 minutes.

Chilled Asparagus (page 108) makes an interesting
vegetable salad.   *4 to 6 servings.*

SWISS TUNA ROMANOFF

    1 package (5.5 ounces) noodles Romanoff
    1 can (6½ ounces) tuna, drained
    1 cup shredded Swiss cheese (about 4 ounces)
    1 tablespoon snipped chives

Heat oven to 350°. Prepare noodles Romanoff as directed on package except—increase milk to ½ cup. In
ungreased 1½-quart casserole, layer half the noodles,
all the tuna and cheese and remaining noodles. Sprinkle
with chives. Cover tightly; bake 15 to 20 minutes.

    Add a pretty and colorful garnish of green grapes.

4 servings.

CRAB LOUIS

    2 cans (7½ ounces each) crabmeat
      Louis Dressing (below)
    4 tomatoes, quartered
    4 hard-cooked eggs, quartered
      Ripe or green olives
    4 cups bite-size pieces salad greens, chilled

Drain crabmeat and remove cartilage; chill. Prepare
Louis Dressing. Arrange crabmeat, tomatoes, eggs and
olives on greens. Pour Louis Dressing on salad.

4 servings.

LOUIS DRESSING

    ¾ cup chili sauce
    ½ cup mayonnaise or salad dressing
    1 teaspoon instant minced onion
    ½ teaspoon sugar
    ¼ teaspoon Worcestershire sauce
      Salt to taste

Mix all ingredients. Cover; chill 30 minutes.

Substitution

    For canned crabmeat: 2 packages (6 ounces each)
frozen cooked crabmeat, thawed.

FISH STICKS WITH CUCUMBER SAUCE

1 package (16 ounces) frozen fish sticks
¼ medium cucumber
1 teaspoon salt
½ teaspoon lemon pepper
1 cup unflavored yogurt

Cook fish sticks as directed on package. Cut unpared cucumber into 1-inch pieces. Chop in blender, watching carefully; drain thoroughly. (Or cucumber can be finely chopped by hand.) Stir cucumber and seasonings into yogurt. Serve sauce with fish.   *6 servings.*

SEAFOOD AND RICE

3 cups cooked seafood* (large pieces)
¼ cup butter or margarine
2 tablespoons lemon juice
1 can (10¾ ounces) condensed cream
   of shrimp soup
1 cup milk
3 cups cooked rice
¼ cup buttered bread crumbs

Cook and stir seafood in butter until heated through. Stir in lemon juice, soup and milk; heat through, stirring frequently. Serve on rice; sprinkle with bread crumbs.   *4 or 5 servings.*

---

* *Use crab, shrimp, lobster or a combination.*

WELSH RAREBIT

    1 can (10¾ ounces) condensed Cheddar
      cheese soup
    ⅓ cup milk
    ¼ teaspoon dry mustard
    ¼ teaspoon Worcestershire sauce
      Dash pepper
    4 slices toast, buttered

Heat all ingredients except toast. Pour about ⅓ cup
sauce on each slice of toast.   *2 servings.*

CHEESE SOUFFLÉED PEPPER SHELLS

    3 large green peppers
    1 package (12 ounces) frozen cheese soufflé, thawed

Heat oven to 325°. Cut peppers lengthwise in half;
remove seeds. Arrange pepper shells in ungreased
baking pan, 13x9x2 inches. Pour soufflé into shells.
Bake uncovered 1 hour or until knife inserted in center
comes out clean.

    Nice with Best Tossed Salad (page 94) and Corn
Bread (page 145).

VARIATION

■ *Ham-Cheese Souffléed Pepper Shells:* Before baking,
sprinkle ½ cup finely diced cooked ham on cheese soufflé
in pepper shells.

Snacks

FRUITY CEREAL SQUARES

 1 package (3 ounces) fruit-flavored gelatin
 ⅓ cup light corn syrup
 2 tablespoons butter or margarine
 4 cups fruit-flavored corn puffs cereal

Butter baking pan or dish, 9x9x2 inches. In large saucepan, mix gelatin (dry), corn syrup and butter. Heat to boiling over medium heat, stirring constantly. Remove from heat; stir in cereal until evenly coated.

With buttered back of spoon, spread mixture in buttered pan. Cover; chill until set, about 30 minutes. Cut into squares.   *3 dozen squares.*

Note: Chill the candy to set it, but store at room temperature.

PEANUTTY SQUARES

 ¼ cup butter or margarine
 3 cups miniature marshmallows
 ½ cup peanut butter
 4 cups O-shaped puffed oat cereal
 1 cup salted peanuts

Butter baking pan, 9x9x2 inches. In large saucepan, melt butter, marshmallows and peanut butter over low heat, stirring until smooth. Remove from heat; mix in cereal and peanuts until evenly coated.

Spread mixture quickly in buttered pan. Cool; cut into squares.   *16 squares.*

Substitution

For miniature marshmallows: 32 large marshmallows, quartered.

CHOCOLATE-O BARS

    ½ cup light corn syrup
    1 package (6 ounces) semisweet chocolate pieces
    1 teaspoon vanilla
    4 cups chocolate-flavored corn puffs cereal

Butter baking pan, 9x9x2 inches. In medium saucepan, heat syrup to boiling. Remove from heat; add
chocolate pieces and vanilla, stirring until chocolate is
melted. Mix in cereal until coated

    With buttered back of spoon, spread mixture in but-
tered pan. Cool 1 hour; cut into bars.   *3 dozen bars.*

OVEN CARAMEL CORN

    3¾ quarts (15 cups) popped corn
    1 cup brown sugar (packed)
    ½ cup margarine or butter
    ¼ cup light corn syrup
    ½ teaspoon salt
    ½ teaspoon soda

Heat oven to 200°. Divide popped corn between 2
ungreased baking pans, 13x9x2 inches. Heat sugar,
margarine, corn syrup and salt, stirring occasionally,
until bubbly around edges. Continue cooking over medium heat 5 minutes.

    Remove from heat; stir in soda until foamy. Pour
on popped corn, stirring until corn is well coated. Bake
1 hour, stirring every 15 minutes.

CARAMEL CRUNCH

28 vanilla caramels
2 tablespoons milk
2 cups O-shaped puffed oat cereal
1 cup Spanish peanuts

Melt caramels with milk, stirring constantly until smooth. Mix cereal and peanuts in large bowl. Pour melted caramels on cereal mixture; stir until evenly coated.

With buttered hands, shape mixture into 1-inch balls. Cool on waxed paper.   *About 2 dozen candies.*

"TARTARE STEAK" APPETIZERS

½ pound ground sirloin
1 egg
1 green onion, finely chopped
½ teaspoon salt
2 dashes red pepper sauce
Soft butter or margarine
5 slices bread

Mix meat, egg, onion, salt and pepper sauce. Set oven control at broil and/or 550°. Butter one side of each bread slice. Broil 3 inches from heat until bread is toasted. Turn; cover unbuttered side with meat mixture. Broil 1 to 2 minutes for rare, 2 to 3 minutes for medium. Cut each bread slice into 9 bite-size pieces.

45 appetizers.

To Charcoal-grill: Cover unbuttered side of bread with meat mixture. Carefully spread butter on meat mixture. Place bread side down 2 inches from medium coals; cook about 1½ minutes or until bread is toasted. Turn; cook 1½ minutes longer.

MEATBALLS MUSHROOM

>   1 pound ground beef
>   1 egg
>   ½ cup dry bread crumbs
>   ¼ cup milk
>   2 tablespoons instant minced onion
>   1 teaspoon salt
>   ⅛ teaspoon pepper
>   1 package (¾ ounce) mushroom gravy mix

Mix all ingredients except gravy mix. Shape mixture into 1-inch balls; place in ungreased jelly roll pan, 15½ x 10½ x 1 inch. Bake uncovered in 400° oven 8 to 10 minutes or until brown.

While meatballs bake, prepare gravy mix as directed in large skillet. Stir in meatballs until all are coated.
35 meatballs.

Substitution

For instant onion: ⅓ cup minced onion.

LONDON BROIL APPETIZER

>   1-pound flank steak, scored
>   1 cup rosé
>   1 teaspoon salt
>   ½ teaspoon rosemary leaves
>   ¼ teaspoon pepper

Place steak in shallow glass dish. Combine remaining ingredients; pour on meat. Cover; refrigerate several hours, turning meat occasionally.

Set oven control at broil and/or 550°. Remove steak from marinade. Broil 2 to 3 inches from heat 4 minutes. Turn; broil 3 to 4 minutes longer.

Cut meat at an angle across grain into thin slices. If desired, salt before serving. Serve on thin rounds of rye or French bread.   *6 to 8 servings.*

Substitution

For rosé: 1 cup cranberry cocktail.

MARINATED SHRIMP

    1½ teaspoons salt
      1 package (12 ounces) frozen cleaned raw shrimp
      1 cup oil and vinegar salad dressing
      1 bay leaf, crushed

Heat 2 cups water and the salt to boiling. Add shrimp; heat to boiling. Cook 1 to 2 minutes or until shrimp are tender; rinse quickly under running cold water to cool.

    Mix shrimp, salad dressing and bay leaf in glass bowl. Cover; refrigerate at least 2 hours.

Substitution

    For frozen shrimp: 2 cans (4½ ounces each) medium shrimp, rinsed and drained.

MEXICAN DIP

      1 can (10¾ ounces) condensed Cheddar cheese soup
    ½ cup finely chopped tomato
      3 tablespoons finely chopped green chili peppers
      2 green onions, finely chopped

Heat all ingredients over low heat about 15 minutes, stirring frequently.   *1¾ cups.*

HOT CURRIED CRAB DIP

      2 packages (8 ounces each) cream cheese, softened
      2 teaspoons curry powder
      1 can (7½ ounces) crabmeat, drained and cartilage
        removed

Heat oven to 375°. In small mixer bowl, beat cream cheese and curry powder. Stir in crabmeat. Turn into ungreased baking dish. Bake about 20 minutes. *3 cups.*

FRESH VEGETABLE RELISHES

Prepare a variety of the vegetable relishes below. Keep crisp in ice and water in refrigerator until serving time. Arrange in a large bowl filled with crushed ice. Delicious with a cheese dip.

Broccoli Buds and Cauliflowerets: Break head of broccoli or cauliflower into bite-size flowerets.

Carrot Curls: With vegetable parer cut carrot lengthwise into paper-thin slices. Roll up and fasten with picks. (Remove picks before serving.)

Cucumber Petals: Run tines of fork down length of unpared cucumber. Cut crosswise into very thin slices.

Green Onions: Remove any loose layers of skin. Trim, leaving about 3 inches of green.

Radish Fans: Remove stem and root ends from large radishes. Make thin crosswise cuts almost through radishes.

SHRIMP DIP

    2 tablespoons milk
    1 teaspoon lemon juice
    1 teaspoon Worcestershire sauce
    ½ teaspoon garlic salt
    ¼ teaspoon dill weed
    1 cup creamed cottage cheese
    1 can (4½ ounces) broken shrimp, rinsed
      and drained

Place all ingredients except shrimp in blender. Blend on high speed until smooth and creamy, about 2 minutes. Pour into small bowl. Stir in shrimp. Cover; refrigerate at least 1 hour.   *About 1½ cups.*

VARIATION

■ *Yogurt-Shrimp Dip:* Substitute 1 cup unflavored yogurt for the milk and cottage cheese; stir together all ingredients.

VEGETABLE DIPPERS WITH HOLLANDAISE DIP

1 package (about 1½ ounces) hollandise sauce mix
1 pound fresh asparagus
10 small cherry tomatoes

Prepare hollandaise sauce as directed on package; chill. Chill vegetables. Serve sauce as a dip. *4 servings.*

Substitution

For asparagus: 1 can (16 ounces) vertical-pack whole green beans, drained.

GUACAMOLE DIP WITH TACOS

1 can (7¾ ounces) frozen guacamole dip, thawed
¼ teaspoon cumin
4 drops red pepper sauce
1 package (5½ ounces) frozen cocktail tacos

Blend guacamole dip, cumin and pepper sauce. Heat tacos as directed on package; serve with dip.

4 or 5 servings.

DEVILED HAM ROLL

1 can (4½ ounces) deviled ham
3 tablespoons finely chopped pimiento-stuffed olives
1 package (3 ounces) cream cheese, softened
1 teaspoon prepared mustard

Mix deviled ham and olives; chill until firm. Shape mixture into a roll. Blend cream cheese and mustard; spread over ham roll. Cover; chill at least 2 hours. Serve with crackers.   *4 to 6 servings.*

SALAMI WEDGES

Soften 1 package (3 ounces) cream cheese; spread cheese on 9 large salami slices. Stack spread slices and top with a plain slice of salami. Cover and chill. To serve, cut into 12 wedges. If desired, garnish each wedge with a pimiento-stuffed olive, pearl onion or cherry tomato on a wooden pick.   *12 appetizers.*

VARIATION

■ *Bologna Wedges:* Add 1 tablespoon prepared mustard to the cream cheese; use only 5 slices large bologna.

LIVERWURST TIDBITS

½ pound liverwurst, softened
1 clove garlic, crushed
½ teaspoon basil leaves

Mash liverwurst with fork; mix in garlic and basil. Shape by teaspoonfuls into balls; chill.   *36 tidbits.*

CRABMEAT SPREAD

1 can (7½ ounces) crabmeat, drained
    and cartilage removed
½ cup mayonnaise or salad dressing
2 tablespoons celery flakes
1 tablespoon lemon juice
2 teaspoons instant minced onion
¼ teaspoon salt
    Dash paprika

Mix all ingredients. Cover; refrigerate at least 2 hours. Serve with crackers.   *1½ cups.*

Substitution

For instant onion: 2 tablespoons minced onion.

CHEESEY-O'S

⅓ cup butter or margarine
⅓ cup grated Parmesan cheese
5 cups O-shaped puffed oat cereal

Heat oven to 300°. In oven, melt butter in baking pan, 13x9x2 inches. Stir in cheese. Mix in cereal. Bake 10 minutes.   *5 cups.*

PARMESAN SNACKS

2 tablespoons butter or margarine
½ teaspoon onion salt
½ teaspoon dry mustard
4 cups corn puffs cereal
2 tablespoons grated Parmesan cheese

Heat oven to 300°. In oven, melt butter in baking pan, 13x9x2 inches. Stir in onion salt and mustard. Gently mix in cereal until butter is absorbed. Sprinkle with cheese. Bake 10 minutes. Stir; bake 10 minutes longer.   *4 cups.*

GOOD AND EASY GUIDELINES

■

Planning Your Meals— the Good and Easy Way

When you stop to think about it, every meal you serve says a good deal about you. It reflects your cooking know-how, of course. It also shows off your ability to manage money, your knowledge of nutrition, your imagination, your own good taste and that very special feeling you have for your family. To make sure that reflection is a pretty picture, take this little refresher course.

PLANNING AHEAD

. . . or how to coordinate three meals a day with ease and expertise. The first thing to do is organize, your thoughts and your menus.

Begin with the Basic Four. You're concerned about your family's health, of course; so safeguard it. Get the Basic Four Food Groups down pat, and plan your meals around them. Here's what you need, every day, for your full share of good nutrition.

Meats: 2 or more servings
(This group includes poultry, fish, eggs, dried beans or peas and peanut butter.)

Vegetables and Fruits: 4 or more servings
(Plan on serving one dark green or yellow vegetable every other day, one citrus fruit each day.)

Milk: 2 or more cups for adults;
3 or more for children and teenagers.
(This group also includes cheese and ice cream.)

Breads and Cereals: 4 or more servings
(Make sure they're whole-grain, enriched, restored or fortified.)

Note: Don't forget fats, sweets and extra servings—they provide additional food energy and other food values.

You can be flexible though. For example, those two servings of meat per day can be scheduled any way you like. If your family goes for hamburgers at breakfast—why not? If they won't drink fruit juice in the morning but they will buy it as a dinner appetizer—then switch. What matters most is that they get their quota of the Basic Four Foods each and every day.

Think Through the Menus. Plan them by the day or by the week, whichever is easier. Either way, try putting things down on paper. Then you can see at a glance how breakfast, lunch, dinner and in-between snacks balance out.

If you start your thinking with the main-meal meat, the high-powered protein food, the rest of the plan will fall right into line. Besides, you'll know better where you stand with the budget. And stop and think. Can you double up on the meat and plan for a repeat performance?

Then consider your side-dish strategy. Round out the meal with a vitamin-rich salad and/or colorful vegetables. Think about potatoes, noodles, homey breads. And keep things pretty—mix colors, contrast textures, vary shapes and sizes.

Give the same careful attention to your other meals. When it comes to breakfast, plan to do something different. For lunches that travel, be sure to tuck in some sweets—that's one way you can try to control the amounts. For snacktime, push the fruit and vegetable munches.

Point of emphasis: variety is the secret of success

in the care and feeding of a family. Keep an eye out for the latest convenience foods. Use our recipes and suggestions to introduce new ideas, but experiment on your own, too.

Now take a look at the total picture. Did you get in enough meat? Enough milk? Do all the servings add up according to the Basic Four Food Groups? Good planning! Easy, too.

EXERCISING ECONOMY

. . . or how to stretch your minutes *and* your food dollars.

☐ Keep a running shopping list. Jot down items as you run low, or as they come to mind. When you're tempted to buy on impulse, ask yourself: "Do I really need it? Will my family eat it?" Remember, food that doesn't get eaten is money *and* nutrition down the drain.

☐ Check the food pages in your newspaper and shop for bargains. But if the bargain takes you across town, be aware that it costs you money to get there. On days when you plan to stock the freezer, it may be well worth the trip. Other days, convenience may count more.

☐ Follow a shopping route, in the order of your menu plot. Buy meat first, depending on the day's best buy. Then match up vegetables and salad items. Move on to desserts and snacks. See how well-plotted shopping aids well-balanced eating.

☐ Brush up on your arithmetic. Check out package sizes and the cost-per-serving; buy the one that's best for your needs—small, regular, even extra large. This is true for meat, too. The lower-priced bone-in cut may well end up costing more than the seemingly higher-priced boneless cut, which allows an extra serving.

☐ Follow the seasons for fruits and vegetables. You can tell when they're in season by the lower prices and the plentiful supply.

☐ Read and heed package directions. The manufacturers of convenience foods have tested their products exhaustively; they *know* which procedures will yield the best results. Look for new recipe ideas on the packages, too.

☐ Remember that time is money, and convenience foods may well save you both.

SERVING WITH STYLE

. . . or how to set the stage to double the pleasure of family meals.

Revamp the Routine. Everybody likes change— even in serving patterns. Sometimes serve from the kitchen, other times go family style. Or give Dad the honors with the head-of-the-table treatment. Buffet service lets youngsters learn to serve themselves—and it gives them a good excuse for not sitting still.

And here's a cagey way to make sure hot foods get eaten while they're still hot. Call the gang together for a just-before-dinner appetizer. Something simple will do—like tomato juice with carrot and celery sticks, or hot bouillon with crisp crackers.

Be Dashing with Dishes. Mix and match colors and textures. Red pottery plates with white china cups and saucers are fun. Match up one shade of green dishes with another. Or set out plates in a rainbow of colors. Soups and cereals can be served in mugs as well as bowls. Fruits and puddings look elegant in wine glasses.

Try a New Cut of Cloth. Switch from place mats to trays to a table runner to a conventional cloth in a gay color or splashy print. Think about a roll of gift-wrap paper, the narrow size, for slashing off a special-treat runner. Or use contact fabric for cutting out place mats in a pattern. Brighten the scene with colorful napkins—those great big paper ones as well as the fabrics.

Show Off with Work-savers. Serve from attractive triple-treat casseroles that go right from freezer to oven to table. Let everyone share in the cooking with do-it-at-the-table helpers such as electric skillets, chafing dishes and fondue pots. And remember those backstage aids that can mean so much to your good and easy plans: electric blenders, knives and can openers; non-stick finishes on anything and everything. Indeed, good equipment is a good investment.

Spruce Up with a Centerpiece. Pile shiny red apples in a pretty bowl. Pop limes into an apothecary jar. Tuck a bunch of parsley in a demitasse cup, or tiny cherry tomatoes in a straw basket. And for goodness' sake, show off that prized piece of kindergarten art right alongside.

Now you take it from here. Use these ideas as starters, then dream up new ones of your own. You'll find dozens of ways to make do with what you have on hand and come up with imaginative, and very personal, treats for the family table. And that's what we call adding a dash of love to good and easy cooking.

Facts About Freezing—the Good and Easy Way

	MEATS AND POULTRY	FISH AND SEAFOOD	STEWS, SAUCES AND CREAMED DISHES
MAXIMUM STORAGE TIME	Red Meat: 4 months Corned Beef, Sausage: 2 weeks Poultry and Game: 2-3 months	3-4 months	3-4 months
FREEZING TIPS	Uncooked: Trim off excess fat (to conserve space, remove bones). Do not salt before wrapping. Cooked: Leftover roasts and Swiss steak freeze satisfactorily for a short time.	Clean; wash, drain and wrap. For small fish, cover with water in leakproof container.	Do not overcook; cool quickly. (Fats tend to separate but will usually recombine.) Leave headspace in freezer container.
THAWING AND REHEATING TIPS	Thaw wrapped uncooked or cooked meats in refrigerator. Uncooked meats may stand at room temperature *just* until defrosted and then be cooked immediately.	Thaw under running cold water in original wrap. Cook while still chilled. If only partially thawed, cook a little longer at a lower temperature.	Partially thaw at room temperature to prevent scorching. Heat in double boiler 30 to 40 minutes. Add liquid if necessary; keep stirring to a minimum.
NOTES	Freeze as soon as possible. Just about all meats freeze well. Do not freeze picnic hams, canned hams or other canned meats. Do not freeze fried foods.	Cooked shrimp can be frozen; shrimp cocktail and shrimp creole can also be frozen but no longer than 6 weeks.	Cool quickly by partially submerging the saucepan in large pan of ice and water. Potatoes do not freeze well; add when thawing. Keep spice level low.

	EGGS (UNCOOKED)	RICE, BAKED BEANS AND PASTA DISHES	BREADS
MAXIMUM STORAGE TIME	9 months	3 months	Quick Breads (biscuits, muffins, nut breads, waffles): 2-3 months Yeast Breads: 9 months
FREEZING TIPS	Stir eggs and egg yolk with a fork. Add 1 tablespoon sugar or corn syrup or ½ teaspoon salt per cup before freezing. For yolks, add 2 times the salt or sweetener recommended for whole eggs.	Cook only partially; cool quickly. Freeze in casserole or in freezer container.	Bake before freezing. (Unbaked dough and batters lose some rising capacity.) Stack waffles but separate with wrap.
THAWING AND REHEATING TIPS	Thaw in refrigerator. Or let stand at room temperature *just* until defrosted and then use immediately.	Heat frozen food in covered saucepan (with small amount of butter in bottom) over medium heat. Or place frozen casserole in 350° oven until center is bubbly, about 45 minutes. (Add small amount of liquid if food seems dry.)	Quick Breads: Thaw in wrap at room temperature or warm in 325 to 350° oven. Yeast Breads: Thaw in wrap at room temperature. Or heat in 350° oven 20 to 25 minutes.
NOTES	Whites need no additions— put through a sieve for uniform texture.	Casseroles of this type vary considerably and some loss of flavor may occur.	Heat frozen waffles in toaster. Overwrap bakery bread if it is to be stored longer than 3 months. A 1-pound loaf of bread thaws in about 3 hours.

	CAKES AND CUPCAKES	COOKIES	PIE AND PASTRY
MAXIMUM STORAGE TIME	2-3 months	9-12 months	Baked Shells: 4 months Baked Pies: 4-6 months Unbaked Pies: 2-3 months Chiffon Pies: 1 month
FREEZING TIPS	Bake and cool cakes before wrapping. Confectioners' sugar and fudge frostings freeze best. Boiled are difficult to store—freeze before wrapping. Or insert wooden picks in frosting to prevent wrapping from touching.	Arrange baked cookies in a sturdy box lined with plastic wrap or aluminum foil. Separate each layer with wrap or foil; seal. Package dough for drop cookies in an airtight container, aluminum foil or plastic wrap.	Baked Pies: Cool quickly; freeze, then wrap. Do not freeze custard, cream or meringue-topped pies.
THAWING AND REHEATING TIPS	Thaw frosted cakes, loosely covered, in the refrigerator. Thaw unfrosted cakes in original wrap at room temperature 2 to 3 hours. Or place in 250 to 300° oven a short time, but watch closely.	Thaw baked cookies at room temperature for about 10 minutes. Thaw cookie dough until just soft enough to spoon or slice onto baking sheet.	Baked Pies: Thaw unwrapped at room temperature 2 to 4 hours. Or unwrap and let stand a short time, then place on lower shelf in 350° oven; heat just until warm. If using lightweight aluminum pie pans, place on baking sheet.
NOTES	Some frostings and fillings do not freeze well. The frostings change texture; fillings make the cake soggy.	Both cookie dough and baked cookies can be frozen.	Best to freeze baked pies—the bottom crust of an unbaked pie may absorb juices from filling and become soggy.

If you're interested in streamlining your cooking and serving chores without short-cutting flavor and variety, learn to use your freezer—or the freezer compartment of your refrigerator—to its full capacity. Cooking for the freezer is simply a matter of habit, and a very good habit at that. It can save you time. It can save you money. It can save you wear and tear. And these days, that's a lot of savings.

We've given you some specific freezing recommendations in the chart pages 290–292, but here are some general guidelines for your freezer "savings bank":

1. Start with top-quality foods. Freezing will never make them any fresher or better than they were to begin with.

2. Remember that superior packaging and wrapping materials go a long way toward insuring a top-drawer product. Best materials include heavy-duty aluminum foil, heavy-weight plastic wrap and freezer bags or containers. These are all good because freezer wraps and containers should be airtight, moisture- and vapor-proof. They should also be convenient to use and occupy as little space as possible.

3. Wrap food securely in an airtight package—unless recipe directions indicate otherwise.

4. Before freezing cooked food, cool quickly.

5. Don't refreeze thawed foods.

6. Freeze in family-size packages or individual portions.

7. Clearly label each package (freezer tape and magic marker are good for this) with the contents, number of servings and expiration date. Rotate packages so the nearest-to-expiration-date foods are near the front.

8. Store food at 0° or lower (unless directions specify otherwise); the temperautre will affect the quality of the food. In fact, it's a good idea to keep a freezer thermometer in the compartment to be sure the temperature's low enough.

Following are some estimated maximum storage times for other freezer-ready foods:

Food	Storage Time
Butter	6 months
Canapés	1 month
Candies	1 year
Cheese (small amounts)	6 months
Ice Cream	3 weeks
Vegetables	1 year

Carving—the Good and Easy Way

Beef Standing Rib Roast

■ Start with large side down. (If necessary, remove wedge-shaped slice from large end so roast will stand firmly.)

■ Insert fork firmly below first rib; cut horizontal slices from the outside of roast toward the rib side.

■ Cut several thin slices or one or two thick slices, if you prefer. Then cut down along inner side of rib bone. (Cut as close to the bone as possible.) As each slice is released, slide knife under it and lift to plate.

Beef Blade Pot-roast

■ Cut between muscles and around bones (bones are easily removed). Remove one section of pot-roast at a time.

■ Turn section so grain runs parallel to platter; carve across the grain. (Slices should be about ¼ inch thick.)

Porterhouse Steak

■ Start with bone at carver's right. Cut closely around bone and remove.

■ Carve 1-inch-wide slices across the full width of steak. Carve thick steaks on the diagonal.

Pork Loin Roast

■ First remove backbone by cutting between rib ends and backbone.

■ With rib side toward carver, cut slices on each side of rib bones. (Every other slice will have a bone.)

Whole Ham

■ Start with the fat side up and shank facing right; cut a few slices from the thin side. (The thin side will face carver if ham is a left leg and away from carver if ham is a right leg.)

■ Turn ham to rest on cut side, where slices were removed. Make vertical slices down to bone. Then run knife horizontally along bone to release slices.

■ Or make only the first and last vertical slice and run knife along bone to release the section intact; then slice.

Leg of Lamb

■ With shank bone to carver's right, cut a few lengthwise slices from thin side.

■ Turn to rest on cut side. Make slices down to bone.

■ Cut horizontally along bone to release slices (as for a whole ham, see page 296).

Turkey or Chicken

■ Start with legs at carver's right. Gently pull leg away from body and cut through joint between leg and body. Remove leg to another platter or board. Cut through leg between drumstick and thigh; slice meat parallel to the bone.

■ Make a deep horizontal cut into breast, just above wing. Insert fork firmly in top of breast; starting halfway up breast, carve thin slices down to the cut, working upward.

APPROXIMATE METRIC EQUIVALENTS

Quantity	Multiplied by	Equals
Teaspoons	5	Milliliters
Tablespoons	15	Milliliters
Fluid Ounces	30	Milliliters
Fluid Ounces	0.03	Liters
Cups	240	Milliliters
Cups	0.24	Liters
Pints	0.47	Liters
Quarts	0.95	Liters
Ounces	28	Grams
Pounds	454	Grams
Pounds	0.45	Kilograms
Inches	2.5	Centimeters
Fahrenheit temperature	5/9 (after subtracting 32)	Celsius temperature (exact)

Index

Almond(s)
  chocolate fondue, 152
  drops, 175
  flatbread, 144
  shortbreads, 166
  toasted, bonbons, 175
Ambrosia
  honey bee, 211
  salad, 104
Appetizers, 278–284. *See also*
      Dip, Soup(s).
  melon and prosciutto, 213
  quiche Lorraine, 225
Apple
  cheese pie, 193
  crisp, 150
  dumplings, mock, 216
  pandowdy, 194
  pie, fix-ups for, 193
  raisin stuffing, 62
Applesauce
  bars, 167
  cinnamon salad, 102
  mock apple dumplings, 216
Apricot(s)
  marshmallow, 215
  nectar, mulled, 242
Artichokes and peas, 107
Asparagus
  à la Polonaise, 108
  chilled, 108
  with cheese sauce, 108

Bacon, 230
  and onion noodles, 129
  Canadian-style, 231
  fan-tans, 143
Banana(s)
  baked, 215
  cake, 178
  cream pie, 200
  orange frost, 245
  pineapple salad, 106
Barley
  and lamb casserole, curried, 53
  Mexi-barley, 138
  pilaf, 138
Bars, 163, 165, 166, 167, 168
Bean(s)
  and rice, Caribbean, 136
baked, speedy, 92
  casserole, deluxe, 109
  chili, lazy man's, 91
  country cassoulet, 91
  salad, bright, 99

  soup, south-of-the-border, 252
Beef, 3–25
  and dressing bake, sliced, 74
  and mushroom salad, 264
  broiled, 7
  California roast, 5
  corned. *See* Corned beef.
  cranberry-pepper roast, 6
  cube steak Stroganoff, 11
  dried, casserole, 17
  ground. *See also* Hamburger(s).
    baked meat sandwich, 36
    chili con carne, 24
    chow mein casserole, 266
    country-style hominy, 23
    giant burger, 25
    meat loaf, baked, 20
    meatball stew, 20
    meatballs, baked, 19
    meatballs, mushroom, 279
    sloppy Joes, 259
  London broil, 11
    appetizer, 279
  mushroom, 13
  pie, savory, 16
  pot-roast in foil, 6
  roast, 3
  round steak, barbecued, 9
  shepherds' pie, 54
  short ribs, braised, 12
  sirloin Stroganoff, 265
  steak
    charcoal-grilled, 9
    pepper, Bordelaise, 10
    supper in foil, 10
    teriyaki, 7
  stew
    good brown, 14
    lunch, 265
    oven, 15
    piccalilli, 15
    Stroganoff, 16
  Swiss steak, 12
  "tartare steak" appetizers, 278
Beets
  savory, 111
  sweet and sour, 111
Beverages. *See also* Coffee
      (beverage), Milk(s).
  apricot nectar, mulled, 242
  banana orange frost, 245
  blender breakfast combos, 244
  breakfast, 242–247
    punch, 242
  cranberry frost, 208

Beverages (continued)
  dessert, 205–208
  fruit fizz, 207
  ice-cream soda, 207
  orange
    eggnog, 245
    freeze, 208
    frost soda, 208
    juice, sparkling, 242
  peach cup, creamy, 208
  strawberry cream, 207
  sunny sipper, 246
  tea, spiced, 207
  tomato bouillon, 244
Biscuit(s)
  fan-tans, 142
    bacon, 143
  quick bread, 145
  rich dinner, 141
Blackeye peas
  creamy, 118
  hopping John, 137
Blueberry
  cobbler, 152
  orange bread, 238
Bologna
  meat 'n potato roll-ups, 228
  meat roll sandwich, 253
  pineapple-cherry, 43
  wedges, 283
Breads. See also Biscuit(s),
    Muffin(s), Rolls, Toast.
  breakfast, 233–241
  dinner, 140–145
Broccoli
  and creamed onions, 116
  and spinach, 118
  elegant, 112
  green rice, 137
  'n chips, 112
Brownie(s)
  fudge cake, 180
  sour cream, 162
  variations for, 162
Brussels (sprouts)
  and carrots salad, 98
  and cauliflower, 114
  and spaghetti, saucy, 132
  sauté, 112
Bulgur pilaf, 139
Bun(s)
  burger, barbecued, 259
  sticks, 140
Butter pecan cookies, 167
Butters for vegetables, 107
Butterscotch
  broiled topping, 192
  crunch cake, 178

Cabbage
  blender coleslaw, 96

Bohemian, 113
  tomato skillet, 121
Cake(s), 177–187. See also
    Coffee cake.
  brownie fudge, 180
  butterscotch crunch, 178
  chocolate chip angel, 184
  cotton candy angel, 183
  country loaf, 181
  cupcakes, busy day, 179
  date, quick, 182
  devils food
    party, 179
    variations for, 179
  fudge, triple, 180
  fudgy pecan pudding, 182
  graham cracker torte, 184
  Hawaiian cream pie, 181
  lemon, triple, 182
  orange-raisin, blender, 185
  peanut butter, 178
  pistachio, mock, 184
  pound, variations for, 183
  root beer angel, 183
  sandwiches, 181
  spice, 187
  strawberry Chantilly torte, 177
  white, variations for, 177
  yellow, variations for, 178
Candies, 172–176
  caramel
    corn, oven, 277
    crunch, 277
  chocolate-O bars, 277
  fruity cereal squares, 276
  peanutty squares, 276
Caramel
  corn, oven, 277
  crunch, 278
  glazed sweet potatoes, 128
  peach crisps, 151
  rolls, 236
Carrot(s)
  and Brussels salad, 98
  bouillon, 113
  hot vegetable relishes, 113
  nuggets and snow peas, 117
  orange muffins, 237
Cassoulet, country, 91
Cauliflower
  and Brussels sprouts, 114
  and peas, dilled, 117
  and spinach noodles, 129
  orange salad, 104
Cereal(s)
  breakfast bars, 218
  hot
    fruited, 216
    stir-ins for, 217
  mock apple dumplings, 216
  peanut mallow chews, 217

Cereal(s) (continued)
  'n soup, 216
  squares, fruity, 276
  sweeteners for, 219
  toppings for, 218
Cheddar egg bake, 90
Cheese. See also Parmesan.
  and fruit tray, 146
  and ham oven omelet, 226
  and hash grill, 256
  apple pie, 193
  bake, puffy, 227
  Cheddar egg bake, 90
  cheesey-O's, 284
  club sandwich, 260
  egg roll, 227
  fondue, jiffy, 87
  pop-ups, 234
  potato casserole, 123
  potatoes, 123
  puffs, 142
  quiche Lorraine, 225
  souffléed pepper shells, 275
    ham, 275
  spinach soufflé, 88
  Swiss, and ham sandwiches,
    grilled, 256
  Swiss tuna Romanoff, 273
  topped pork cutlets, 34
  vegetable chowder, 248
  Welsh rarebit, 275
Cheeseburgers, 257
Chef's salad, 269
Cherry(ies)
  butter frosting, 190
  chocolate parfait, 153
  chocolate cake, 179
  cobbler, 152
  milk shake, 247
  opera fudge, 172
  pie
    fix-ups for, 195
    orange, 195
    supreme, 158
Chicken, 61–69
  à la king, 270
  and macaroni casserole, 69
  and macaroni salad, 271
  and shrimp, speedy, 271
  and wild rice casserole, 76
  bake, 65
  barbecued, 66
  broiled, 68
  can-opener combo, 69
  crusty-curried, 64
  divan, 75
  fixup, barbecued, 67
  fried, 63
    Maryland, 64
  garlic chip, 65
  giblets, 62

  golden Parmesan, 65
  in a pot, 62
  Islander, 66
  livers with mushrooms, 229
  oven-fried, 64
  roast, 61
  salad
    fruited, 76
    hot, 269
  stewed, 67
  stuffing for, 62
Chili
  beans, lazy man's, 91
  casserole, 266
  con carne, 24
  Coney Island hot dogs, 255
  dogs, 46
  easy, 259
Chocolate
  bonbons, 174
  butter frosting, 191
  butter nut frosting, 191
  cherry parfait, 153
  chip
    angel cake, 184
    bars, 166
    cookies, 169
    ginger drops, 162
  fondue, 152
  frosting, variations for, 188
  fudge, 172
    sauce, 246
  ginger drops, 162
  glaze, 191
  milk
    hot, 247
    shake, 246
  mint parfaits, 159
  nut
    creams, 176
    fudge, 172
  O bars, 277
  pears au chocolat, 148
  pie, rich, 201
  refrigerator cookies, 165
Chowder. See Soup(s)
Chow mein casserole, 266
Cinnamon
  applesauce salad, 102
  coffee, red-hot, 205
  fruits, 214
  rolls, 236
Clam
  and tomato bisque, 250
  corn chowder, 251
  potato chowder, 251
Cobbler
  blueberry, 152
  cherry, 152
  peach, 152

Cocoa
   butter frosting, 191
   cereal milk shake, 244
   continental, 247
   flavored coffee, 247
   frosting, creamy, 180
Coconut
   broiled topping, 192
   ginger drops, 161
   pudding, 154
   rice, 134
   toffee bars, 168
Coffee (beverage)
   à la mode, 206
   café Mexican, 206
   California, 206
   cocoa-flavored, 247
   demitasse, 205
   Irish, 206
   mocha dessert, 205
   red-hot cinnamon, 205
Coffee cake. See also Sweet rolls.
   peanut butter and jelly, 235
   streusel, 235
Coleslaw, blender, 96
Cookie(s), 161–171
   almond shortbreads, 166
   applesauce bars, 167
   brown sugar pecan rounds, 170
   brownies
      sour cream, 162
      variations for, 162
   butter pecan, 167
   chocolate chip, 169
      bars, 166
   coconut-toffee bars, 168
   crumb crust, 203
   date bars, variations for, 163
   fudge crinkles, 164
   gingerbread drops, and
      variations, 161
   golden good bars, 165
   pat crust, 204
   peanut break, 171
   peanut butter, 163
   pineapple
      coconut, 170
      raisin, 170
   Polynesian, 170
   refrigerator, 165
      chocolate, 165
      dessert, 157
   salted peanut, 171
Corn
   and cucumber, creamy, 114
   bread, 145
   caramel, oven, 277
   clam chowder, 251
   hamburger bake, 21
   muffins, 145
   sesame sauté, 115

   sticks, 145
   soup, cream of, 248
Corned beef
   grilled Reuben sandwich, 255
   hash, eggs on, 222
   potato pancakes, 240
   Rachel sandwich, 255
   stew, 18
Crab (meat)
   dip, hot curried, 280
   Louis, 273
   spread, 283
Cranberry
   frost, 208
   pepper roast, 6
Crumpets, jam, 233
Cube steak Stroganoff, 11
Cucumber
   and corn, creamy, 114
   relish mold, 99
   salad, marinated, 97
   sauce, 48
Cupcakes, busy day, 179
Currant-raspberry compote, 213

Date
   bars, variations for, 163
   nut ginger drops, 161
   pineapple dessert, 149
Demitasse, 205
Denver sandwiches, 262
Desserts, 146–208. See also
      Cake(s), Cookies, Ice
      cream, Pie(s), Puddings.
   apple crisp, 150
   bananas, baked, 215
   blueberry cobbler, 152
   caramel peach crisps, 151
   cherries supreme, 158
   cherry cobbler, 152
   chocolate fondue, and
      variations, 152
   cookie refrigerator dessert, 157
   fruit. See also names of fruits.
      and cheese tray, 146
      compote, dried, 213
      compote, hot, 150
      delight, 153
      dessert freeze, 157
      in sour cream, 148
      kabobs, broiled, 150
      slices, frozen, 212
      with yogurt, 211
   fruited sherbet, 147
   grapefruit
      broiled honey, 214
      minted, 147
   honey bee ambrosia, 211
   lemon sherbet, creamy, 159
   marshmallow apricots, 215
   peach cobbler, 152

Desserts (continued)
pears
au chocolat, 148
ruby-jeweled, 149
pineapple
date dessert, 149
zip, 149
raspberry-raspberry, 156
strawberry(ies)
ice, 156
in sour cream, 148
rhubarb compote, 212
Romanoff, 147
to dip, 147
Deviled ham roll, 282
Dip
crab, hot curried, 280
guacamole, with tacos, 282
hollandaise, vegetable
dippers with, 282
Mexican, 280
shrimp, 281
yogurt, 281
Dried beef casserole, 17

Egg(s)
and ham, creamed, 90
bake, Cheddar, 90
breakfast, 220–227
continental, 88
foo yong, 89
fried, 222
ham and cheese oven omelet, 226
Mexicali, 224
on corned beef hash, 222
potato scramble, 223
puffy cheese bake, 227
quiche Lorraine, 225
roll, cheese, 227
rolled, 227
scrambled, 222
shirred, 220
Eggnog, orange, 245
Eggplant, oven-fried, 115

Finnan haddie, 229
Fish, 77–86. See also names of
fish and seafood.
almondine, 81
baked, 77
broil(ed), 79
Italiano, 80
parsleyed, 78
oven-fried fillets, 82
paella, skillet, 84
panfried, 81
poached, 79
seafood and rice, 274
stick(s)
breakfast, 230

crispy, 80
lime-glazed, 80
orange-glazed, 80
with cucumber sauce, 274
with mushrooms and
pecans, 81
Fondue
cheese, jiffy, 87
chocolate, 152
Frank rolls, baked, 259
Frankfurter(s)
casserole, 45
chili dogs, 46
chowder, 267
Coney Island hot dogs, 255
Creole wieners, 45
French toast
oven, 240
waffled, 240
Frosting(s). See also Topping.
butter, 190, 191
chocolate
glaze, 191
variations for, 188
white
creamy, variations for, 188
fluffy, variations for, 189
Fruit(ed) (s). See also names of
fruits.
and cheese tray, 146
and pork skillet, 34
breakfast, 211–215
cereal
hot, 216
squares, fruity, 276
chicken salad, 76
cinnamon, 214
compote
dried, 213
hot, 151
delight, 153
dessert freeze, 157
desserts, 146–152
fizz, 207
ginger drops, 161
honey bee ambrosia, 211
hot breakfast, 214
in sour cream, 148
kabobs, broiled, 150
'n rice dessert, 154
salad. See also Salad(s).
freeze, 157
macaroni, 105
sherbet, 147
slices, frozen, 212
turkey salad, 76
with yogurt, 211
Fudge(y)
balls, peanut butter, 174
cake
brownie, 180

Fudge(y) (*continued*)
  triple, 180
  chocolate, 172
  clusters, 173
  crinkles, 164
  opera, 172
    cherry, 172
  pecan pudding cake, 182
  sauce, chocolate, 246

Garlic
  chip chicken, 65
  French bread sticks, 140
Giblets, 62
Gingerbread drops, 161
Glaze
  brown sugar, 181
  chocolate, 191
  orange, 37
Graham cracker
  crust, 204
  torte, 184
Grapefruit
  crunchy broiled, 214
  honey broiled, 215
  minted, 147
Grasshopper pie, 201
Gravy, pan, 30
Green beans
  and bacon, 109
  Italian
    and carrot nuggets, 117
    mushroom, 111
Guacamole dip with tacos, 282

Halibut with vegetables, 78
Ham
  and eggs, creamed, 90
  and macaroni casserole, 69
  and noodle cooler, 267
  baked, 36
    glazed, 37
  broccoli sandwiches, 261
  casserole, 41
  cheese
    souffléed pepper shells, 275
    oven omelet, 226
  dinner
    layered, 42
    Tahitian, 40
  'n hash, 267
  'n limas, 39
  slice, smoked, 39
  waffles, 238
Hamburger(s), 257–259. *See also*
      Beef, ground.
  bake hearty, 23
  baked frank rolls, 260
  barbecued burger buns, 258
  breakfast burgers, 228
  California, 257

casserole, complete, 22
cheeseburgers, 257
corn bake, 21
freezer burgers, 258
giant burger, 25
gourmet burger, 25
maké-ahead mix, barbecued,
    259
panfried, 257
sloppy Joes, 259
spread-a-burger, 260
Stroganoff, 24
Hash
  and cheese grill, 256
  corned beef, eggs on, 222
  ham 'n, 267
Hollandaise
  dip, vegetable dippers with, 281
  onions, 115
Hominy, country-style, 23
Hopping John, 137
Horseradish sauce, 3

Ice, strawberry, 156
Ice cream
  chocolate-mint parfaits, 159
  individual baked Alaska, 160
  peach Melba, party, 159
  soda, 207
  sundae waffles, 158
  waffles, 158

Jam
  crumpets, 234
  grill, 233

Kabobs, broiled fruit, 150

Lamb, 47–54
  and barley casserole, curried,
      53
  chops
    broiled, 50
    charcoal-grilled, 52
    mixed grill, 52
    princess, 51
  leg of, Swedish, 49
  ossobuco, 53
  patties, best broiled, 50
  pie, savory, 16
  roast, 47
  shepherds' pie, 54
Lemon
  cake, triple, 182
  dressing, creamy, 94
  pudding
    shells, 155
    cake pie, 199
  sherbet, creamy, 159
Lima beans
  'n ham, 39

Lima beans (continued)
   hickory, 110
   perky, 110
Lime-glazed fish sticks, 80
Liver, 18
   and onions, 19
   Creole, 19
Liverwurst tidbits, 283
Lobster
   chowder, 251
   Newburg, jiffy, 83
London broil, 12
   appetizer, 279
Louis dressing, 273

Macaroni
   and chicken
      casserole, 69
      salad, 271
   and ham casserole, 69
   and tuna salad, 271
   and turkey
      casserole, 69
      salad, 271
   fruit salad, 105
   tomatoed, 133
Marguerites, 173
Marmalade pinwheels, 235
Marshmallow
   apricots, 215
   puff squash bake, 120
Meat. See also specific kind.
   loaf, baked, 20
   'n potato roll-ups, 228
   pie(s). See Pie(s), meat.
   roll sandwiches, 253
   sandwich, baked, 36
Meatball(s)
   baked, 19
   mushroom, 279
   stew, 20
Melon and prosciutto, 213
Meringue, brown sugar, 192
Milk(s)
   flavored, 245
   hot chocolate, 247
   shake
      cherry, 247
      chocolate, 246
      cocoa-cereal, 244
      pineapple, 247
      strawberry, 247
Mincemeat
   ginger drops, 161
   pie, fix-ups for, 198
Mint(ed)
   chocolate
      fondue, 152
      shake, 246
   grapefruit, 147
Mixed grill, 51

Mocha
   butter frosting, 191
   chocolate shake, 246
   dessert coffee, 205
Molasses pandowdy, 194
Muffin(s)
   carrot-orange, 237
   chive dinner, 142
   corn, 145
   English, dinner rounds, 141
   jam crumpets, 234
   Parmesan rounds, 141
Mushroom
   corn soup, 243
   herb rice, 134
   Italian green beans, 111
   meatballs, 279
   pilaf, 136
Mustard tomato sauce, 26

Noodle(s), 129–133
   and ham cooler, 267
   and spinach combo, 131
   bacon and onion, 129
   Roma, 131
   Romanoff, stir-ins for, 131
   spinach and cauliflower, 129
   stir-ins for, 130
   Swiss tuna Romanoff, 273
   tangy, 130
   tuna dinner, 86

Okra and tomato salad, 98
Onion(s)
   and broccoli, creamed, 116
   and potatoes, broiled, 116
   hollandaise, 115
Orange
   and onion salad, 105
   blueberry bread, 238
   butter frosting, 190
   carrot muffins, 237
   cauliflower salad, 104
   cherry pie, 195
   eggnog, 245
   freeze, 208
   frost soda, 208
   glaze, 87
   glazed fish sticks, 80
   juice, sparkling, 242
   nut waffles, 238
   pecan bread, 237
   raisin cake, blender, 185
   rice, 134
   rolls, 236
Oyster stew, 243

Paella, skillet, 84
Pan gravy, 30
Pancakes, 239, 240, 241
Papaya, 212

Parmesan
  chicken, golden, 65
  French sticks, 140
  rounds, 141
  snacks, 284
  supper bread, 144
Parfait(s)
  chocolate-cherry, 153
  chocolate-mint, 159
Pastry, electric mixer, 202
Peach
  cobbler, 152
  crisps, caramel, 151
  cup, creamy, 208
  Melba, party, 159
Peanut(ty)
  break, 171
  cookies, salted, 171
  ginger drops, 161
  mallow chews, 217
  pop-ups, 234
  squares, 276
Peanut butter
  and jelly coffee cake, 235
  cake, 178
  cookies, 163
  frosting, 190
  fudge balls, 174
  ginger drops, 161
Pears
  au chocolat, 148
  ruby-jeweled, 149
Peas
  and almonds, 117
  and artichokes, 107
  and cauliflower, dilled, 117
  blackeye
    creamy, 118
    hopping John, 137
  green and gold salad, 97
  snow, and carrot nuggets, 117
  with celery and onion, 116
Pecan
  bread, orange, 237
  pie, 197
  pudding cake, fudgy, 182
  rounds, brown sugar, 170
  stuffing, 62
Pepper shells
  cheese souffléed, 275
  ham-cheese souffléed, 275
Pepper steak Bordelaise, 10
Peppermint creams, 175
Perfection salad, 99
Piccalilli stew, 16
Pie(s), dessert, 193–204
  apple
    cheese, 193
    fix-ups for, 193
    pandowdy, 194
  banana cream, 200

berry basket, 196
cherry
  fix-ups for, 195
  orange, 195
chocolate, rich, 201
crusts
  cookie crumb, 203
  cookie pat, 204
  graham cracker, 204
  grasshopper, 201
lemon pudding cake, 199
mincemeat, fix-ups for, 198
molasses pandowdy, 194
pastry, electric mixer, 202
pecan, 197
pineapple, perfect, 196
pumpkin, fix-ups for, 198
raspberry, 194
strawberry cream, 200
Pie(s), meat
  beef, savory, 16
  lamb, savory, 17
  shepherds', 54
  veal, savory, 17
Pineapple
  banana salad, 106
  braised drumsticks, 74
  cheese mold, 101
  cherry bologna, 43
  coconut cookies, 171
  date dessert, 149
  marshmallow slaw, 96
  milk shake, 247
  pie, perfect, 196
  Polynesian cookies, 169
  raisin cookies, 171
  stuffed spareribs, 32
  zip, 149
Pizza
  mock, 259
  rice, 87
Polish sausage boil, 44
Pork, 26–46
  and fruit skillet, 34
  and rice, Chinese, 35
  baked meat sandwich, 36
  broiled, 28
  chop(s)
    braised, 30
    dinner, 28
    Mexican, 29
    stuffing-topped, 29
  city chicken, seasoned, 57
  cutlets, cheese-topped, 34
  ribs, barbecued, 31
  roast, 26
  spareribs. See Spareribs.
  subgum, 35
  tenderloin patties supreme, 33
Potato(es), 123–128
  and onions, broiled, 116

Potato(es) (continued)
  au gratin, stir-ins for, 125
  bake, golden, 124
  cheese, 123
    casserole, 123
    clam chowder, 251
  mashed, stir-ins for, 124
  O'Brien, 125
  pancakes, 239
  salad, scalloped, 127
  scalloped
    "and," 40
    creamy, 126
    variations for, 126
  scramble, 223
  soup, creamy, 252
  sweet. See Sweet potato(es).
  tuna scallop, 272
Pot-roast in foil, 6
Prosciutto and melon, 213
Puddings, 153–155
Pumpkin pie, fix-ups for, 198

Quiche Lorraine, 225

Raisin
  nut ginger drops, 161
  orange cake, blender, 185
Raspberry
  pie, 194
  raspberry, 156
Ravioli-sausage casserole, 41
Rhubarb-strawberry compote, 212
Ribs, barbecued, 31. See also
    Spareribs.
Rice, 134–139
  and beans, Caribbean, 136
  and pork, Chinese, 35
  and spaghetti, Italian, 132
  and tuna melange, 86
  coconut, 134
  curried, 135
  frozen, in combination, 134
  green, 137
  hopping John, 137
  medley, 135
  mushroom
    herb, 134
    pilaf, 136
  'n fruit dessert, 154
  orange, 134
  oven steamed, 134
  pizza, 87
  skillet pilaf, 136
  Spanish, 268
    with sausage, 268
  wild. See Wild rice.
Rolls. See also Sweet rolls.
  cheese puffs, 142
  herb-topped, 141
  twin pan, 143

Root beer angel cake, 183
Rye fingers, sesame, 140

Salad(s), 93–106
  ambrosia, 104
  asparagus, chilled, 108
  bean, bright, 99
  beef and mushroom, 264
  Brussels and carrots, 98
  chef's, 269
  chicken
    and macaroni, 271
    fruited, 76
    hot, 269
  cinnamon-applesauce, 102
  coleslaw, blender, 96
  cucumber
    marinated, 97
    relish mold, 99
  frozen cocktail, 103
  fruit
    freeze, 157
    macaroni, 105
  green
    and gold, 97
    and white, 95
  ham and noodle cooler, 267
  okra and tomato, 98
  orange
    and cauliflower, 104
    and onion, 105
  perfection, 101
  pineapple
    banana, 106
    cheese mold, 102
  potato, scalloped, 127
  seedless grape, 103
  tossed
    best, 94
    with classic dressing, 96
  tuna
    and macaroni, 271
    hot, 270
    on a shoestring, 272
  turkey
    and macaroni, 271
    fruited, 76
    hot, 270
  veal, hot, 270
  Waldorf
    country-style, 106
    molded, 100
Salad dressings, 93–94
Salami wedges, 283
Salmon
  puff, 85
  steaks, herbed, 82
Sandwich (es), 253–263. See also
    Hamburger(s).
  baked meat, 36

Sauce
  chocolate fudge, 246
  cucumber, 48
  horseradish, 3
  mustard-tomato, 26
Sausage, 231
  and kraut Romanoff, 42
  country cassoulet, 91
  peasants' feast, 44
  Polish, boil, 44
  ravioli casserole, 41
  Spanish rice with, 268
  stuffing, 62
  Yorkshire, 232
Scallop casserole, 83
Scalloped potatoes "and," 40
Schnitzel surprise, 58
Seafood and rice, 274
Sesame rye fingers, 140
Shepherds' pie, 54
Sherbet
  creamy lemon, 159
  fruited, 148
Short ribs, braised, 12
Shortcakes, tomato, 261
Shrimp
  and chicken, speedy, 271
  and peas, creamy, 84
  bisque, 249
  dip, 281
    yogurt, 281
  marinated, 280
  Newburg, jiffy, 83
  skillet paella, 84
  towers, 262
Sirloin Stroganoff, 265
Sloppy Joes, 259
Smoked ham slice, 39
Snacks, 276–284. *See also*
        Appetizers.
Snow peas and carrot nuggets, 117
Soda
  ice-cream, 207
  orange frost, 208
Sole, golden, 77
Soufflé, cheese-spinach, 88
Souffléed pepper shells
  cheese, 275
  ham-cheese, 275
Soup(s), 248–252
  beans, south-of-the-border, 252
  clam
    and tomato bisque, 250
    corn chowder, 251
    potato chowder, 251
  combos, quick, 250
  cream of chicken, herbed, 243
  cream of corn, 248
  herbed, 249
  lobster chowder, 251
  madrilene, sherried, 251

  mushroom-corn, 243
  'n cereal, 216
  potato, creamy, 252
  shrimp bisque, 249
  tomato bouillon, 244
  vegetable cheese chowder, 248
Sour cream brownies, 161
Spaghetti
  and rice, Italian, 132
  and sprouts, saucy, 132
Spanish rice, 268
  with sausage, 268
Spareribs
  baked, 31
  barbecued, glazed, 32
  glazed, 33
  pineapple-stuffed, 32
Spice cake, 187
Spinach
  and broccoli, 118
  and noodle combo, 131
  cheese soufflé, 88
  crunchy creamy, 118
  green rice, 136
  noodles and cauliflower, 129
  sautéed, 119
Squash
  bake
    crusty pecan, 120
    marshmallow puff, 120
  honey-chili, 120
  nutty baked, 119
Stew
  beef, lunch, 265
  corned beef, 18
  good brown, 14
  meatball, 20
  oven, 15
  oyster, 243
  piccalilli, 15
  Stroganoff, 16
Stewed chicken, 67
Strawberry(ies)
  berry basket pie, 196
  Chantilly torte, 178
  cream, 207
    pie, 200
  ice, 156
  in sour cream, 148
  milk shake, 247
  rhubarb compote, 212
  Romanoff, 147
  to dip, 147
Streusel coffee cake, 235
Stuffing
  apple-raisin, 62
  pecan, 62
  sausage, 62
  topped pork chops, 29
Subgum, 35
Submarine sandwiches, 253

Sweet potato(es)
  caramel-glazed, 128
  casserole, 127
  orangé, 128
  skillet-glazed, 128
Sweet rolls
  caramel, 237
  cinnamon, 237
  marmalade pinwheels, 234
  orange, 236
Swiss
  steak, 11
  tuna Romanoff, 273

"Tartare steak" appetizers, 278
Tea, spiced, 207
Teriyaki steak, 7
Toast
  continental brunch, 241
  flavored oven, 233
  French
    oven, 239
    waffled, 239
Tomato(ed) (es)
  and clam bisque, 250
  and okra salad, 98
  baked stuffed, 122
  bouillon, 244
  broiled, 122
  cabbage skillet, 121
  macaroni, 133
  mustard sauce, 26
  shortcakes, 261
Topping(s)
  broiled
    butterscotch, 192
    coconut, 192
    crunchy, 192
  brown sugar meringue, 192
  for cereal, 218
Tuna
  and macaroni salad, 271
  and rice melange, 86
  burgers, 263
  noodle dinner, 86
  on a shoestring, 272
  potato scallop, 272
  Romanoff, Swiss, 273
  salad, hot, 270
Turkey, 70–76
  à la king, 270
  and dressing bake, sliced, 76
  and macaroni
    casserole, 69
    salad, 271
  and wild rice casserole, 74
  can-opener combo, 69

cooking in foil, 71
divan, 75
drumsticks
  deluxe, 74
  pineapple braised, 74
roast, 70
  half, 73
  herbed, 73
  orange, 72
salad
  fruited, 76
  hot, 270

Vanilla
  bonbons, 174
  butter frosting, 190
  fondant, creamy, 175
  nut creams, 176
  pudding, rich, 154
Veal, 55–60
  city chicken, seasoned, 57
  cutlets, breaded, 59
  mustard, 60
  paprika, 56
  pie, savory, 16
  roast, 55
    savory, 56
  salad, hot, 270
  schnitzel surprise, 58
  with tomato sauce, 57–58
Vegetable(s), 107–122. See also
      names of vegetables.
  butters for, 107
  cheese chowder, 248
  dippers with hollandaise dip, 282
  relishes
    fresh, 281
    hot, 113

Waffles
  ham, 238
  ice-cream, 158
  orange-nut, 238
  sundae, 158
Welsh rarebit, 275
Wild rice
  and chicken casserole, 75
  and turkey casserole, 74

Yogurt
  fruit with, 211
  shrimp dip, 281

Zucchini
  herbed, 120
  Italian-style, 121

KITCHEN POWER!

- [ ] COMPLETE BOOK OF MEXICAN COOKING—Ortiz   4107 • 95¢
- [ ] THE COMPLETE BOOK OF PASTA—Jack Denton Scott   5347 • 95¢
- [ ] THE ART OF SALAD MAKING—Carol Truax   5936 • $1.00
- [ ] AMERICA'S FAVORITE RECIPES FROM BETTER HOMES & GARDENS   6368 • $1.25
- [ ] ORIENTAL COOKING—Myra Waldo   6482 • $1.25
- [ ] YOGA NATURAL FOODS COOKBOOK—Hittleman   6885 • $1.25
- [ ] THE ART OF JEWISH COOKING—Jennie Grossinger   7033 • $1.25
- [ ] THE ART OF FRENCH COOKING—Fernande Garvin   7045 • $1.00
- [ ] THE ART OF FISH COOKING—Milo Milorandovich   7052 • $1.00
- [ ] COMPLETE BOOK OF WINE COOKERY—Waldo   7080 • $1.25
- [ ] THE SPANISH COOKBOOK—Barbara Norman   7132 • $1.00
- [ ] COMPLETE BOOK OF VEGETABLE COOKERY—Waldo   7321 • $1.00
- [ ] THE GRAHAM KERR COOKBOOK—Galloping Gourmet   7424 • $1.95
- [ ] BETTER HOMES & GARDENS CASSEROLE COOKBOOK   7854 • $1.25
- [ ] FANNIE FARMER BOSTON COOKING SCHOOL COOKBOOK —Wilma Perkins   7934 • $1.95
- [ ] BETTY CROCKER'S COOKBOOK   8108 • $1.95
- [ ] THE ART OF ITALIAN COOKING—Mario LoPinto   8298 • $1.25
- [ ] THE ART OF GERMAN COOKING—Betty Wason   8714 • $1.25

How's Your Health?

Bantam publishes a line of informative books, written by top experts to help you toward a healthier and happier life.

Facts at Your Fingertips!

Bantam Book Catalog

It lists over a thousand money-saving bestsellers originally priced from $3.75 to $15.00 —bestsellers that are yours now for as little as 50¢ to $2.95!

The catalog gives you a great opportunity to build your own private library at huge savings!

So don't delay any longer—send us your name and address and 10¢ (to help defray postage and handling costs).